Hold Onto Your Celestial Dreams

Tools to Help You Safeguard Your Temple Marriage Against Divorce

By Terry Hardy Olsen

Insightful, wonderfully written, and well worth reading. Terry's insights, anecdotes, and easy style make it seem like she's talking directly with you. This book has something for everyone who is dating, newly weds, or been married for any length of time.

– Mike L Hardy – Married 38 years.

I felt so unprepared when my husband and I were married. I knew the timing was right and the person was right but I was not prepared for the challenges of blending traditions and families. My in-laws were recently empty nesters so it has been a challenge for both them and us even though I married a recently returned missionary. We also had his sister, who is the baby in the family, move in with us the week after we were married, so we had a difficult time starting our marriage with a roommate. Now that we are by ourselves, we feel like we are starting over in the intimacy department. Terry offered a ton of insight into what we were going through and how to better develop our marriage. This book along with having the house to ourselves has helped our marriage. We are both so much happier now. She has literally been an answer to our prayers.

- Autumn Carter- Married 1 year and a half

Terry and I have known each other since we were ballroom dance partners at Rick's College in the mid 70's. So when she asked if I would read her book I was thrilled. My wife and I were married in the Manti temple in the late 70's. And to be honest we have had our ups and downs. I don't think any marriage is above needed improvement to make it lasting and loving. This book is full of practical, common sense; scriptural backed ideas that would help any reader improve their eternal marriage if that truly is the honest desire of their heart. I know after reading it, I myself have lots of things I need to improve on. This book brought those things lovingly to my mind, and instilled in me a real desire to work harder to make my marriage better. As you read the book the spirit will whisper to your mind again and again those loving things that will uplift, repair, and help heal any marriage. I would encourage the reader to keep pen and paper close and write down those impressions as the spirit speaks to you. If you do you will find many things that will help improve your eternal lives together. I would highly recommend this book to anyone who is just starting or planning on marriage together or to anyone who has been happily married for 50 yrs. I promise you will find things in this book that will help you make your marriage happier, more loving, and stronger, even eternal, as it was always intended to be.

- Stan Snook - Married 33 years

TABLE OF CONTENTS

Acknowledgements

I feel like John Glenn (the astronaut) who said, "I am not a hero, but I have spent my life in the company of heroes".

To my best friend and sweetheart,

Thank you for your unconditional love and support. Your patience, wise counsel, example and advice have been a valuable resource for me to be able to write my book. You believed in me when I did not, and cheered me on when I felt like giving up. Every day with you, is sweeter than the day before. My love for you grows with each passing day. Being married to my best friend and sweetheart is one of my choicest blessings! The thought of spending eternity with you fills my heart with great joy and happiness.

To my angel mother,

You *showed* me how unconditional love and commitment in marriage could literally bring about miracles in being able to build a Celestial marriage on earth, as well as in the eternities. Your excellent example has helped me to be a much better wife and mother, and given me many ideas to include in this book. If giving even one person the encouragement and hope to keep hanging in there when they did not previously know how they could continue, then hopefully, all you endured, will have been worth it. I am looking forward to the day when I can wrap my arms around you and thank you for all you did to bless my life, and for being one of my best friends and precious mother.

To our sons,

Your excellent examples as husbands, fathers, sons, sons-in-law, and sons of God, along with your dedication and commitment to the Gospel of Jesus Christ, gives your father and me hope that our family will someday be together forever. My life is filled with joy in knowing that my children and their families walk in righteousness.

To our daughters-in-law,

Each of you has brought many blessings to our family through your love and commitment to our sons and grandchildren, as well as us, and the rest of the family. All you do to strengthen the bonds and love between our extended family is greatly appreciated by me and Eric. Thank you for helping me to include being a mother-in-law, as one of my greatest blessings!

To Jim and Renee,

Thanks for being cheerleaders, and for your excellent advice and encouragement. I could not have done this without you! It is a pleasure and an honor knowing you. It is an added blessing to be included in your exceptional and beautiful family tree!

To Autumn Marshall Carter and Andrew Carter,

You and Drew are very dear to us. Autumn, you will never know what it means to Eric and me to be treated like we were your parents (Autumn) when you served your mission. We love the two of you as if you are our own kids. Autumn, there are no words to thank you for your hard work in editing this book. Plus, your encouragement with it is very much appreciated. May God bless both of you as you work towards your happily-ever-afters!

Laura Brotherson (Author of "And They Were Not Ashamed"), Gracia Jones (author of numerous books about Joseph and Emma Smith, as well as historian for the Joseph Smith Jr. and Emma Hale Foundation), Sarah Swann, Kathaleen May, Debbie Jensen Olsen, Stan Snook, Tammy Gerdes, Jim and Danielle Marsh, and many others…in fact, too many to count…whose examples and teachings have contributed to the writings in this book. Thanks for your suggestions and for helping with the editing of this book. It helps to have cheerleaders and tutors when you are working towards your dreams; and each of you have been that and more for me. Each of you has touched my heart in ways you will never know. To you, I say "Thank-you from the bottom of my heart!" However, the One whom I give the most heart felt gratitude is the Lord. He has filled my life with experiences, insights, and understandings in my desire to learn how to build a Celestial marriage. A teacher can know they have been a success when they see their pupil(s) teaching others what they have learned as their student. It is for that reason that I have desired to share what He has taught me, with others.

Introduction

The Introduction usually lays the foundation for the rest of a book, however, too often it is thought of as the "sealed portion", or a bother. So in order to keep the reader from missing my reasons for writing this book, I have moved the reason for writing this book, to the first chapter. Then, to encourage the reader to finish the book, I want to emphasize that each chapter lays the foundation for the next chapter…all the way to the last phrase in the last chapter.

I also want to point out, that even though this book was written for individuals and couples who will be, or have been married in the temple, it can benefit any individual or couple who desires to have a strong and loving marriage that will stand the test of time.

Intellectual Properties (The Church of Jesus Christ of Latter-day Saint's copyright department) has put greater restrictions on the use of quotes by their Church leaders. Therefore, since there are some excellent quotes that I wanted to include in this book, I have summarized what they said, into my own words, and then made references to where the reader can find the quotes or articles so they can read them in their entirety.

Section One

Celestial Dreams Can Become a Reality

Hold fast to your dreams until they become a reality

Chapter One

Two Hearts - One Dream

A number of years ago, my husband and I were blessed with the wonderful opportunity of serving in a singles Ward at Church. Even though most of our experiences were very positive and uplifting, within a few short years, we noticed an unsettling trend as more and more divorced singles started showing up in the university singles Wards (congregations) in our town. Those divorces would be easier to understand if either the husbands or the wives had been unfaithful or abusive. However, in most cases, one or both of the spouses had served a mission for our Church, and all the couples that we knew of, had married in the Temple. To make it even more perplexing, each of the ex-spouses were still active in church and held current temple recommends.

One Sunday, a beautiful single adult from that Ward, expressed her concerns that most of her friends (who had previously married in the temple) were now divorced; and most, if not all, had not yet reached their 25th birthdays! Understandably, she was having serious doubts that even if she found the man the Lord wanted her to marry, there was no guarantee that their temple marriage would last.

I do not know if it was the sound of her voice, or the look in her eyes that got my attention that day, but that was when I realized that I could no longer stand idly by, without trying to do something to make a difference. Therefore, I started praying with all the energy of my heart, to better understand what would cause faithful Latter-day Saint couples to abandon their temple marriages; and to better understand what it takes to build happy and loving marriages that will not only stand the test of time on Earth, but will last throughout the eternities.

Fairytales vs. Real Love

It was not long after starting this journey that I discovered a simple yet common denominator that many faithful Latter-day Saint couples face, even before becoming husband and wife. This seemingly insignificant problem manifests itself when the man or woman assumes that marrying the right person, at the right time, in the right place, *will guarantee* their safe passage into the Celestial Kingdom.

In this Utopia-type-scenario, the powerful feelings of love between the husband and wife, never dim—in-laws are always supportive of the couple's choices—dinners are never late or burned—the house is always spotless and orderly—the dishes magically wash themselves—clothes are always clean, ironed, and put away—there is always plenty of money to pay the bills; and for anything else the couple desires—the cars are always in good running condition, and never in need of new tires—and the children are always obedient and cheerfully volunteer to do household chores, and homework.

Unfortunately, as the sun rises on each new day following the honeymoon, realities that were ignored or downplayed may be noticed. Personal habits, once thought of as cute, are now annoying. Problems with jobs, education, health or family dynamics (often spelled mother and father-in-laws) may weigh heavily. Church responsibilities may require time away from the home and the paycheck does not stretch as far as expected. When any or all of these things occur, one spouse or the other may start to believe that the marriage was a mistake.

Assuming that such problems are limited to those who do not marry in the temple can add to a couple's confusion and mistaken ideas about the realities of married life. The truth is that the Lord meant for there to be opposition in *all* things, even in marriages that appear to be made in Heaven (2 Nephi 2:11).

Another contributing factor to misconceptions that can lead to failed marriages also seems harmless and even highly desired by many. This misconception usually comes from the love affair our society has with fairytales, romantic movies, television, love songs, love sonnets, along with romance novels (all of which are prevalent in our society) that often give the false portrayal of what "true love" is.

Unfortunately, the casualties of war can be found in, as well as out of the Church—from good upbringings, as well as poor ones—from families where there is a good income, to ones that struggle to keep food on the table, and a roof over their heads.

How do I know such an attitude can be a problem? Well, I will tell you; for I speak from experience. My programming started at the mature age of five after seeing the movie "Sleeping Beauty". I had dreams of growing up to become a beautiful princess, complete with an elegant, flowing gown and a sparkling tiara placed on top of my long golden hair; and that a handsome Prince would whisk me away on his white stallion, to his castle in the clouds, where we would live happily-ever-after.

However, by the time I reached the much wiser age of 15, I had replaced my dream of marrying a handsome prince, to that of marrying a handsome returned missionary, who would take me in his VW Bug (like the one in "Herbie the Love Bug" movie) to the temple, where we would be married for time and all eternity…and live happily-ever-after.

Hey, when I was five, I did not know how scarce Mormon Princes were, and when I was 15, VW Bugs were very popular, where I lived in Southern California.

During those days of youthful ignorance, I was sure that the goals for all LDS young women were similar to those espoused in the Young Women's Theme [1], used in the Church today. However, I have added a few phrases to fit my naïve way of thinking back then: As I live the Young Women's values, I will find a handsome returned missionary who will take me to the temple. I will support and sustain my husband in all his callings, which will surely include being a Bishop, Stake President, and/or General Authority, and quite possibly the Prophet. With my eternal companion, I will enjoy the blessings of exaltation, which is better known to starry-eyed teenagers, and some BYU Coeds, as "living happily ever after".

Okay, you can stop laughing now. I really believed those things…and I am confident that some of you deal with the same delusions.

A few years ago, a young bride (that we had known from when she was single) told my husband and me about her impending divorce. When we asked what had happened, she told us that when she was in a singles Ward, it seemed that nearly all her friends were getting engaged and marrying in the temple. Therefore, not wanting to be left off the Temple Marriage-Merry-Go-Round, she and her boyfriend, decided to join in on the fun and excitement.

However, as they moved forward with their wedding plans, she could not get rid of the strong impression that she should not marry him. Nevertheless, her desire to get married outweighed her good judgment, and she went through with her storybook wedding.

Sadly, her assumption that marrying in the temple would magically protect her and her husband from marital problems was not enough to bring about her expectations. It was not long after their first anniversary that her husband announced that he no longer wanted to go to church, and then came his dreaded announcement, that he wanted a divorce. She begged him to go with her to counseling. However, it proved to be futile; his mind was made-up.

She then told us how she realized that her impatience and unwillingness to seek for and follow the promptings she had received from the Lord had gone against everything she knew to be right. Even though she could pick up the pieces, and let the power of the Atonement heal her broken heart and shattered dreams, she could not go back and redo the unwise choices she had made.

I would like to say that her scenario is not a common one. However, I believe there are elements in what she and her husband went through, that are common in far too many temple marriages that end in divorce.

Ideally, young adults (and not so young adults) who marry in the temple should not be spiritual lightweights when it comes to understanding and applying gospel principles in their lives; as being worthy of one requires a serious commitment to living the Gospel of Jesus Christ. Yet, far too many of these "gospel-savvy" men and women lack the commitment and/or a willingness to make it through their first few years of marriage. Therefore, it seems that being well versed in and committed to living the Gospel is not always enough to help couples stay together.

During the time my husband and I served in that singles Ward, there were close to 60 couples who met, fell in love, and married in the temple. You know the typical scenario: Valiant missionary returns home from his mission, where he served with honor. He attends an Institute or church activity where he sees the girl of his dreams across the room. He musters up the courage to cross the room to ask her name. Then, as she and he gaze into each other's eyes for the first time, they find themselves asking, "Haven't I seen you somewhere before?"

Okay, you can stop gagging. It happens more times than most guys would like to admit, but many girls seem to think it should happen that way every time!

For you men who may not understand the mental workings of the female mind, it is far too common when she gets engaged for the woman to imagine that no other couple has ever loved as deeply as she and her fiancé. In addition, it us usually the woman (but sometimes the man) who is sure that her and her fiancé's union will produce the most valiant stripling warrior sons that ever lived; and that their daughters will resemble Ruth (Ruth 1-4); and Esther (Esther 1-10) from the Old Testament, whose devout faithfulness to God, set a sterling example, that many young women want to emulate.

Okay, maybe not all women or men think that way. However, if I am wrong, then why are there so many young brides who admit to having planned their dream weddings long before they meet the man of their dreams? Moreover, why do so many wedding receptions reflect the princess theme? In addition, why are stories and paraphernalia about princesses, so popular among girls and young adult women? I have watched in amazement as female toddlers get all starry-eyed when they see movies and anything to do with princesses. Moreover, I have heard mothers tell how their young daughters refuse to wear anything except princess clothing. Okay, I admit it, if those clothes had been available when I was a child I would have been the same way.

Furthermore, it is normal for every new father and mother to treat each of their children as if they are the most handsome/beautiful; and smartest and most talented children that ever came to Earth.

Even the best marriages can be very difficult and fraught with discord from time to time. However even ones that start out on shaky grounds, can also experience happiness and unspeakable joy, if they will stay committed to doing the things that will help to build and strengthen their marriage bonds.

President Spencer W. Kimball (12th President of the Church), said every husband and wife can experience "exultant ecstasy" that is beyond anything they can comprehend.[2] *Exultant,* is the "act or condition of rejoicing greatly" (Dictionary.com); and *ecstasy* is "a state in which the mind is elevated above the reach of ordinary impressions, as when under the influence of overpowering emotion; an extraordinary elevation of the spirit" (Dictionary.com); or "poetic inspiration, mental transport or rapture from the contemplation of divine things" (Webster's Dictionary).

Wow! Those two words capture the depths and heights of what inspires some of the most endearing love songs and poetry. And it is not surprising, that those delicious feelings have been known to cause love-struck lovers to behave in ways that no normal, rational person would ever be caught doing. Yet, when those intoxicating emotions take over one's mind and heart, it is unconscionable to think they will ever fade. And, to my knowledge, I do not believe anyone one has ever tried to come up with an immunization, nor a cure, for being bitten by the "love bug!

So then, why is it, when the newly weds first experience the pain of trying to blend their diversities, or their weaknesses and/or lack of maturity takes their toll, their memory of having felt those exhilarating feelings, fade quickly; and rather than figuring out what to do to repair, build and strengthen their marriage bonds, they too often toss their marriage in the garbage pail like they would a crumpled piece of paper.

Is it too hard, or is it an Unwillingness to Keep Trying?

How many times have you heard someone say, "It's too hard!"? Where would we be if the Lord had decided the Atonement was too hard? He could have easily chosen not to go through with it, using the excuse that so few of His brothers and sisters would appreciate His priceless gift. Yet, He went through with it because He knew His Father expected Him to, and because of His great love for every person…even the imperfect and ungrateful ones.

Ponder if you will, on the great blessings that have come to you and all mankind because of the Savior's choice to go through with the Atonement and death when it felt like it was too hard.

The pain and suffering every spouse endures as they work towards becoming Celestial husbands and wives will pay big dividends, not only in this life but also throughout the eternities.

To *endure,* means to "undergo hardship without giving in"; or "remaining firm under suffering or misfortune with out yielding" [3]

So I ask again, why would a couple who has made the valiant effort to marry the right person, in the right place, at the right time, choose instead to abandon their hopes and dreams of being together forever, just because it is hard at times?

When trials, heartaches, and disappointments make me feel like giving up, it helps me to remember the words to Michael McLean's popular song…"Hold On, The Light Will Come" [5].

The Cement That Binds Hearts

Not long ago, while talking with a young wife and mother, I had what I like to refer to as an "A-ha moment" as she was telling how difficult hers and her husband's first few years of marriage had been. They had come from very different upbringings, and both had strong personalities, which often clashed. As you can imagine, those diversities caused some serious challenges for both of them.

When I asked what helped her to stay in the marriage when things got so rough, she told me how there were times when she did not want to keep trying, but she remembered that she and her husband had committed, before their wedding day, that divorce would never be an option.

They are an inspiration to me that any couple who will commit to do so, can build a marriage that not only will last the eternities, but can also find great joy in the journey.

If more couples, who have made sure to marry the right person, in the right place, at the right time, would make the commitment to each other and the Lord, that divorce will never be an option, and then will sincerely and prayerfully seek to find the answers to help them keep their commitment, then more couples would see their eternal hopes and dreams become a reality.

You, or someone you know, may be divorced or headed for divorce; on the other hand, you may be in a good marriage but want to know how to keep it strong, and/or help it to grow into the marriage that you dreamed of before you got married. You may be single and want to learn what it takes to build a strong marriage that can weather the storms of life for when you do get married, so you do not have to worry about going through the pain and heartache of a failed marriage. You may be working towards marrying, or being sealed in the temple after marrying civilly. No matter what your reason(s) for thumbing through or reading this book, it is my sincere hope and prayer, that something in it will help you or someone you know, be able to find answers in how to build a Celestial marriage that can last through time and the eternities.

In her talk, "God Needs a Powerful People", Sheri Dew told how after her talks people often tell her that she said exactly what they needed to hear. When she asked what she said, they said something she did not remember saying. She claims it is the Spirit who does the teaching in those situations. I know it to be true, because I have noticed when I am reading scriptures, or listening to something spiritual in nature it is very common for enlightenment to come to my mind and heart that may not have anything to do with what I am reading or listening to.

I want to add a word of caution here. Do not become discouraged if your spouse, future spouse, or family member, does not get the same message(s) or inspiration from a prayer, a talk, or a passage of scripture that you get. We are all at different levels of progression, and learn differently. Sometimes, one person puts in the effort to gain the answer, and the other does not. The diversity does not necessarily mean that one spouse or family member is more righteous than the other is. However, in 1 Nephi 15:2-11, the account is told about Nephi's overhearing his brothers Laman and Lemuel disputing over some things their father had said to them that were hard for them to understand. Nephi asked them if they had inquired of the Lord; they responded "We have not, because the Lord maketh no such thing known to us."

Look at the disastrous results that came to Laman and Lemuel and countless generations who followed them because of their hard hearts and unwillingness to simply *ask* the Lord.

The Lord Is the Teacher; I Am Only the Student Who Is Willing To Share What He Has Taught Me

I do not consider myself an expert in what I have shared in this book. The Lord is the expert; I am only the student, willing to share with others the answers and insights He has helped me to find.

Therefore, this book is devoted to you the reader, to be able to find answers and tools that the Lord has provided for all of His children. As you read, you will more than likely see many things you already know and have a strong testimony of. You may even be tempted to put the book down, thinking it has nothing to offer you. However, I would suggest that you continue to read and study every part of this book, as it is filled with reminders of whom we are and why we came to Earth. You may also be surprised at what the Spirit will teach you that is not contained in this book.

I would suggest that you keep a journal and notes of impressions that come to your mind and heart, as you read from these pages, and as you ponder on what you have learned. Refer back to your notes and this book from time to time, because they will bring back to your memory things you may have forgotten or were not ready to be taught the time you read it before.

I feel confident that there is something in this book for everyone who wants to be able to safeguard against the pitfalls that can lead to divorce, as well as seeing their hopes and dreams for eternity, to become a reality.

Notes:
1. Young Womens Theme for The Church of Jesus Christ of Latter-Day Saints
2. President Spencer W. Kimball, First Presidency Message, "Oneness in Marriage", *Ensign*, March 1977
3. Websters-Online-Dictionary.org
4. Dictionary.com
5. Michael McLean, "Hold on the Light Will Come"

Chapter Two

Begin with the End in Mind

Years ago, when I served in a Stake Young Women's Presidency, we decided to have an activity to help the youth and their parents gain stronger testimonies of the Plan of Salvation. To begin the activity, we had all the youth and their parents gather in the Chapel where they were presented two plans. A man who represented Jesus presented one plan, and a man who represented Lucifer presented the other.

The youth and their parents (not being instructed beforehand whom the men represented) were allowed to choose the plan they wanted to follow. Fortunately, they all chose Christ's plan, even though the man who represented Lucifer presented a very compelling plan.

The youth and their parents were then instructed to go to the gym (which represented earth life) where there was a carnival atmosphere with all sorts of game booths. The games that were spiritual in nature rewarded white tickets to the participants. The games that were just for fun, but did not have much substance, rewarded blue tickets, and the games of chance, rewarded red tickets.

During the event, a person (that happened to be the man who had represented Lucifer) went around offering to exchange anywhere from 3-10 of his colored tickets for one white ticket. I got a chuckle when one of the adult women jumped at the chance to exchange the few white tickets she had for the handful of colored tickets she was being offered. However, she no sooner held out her tickets to exchange them when one of the youth came up to her and with a shriek said, "Don't you know who that is? He is Satan!"

Her timing was perfect and spontaneous as the young woman had figured out, on her own, the meaning of the tickets.

There was another person dressed in a black hooded cape and carrying a large staff who represented the Grim Reaper. It was his job to go around the room tapping different individuals on the shoulder and instructing them to take their tickets and go quietly to the chapel where they were to find their Bishop.

Each participant's Bishop counted their tickets and informed them which color of ticket they had the most of, still not explaining what the tickets represented. The youth and their parents were then instructed to find a seat in the chapel where they were to sit reverently until further instructions were given.

Once all the participants were in the chapel, they were then lead in groups to three different rooms. The first room was dimly lit with worldly looking people in it. The young men were instructed to sit on one side of the room, while the young women were instructed to sit on the other side of the room. Then, one of the actors said he was a member of The Church of Jesus Christ of Latter-day Saints. He had served a mission and married in the temple, and was active in the church for a good number of years. He told how he thought it was no big deal when a cashier had given him too much change, so he kept the money. He said he thought nothing of taking pens from work, and that he was not completely honest when he filed his income taxes. He said he did not see how these decisions were hurting anyone, but then he started finding excuses for not going to the temple, and then he started staying away from church. His wife and kids begged him to go with them, but he continued to come up with excuses for his behavior and attitudes. Then one day, without warning, he died and found himself in a place he had never expected to be. He began to sob when he told how his wife had met and married another man who honored his priesthood. He buried his face in his hands as he told how she had chosen to break her temple sealing to him, choosing instead to be sealed to her second husband. Then, through his sobs, he told how he wished he had taken the Gospel more seriously, but now it was too late.

In the next room, there was a very pleasant setting where church hymns were being played. A picture of the Savior was on the end table next to the couch. However, once again we had the young men sit on one side of the room, and the young women on the other side of the room. One of the women told the group how she had worked hard to become an accomplished concert pianist; and how she had turned down the proposal of marriage with a man she loved because she did not want to give up her career, and did not want to have any children because she could not stand the sound of crying babies. Then, with tears in her eyes, she told how she would give anything to hear the cry of a baby, as there were no babies in the kingdom that she had been assigned to.

She then perked up as she told how Jesus came to visit them every so often, and how glad she was to see Him. Nevertheless, there was a look of sadness as she told how sorry she was each time He had to leave because she knew she could not go where He dwelt. Then, with a trembling voice, she told how much she missed her parents, siblings, and Heavenly Mother and Father. She told how it broke her heart that she could never see them again as they were all in the Celestial Kingdom, and she was not allowed to go there.

Upon leaving that room, I overheard the conversations of the youth and parents as they discussed what they had experienced so far. Some of the participants had figured out the significance of the tickets and were frustrated that they had not made better choices in the carnival setting; yet others were just having a good time and were clueless about the correlation of the things they had experienced up to that point. It was interesting to compare the comments and attitudes of that evening with how many of us view our earthly experiences...some get it and some are clueless as to why we are here, and what awaits us on the other side of the veil.

As each group entered the last room, a wonderful missionary couple (dressed in Sunday clothes) who represented our Heavenly Father and Mother, went up to each person as they entered the room and wrapped them in their arms, telling them how much they had missed them and were glad they had made it home.

A young girl went up to one of the young men in my group and gave him a hug, telling him how grateful she was when he and his Home Teaching companion had come when she was critically ill. She told how the priesthood blessing they gave her helped her get well.

Next, a man went up to a father and his son, telling them how much it meant when his wife had died, that they and the rest of their family were there for them, offering food, housework, yard work and help with the kids. He told how it helped him in his darkest hours to realize he was not alone.

Others went up, giving hugs and shedding tears of joy as they thanked the youth and their parents for bringing them the Gospel. It was wonderful to see families with their *children and babies* in that room. It was also wonderful to see the men and women together as husbands and wives, not as single people.

I could not help but feel like we were being allowed a brief glimpse of what it will be like for those who enter the highest degree of the Celestial Kingdom. As I was taking in the wonderful scene that was being played out before my eyes, I overheard one of the youth tell her mother, "This is where I want to be, so we can be with (her brother who had died a few weeks before)". Her mother agreed as they embraced and started to cry. This was for real. They were not acting. The girl's brother died a few weeks before when he was electrocuted while unscrewing a burned out light bulb in the pool he was swimming in.

After leaving that room, the youth and their parents were instructed to enter the chapel where they were to sit reverently while pondering on the things they had experienced, and while awaiting further instructions. When all the participants were seated in the chapel, a speaker gave a powerful talk on the Plan of Salvation and how it relates to each of us. After he was finished, we then encouraged the youth and their parents to share their testimonies about their experiences that evening. It was inspiring to see the transformation of the youth, where only a few hours before, their only focus was on being teenagers and having a fun time, who, a few hours later, were sharing powerful testimonies of what the Plan of Salvation meant to them.

If we will begin with the end in mind each day, and stay committed to those choices, we will find treasures, yea even hidden treasures and joy that will go beyond our mortal understanding.

Our Decisions Will Determine Our Eternal Destination

This life is like a speck of dust in comparison with the vastness of eternity. Yet the decisions we make in this life will determine our eternal destination. An airline pilot who allows his plane to get off course by a few degrees can end up far from his intended destination. In comparison, if we allow ourselves to think some of our choices are no big deal, then even one that seems harmless, if left unchecked, has the potential to lead us to spiritual suicide.

I was deeply saddened as I listened to a woman in a Ward I was visiting recently tell how it took her daughter's trying to take her own life for them to decide it was time to start having family prayer and go back to church.

Why does it take a crisis like that to wake us up? Too often the damage is so deeply ingrained that overcoming the incorrect attitudes and behavior is too much for family members to handle. So why not decide today (if you haven't already done so) to be completely committed to making righteous choices that will insure a much better eternal outcome for you and your loved ones.

President Spencer W. Kimball made up his mind early in life that he would obey the Word of Wisdom and keep himself unspotted from the world. It was because of making those decisions early in his life, and his commitment to stick with them, that he did not have to struggle with what to do when he was later faced with those temptations that might have otherwise derailed him.

The Lord qualifies His leaders' one choice and one decision at a time. The need for courageous and valiant standard-bearers is needed now more than at any other time in the history of the world. The storms and temptations will continue to intensify as we draw closer to the Second Coming. There may be times when it may seem like there is no way to hang on…but hang on we must at all costs, for our very lives and salvation may depend on that last ounce of courage and determination we exert.

Shortly before graduating from high school, I attended a youth conference where we were instructed to write down the qualities we wanted in a spouse. On the same paper, we were asked to include a description of the type of home we expected to have ten years down the road.

As I wrote my list, it helped to think of my eternal goal of obtaining the highest degree of the Celestial Kingdom. It was reassuring when I came across and reread that list recently, to see that none of my goals included marrying a handsome prince, riding a white stallion, driving a VW Bug, or paying the mortgage on a castle in the clouds. I am grateful that somewhere between the time that I was five until I turned 18 that I gained a better understanding, as well as stronger convictions, about the qualities I wanted in an eternal companion. Making those goals early in my life has helped to make my and my family's journey towards the Celestial Kingdom a more sure-footed one.

Think about the temple recommend interviews you have been through as a youth and as an adult. Do you recall anywhere in the interviews where you were asked what you are doing to obtain riches, or to be more beautiful or handsome? You will never be asked those things, because those are not prerequisites for entering the Temple or the Celestial Kingdom.

If you are interested in what I wrote on my list for what I was looking for in a spouse, and the type of home I wanted, read on:

1. He has to put the Lord first in his life and have a close relationship with Him.
2. He should have served as a valiant missionary.
3. He will have a strong testimony of the Gospel of Jesus Christ.
4. He should be committed to reading and studying scriptures daily.
5. I have to have a sure testimony that he is the one the Lord wants me to marry.
6. I want a home where the Spirit will be and peace and harmony are present.
7. I want pictures of the Savior and temples on the walls.

Writing those goals down and being completely *committed* to them (there is that word again), helped me to be able to recognize those qualities in my husband when I met him. It also kept me from settling for someone who did not possess those qualities (not that the other young men I was engaged to lacked those qualities, for they did—you can read those accounts later in this book).

Those goals are even more important to me today than they were back then, because I have seen the benefits and blessings of marrying a man who possessed each and every one of those qualities.

It is interesting that even though I had forgotten (until I found the list recently) that I had included goals about the type of home I wanted, that formulating in my mind, and writing down those goals, helped me know what I wanted when I was looking for pictures to put on the walls of all the homes I have lived in. I am grateful that I had the insight to write what I did when I was young, because having those pictures in our homes has helped to create a more reverent atmosphere and helped keep my family's and my minds focused on the things of eternity.

Chapter Three

True Beauty Comes from Within

President Spencer W. Kimball was very concerned about singles who mistakenly believe that there is only one "soul mate" for them. He referred to such ideology as fiction and an illusion. It is only natural for men and women to desire a marriage relationship that is synergistic (where both are winners), is free of contention, and with someone they feel they are compatible. However, he believed that it is within the reach of any righteous husband or wife to build a happy and lasting marriage if each spouse is willing to work hard for it. [1]

The concern, is that there are those singles that set their sights so high for the type of spouse they are willing to accept, that they are unwilling to allow for imperfections in the least degree; forgetting, or not realizing, that if the tables were turned, few potential spouses would be willing to give them a second glance, because of their imperfections or flaws.

Being unwilling to accept a rose, because of the fear of being pricked by its thorns, will cause the would-be recipient of the precious gift, to miss out on the intoxicating beauty of the delicate, velvety flower.

I fear too much is made out of outward beauty. There is a tragic story written by Oscar Wilde about a man named Dorian Gray, who made a pact with the Devil, where instead of losing his good looks and youthful appearance, a portrait painted of him (that was stored behind locked doors) showed his true age, as well as what his soul looked like.

About the time the portrait was painted, a friend introduced Dorian to literature about immoral and decadent living, which Dorian embraced to the fullest. With each sinful or cruel act, his portrait became more sinister and disfigured, while he retained his wholesome, youthful, handsome features.

After years of immoral and sinful living, Dorian met and fell in love with a beautiful young woman who possessed angelic qualities, so he decided to mend his ways. Upon making that effort, he quickly ran to the room where his portrait hung to see if the features in the portrait had improved. To his horror and anguish of soul, the portrait was even more hideous and disfigured than before. Therefore, not being able to bear it any longer, Dorian picked up a knife and plunged it into the heart of the monstrous figure in the portrait.

Upon hearing his blood curdling screams, his fiancé and servants broke down the door and found him lying dead with the knife in his heart. The portrait had been restored to its former wholesome, handsome and youthful appearance, and Dorian had taken on the horrible features that showed his true age and the corruptness of his soul. I have always thought of that story as an allegory of what true beauty is, and is not.

Isaiah said the Savior did not possess beauty that any man would desire (Isaiah 53:2). Yet there are those that have seen Him who have referred to Him as beautiful. Inner beauty radiates in our eyes and countenances. The Savior is beautiful because of who He is, and how He loves.

When I was a young adult, I knew a young woman that I did not think was very attractive; yet my brother and the other young men in our Ward made over her as if she was the most beautiful woman in the world. It finally got to me and I asked my brother what he saw in her. His response caught me by surprise when he said, "She is beautiful and so lady-like!"

After his comment, I paid close attention to see why he would think those things about her, and it was not long before I too recognized what made her beautiful. I saw that she always had a smile that warmed every heart she came in contact with; she treated everyone she met as if they had great worth. She carried herself with the graceful elegance of a queen, yet she was not arrogant or conceited. Even though she did not dress in the latest fashions, there was something about the way she dressed, that made her stand out from the rest, and gave her the appearance of a person of royal birth.

Contrast that with the handsome man or beautiful woman, who captures the eye of onlookers, whose good looks quickly fade once they open their mouths or allow their true selves to come out of hiding.

Angels in Our Midst – And In a Moment, the Savior Stood Before My Eyes
The big day finally arrived. Cindy had dreamed of this day for years, as she was now old enough to go to college. Along with her college classes, she was able to work in a few classes at the Institute of Religion. While hanging out at the Institute, she quickly made friends who shared similar standards and goals.

One day, when walking into the Institute, she saw a poster announcing a formal dance where the boys were supposed to ask the girls. She started running through a list of young men she would not mind asking her.

As the day of the grand event drew closer, she grew concerned when all of her friends had dates and she did not. She tried to hide the embarrassment she felt, but it was getting harder to conceal, so she decided to study at the library on campus, to make it easier to avoid her friends' questions.

As she was trying to work through some difficult math problems, a young man sat down next to her. She gave no thought to it until she heard a squeaky voice struggling to say her name. As she slowly raised her eyes to see who it was, she had a sinking feeling settle in her stomach as the barely audible voice told how he had been looking all over for her, so he could ask her to the dance. Disbelief filled her mind as she ran through the scenario of spending an evening with J-o-h-n-n-i-e, who was viewed as the most unattractive and boring single adult male at the Institute. In all fairness to her, she never got a good look at his face, as he usually hung his head with his hair hanging in his eyes. So he could have been very handsome, but she would never have known unless a good wind had blown his hair out of his face.

To add to the discomfort of spending an evening with him, she could not imagine having a conversation with him, as they had never said so much as "Hi" to each other, and he usually sat in the back of the classroom, never answering or asking questions. If she said "Yes", this could possibly become one of the longest and most boring nights of her life. Besides, what would her friends say if they saw her with Johnnie? After all, their dates were all handsome and fun to be around. And worse yet, if she were seen on a date with Johnnie, the other young men might think he was her boyfriend, and she might never get asked out again...not that she got asked out that much anyway...but still, her mind kept reeling from all the "what ifs" if she agreed to go to the dance with him.

However, in spite of all the strong repulsion she felt, Cindy had been taught to be Christ-like, so she mustered up all the mental energy she could, while trying to find just the right words to turn him down as nicely as she was able. However, as her mind was racing to find the words, she noticed his terrified eyes, and she realized that she might crush him if she turned him down. Then, before she knew it, she heard herself telling him, "I would love to go with you!"

A sigh of relief came over Johnnie's face as he anxiously shook her hand, and told her when he would pick her up, and then beelined for the door...all before Cindy could retract what she had said.

To keep from being embarrassed when she saw her friends, Cindy enthusiastically told them about the efforts Johnnie went through to find her to ask her to the dance. Then, to keep from seeing their looks of confusion, she started talking about what she was going to wear and how she was going to fix her hair. Her friends then joined in by telling what they were going to wear, and before long the uneasiness was gone and Cindy felt more at ease about her date with Johnnie.

The news quickly spread like wildfire around the Institute about the efforts Johnnie went through to ask Cindy to the dance and how excited she was about going with him ... which happened to be overheard by Johnnie.

The night of the big dance came and Johnnie showed up looking radiant as Cindy opened the door. As he held out his hand to take hers, he gently placed a beautiful corsage on her wrist. Then, while still holding her hand in his, he stood back and caught his breath as he told her she was a vision of loveliness.

Cindy had to do a double take as she gazed upon the handsome, tuxedo-clad young man at her door. Why, this man did not bear much of a resemblance to the trembling question mark of a figure that could barely muster the courage to ask her to the dance. The voice was similar, only it was stronger and more confident than she remembered. The face was definitely one she was not familiar with, but, since he rarely looked up or bothered to brush his hair from his face, how would she know what he looked like? Could Johnnie have chickened out and asked someone else to take his place? If that was the case, the man standing in front of her made no effort to let on that he was anyone other than Johnnie. So, trusting that it was not a joke or a dream, Cindy took Johnnie's arm as he lead her down the walk in front of her apartment. Cindy's knees went weak when they stopped in front of a beautiful white, horse drawn carriage. Could this be a dream? Dream or not, Cindy was elated to be able to go to the dance in a carriage fit for a Queen.

As the coachman drove past the open-mouthed onlookers, Cindy's fears of what the evening would be like started to subside. However, her euphoria was short-lived as the carriage pulled into the driveway of a McDonald's restaurant and stopped in front of the entrance. Then Johnnie stepped out and offered Cindy his hand.

This time, it was she who hung her head. How could he do this to her? What was he thinking? What if someone she knew saw her? How would she endure the embarrassment? What would she say to her friends when they asked where Johnnie took her for dinner? Did Johnnie run out of money and could not afford to take her to a nice restaurant? She would have been happy with him taking her to the dance in a car so he could have afforded to take her to a nice restaurant…yet, as her mind raced for answers to this puzzler, her confusion turned to laughter as Johnnie led her to an elaborate table set for a king and queen.

They were no sooner seated when a maître d' appeared, and handed them an elegantly decorated menu. After looking over their choices, they both decided to order Happy Meals with chocolate shakes.

The time flew by as Cindy and Johnnie talked and laughed…not caring about the curious glances of onlookers. Then, Johnnie looked at his watch and announced that they would be late for the ball. He then stood and held out his hand. Then gently taking her hand in his, he placed it on his arm as they glided out of the restaurant to the awaiting carriage.

Nothing could have prepared her for the gasps and surprised looks of her friends and peers as she and Johnnie walked into the ballroom. Cindy felt like the bell of the ball as one friend after another came up and told her how beautiful she looked. The best part was when they inquired who her handsome date was, and wanted to know what had happened to Johnnie. The gasps were hard to hide as each inquiring mind found out that the handsome and debonair young man was actually Johnnie.

The enchanting evening passed too quickly for Cindy. The carriage ride home was more enchanting than on the way to the dance. The stars shown brighter and music filled the air. As the carriage came to a stop in front of her apartment building, Johnnie quickly jumped out of the carriage and offered Cindy his hand to steady her as she stepped out onto the sidewalk. When they reached the apartment door, Cindy did not have to force a smile, as it came effortlessly. She had had the most memorable and wonderful evening of her life. Then Johnnie, with the manners of a true gentleman, asked if he could kiss her hand.

As Cindy closed the door behind her, she quickly placed the hand that had just been kissed, to her cheek. She gave thanks to the Lord that she had had such a wonderful evening, and that He had helped her to see the diamond in Johnnie.

The magic that took place that night was not just in the memorable evening that Johnnie provided for Cindy, but the transformation that took place in Johnnie and Cindy. What Cindy could not have known the day Johnnie asked her out, was that he had been turned down by numerous young women who thought nothing of the consequences of the heartless ways they rejected him, that he had given up on dating. However, Cindy was different. She had been so nice to everyone she met, that Johnnie thought she might agree to go out with him. When she answered with such enthusiasm, it gave him the courage to get his creative juices flowing. If this was going to be his first and last date, then it was going to be his finest.

Because she chose to follow the example of the Savior, Cindy was able to find the man of her dreams, and Johnnie was able to rise up and let the man of her dreams shine through.

(Cindy and Johnnie are composite characters, whose story represents a compilation of experiences in which individuals were able to see their worth because of the unconditional love and friendship that was shown to them. The selfless efforts of those who are literally saviors on Mount Zion will have lasting affects on countless generations throughout the eternities.)

The Lord taught me a powerful lesson recently when He opened my eyes to a flesh and blood angel in my own life. I have often referred to family members and friends as angels, because of the way they treat others, including me. However, this was different and left a more profound affect on me.

It happened while my husband and I were visiting with one of our sons and his family for the weekend. I was concerned over how much pain our daughter-in-law was in, as even though she was only 7 months pregnant, she looked like she was having twins, or was way past her due date. Nothing she did seemed to bring her relief. Yet, the whole time we were with them she served us, and her husband and their children with love and thoughtfulness.

I could not help but notice how much trouble she was having sitting through Church. Yet, during Sunday School class she glanced over at our son (who was leaning forward in his seat) and gently rubbed his back. When I saw that gesture of love, I could not help but wonder if it was she who desperately needed the back rub. Therefore, during Relief Society, I scooted next to her and had her lean forward so I could rub her back. I wanted to ease her suffering and repay some of what I have watched her do for others (including me) over the years that I have known her.

Then as I sat there, I decided to put my arm around her shoulder. As I did so, feelings of love for her, poured through me. The feelings were so strong that I could not hold back the tears that were welling up in my eyes.

Then it dawned on me that the feelings that were flowing through me were coming from the Lord. He gave me a brief, yet life-changing glimpse into how deeply He loves that precious daughter-in-law. He also showed me how He views her selfless acts of love and service for her family and others. I am not sure most of the recipients of her acts of love even know of the sacrifices she makes to serve them.

As I pondered over that experience on the drive home, it came to my mind that the Lord had taught me, through her, what it means to be on the *errand of angels*. I learned in a greater degree that day, that angels are not always someone from the other side of the veil that come to our aid; as often, they are someone who is no different than you or I, that recognizes a need, and quietly fills it.

We all have the power of Angelhood within us. Is that even a word? If not, it should be, because it helps us realize the divine role of all angels, even ones in mortal bodies.

Even the least of us can be anxiously engaged in the "errand of angels". All it takes is seeing a need and filling it. No act of kindness or service is too small or unimportant to the Lord. Besides, it is often through those tiny acts of service and love that the greatest blessings come. Never underestimate the blessings that the Lord is able to bestow through our simple but heart felt acts of love and service.

If you do not think your efforts matter to anyone, then think of small and simple acts of kindness that have been shown to you…even and especially when you feel you least deserved them.

To put it another way, the errand of angels is one of the ways our Savior shows His love for all of His children.

Walking In another Person's Footsteps

Let's look at it from the other side of the spectrum. How have you felt when you were being ignored, or like you were not good enough for someone else? Years ago when I was single, I visited a married friend's Ward. After Sacrament Meeting, she introduced me to the Stake Young Adult President. He took me to the classroom where the Young Adult Sunday School class was being held and told me he had some business to attend to, and that was the last I saw of him.

There were only one or two other single adults in the tiny town I lived in, so I was excited to be able to attend a Sunday School class that was filled with singles that were my age. Yet, as the seats began to fill, not one person acknowledged my presence. I assumed the reason might have to do with there being a steady flow of new people. However, as the teacher opened the class, no one other than two people on the other side of the room, were introduced as being new to the class.

I fought hard against the mounting feeling that I might be invisible to all those in the room. However, I started losing the battle when the girls sitting on either side of me seemed oblivious that anything other than a chair was between them. I think it would have been less humiliating, if they had simply asked if I would move over so they could sit next to each other...as each time they leaned over me to whisper to each other, it was a painful reminder that I was indeed being ignored!

My suspicions were confirmed, when a sign up sheet was handed to the girl sitting to my left, and then she handed it over me to the girl on my right, without asking me if I wanted to see it. For the first time in my life, I knew what Claude Rains must have felt as the Invisible Man!

I got through that painful ordeal. However, it instilled in me an ever-present desire to always be aware of the new (or even familiar) face in the crowd who needs to be acknowledged and made to feel welcome. I love the hymn "As Sisters in Zion", because it is a reminder to me that the errand of angels is given to all of Father in Heaven's children, not just to women.

Imagine what the world will be like during the Millennium when every person on the earth will be on the errand of angels.

To you, who are still single, translate the errand of angels, into your relationships with other singles that you associate with at church, the Institute, at school, and in the work place. Even if you have no intention of marrying the person, imagine what your Christ-like efforts will do for them. You may be the only person they feel is a true friend, and your efforts to help them see their worth to the Lord and others, may be the catalyst needed for them to soar to their Celestial potential.

When my husband and I were serving in the singles Ward, there were less active singles that showed up to church looking shy and uncomfortable, who were quickly befriended by the other singles in the Ward who invited them to go to their Sunday night get-togethers. That act of friendship made it easy for the new people to become a part of their close-knit group. It was not long before they became active in church, and before the school year had ended, it was gratifying to see most of them either go on missions, or marry in the temple. To my knowledge, most of them are still active in the Church today, and continue to stay close to those who fellowshipped them.

Can you see why the errand of flesh and blood angels is desperately needed in a world where the love of God is diminishing? When we feel needed, accepted, and like we have great worth to others (especially to our eternal companion's), it is easier to feel our worth to the Lord.

Now, imagine a marriage where a husband and wife, along with their children, serve each other through daily selfless acts of love. Such a home would truly be a Heaven on Earth!

Something to remember is, no matter how simple or unimportant the task may seem, we should never forget that those we serve, are all gods and goddesses in embryo.

Those simple acts of kindness may be the spark that will light the candle within the recipient that will burn bright, to light the way that others, as well as future generations, will want to follow. Think of it this way, what we do for others is the same as doing it for the Lord (Matthew 25:40).

Notes:

1. "Marriage and Divorce" – Spencer W. Kimball, BYU Devotional Address given on 7 September 1976

Chapter Four

Dating – Nothing Ventured – Nothing Gained

I knew a returned missionary, who continued to wear his missionary nametag as if it were his badge of honor. He also spent a good amount of his time going on splits with the missionaries. It was admirable that he wanted to continue to share the Gospel with others, and I have no doubt that the missionaries appreciated his being willing to help them out. But, he was no longer a full-time missionary, and he needed to get a job, go to school, and *start dating*.

Fortunately, there was a very wise and courageous young woman in the young adult group he "hung out" with, who gave him a book, "Dating No Guts No Glory". It seemed to be just what he needed, as reading it gave him the courage to start dating and getting back into civilian life again.

It was from his associations with his young adult friends that he met and fell in love with the beautiful young woman, who is now his wife.

Asking a young woman to go on a date, can be a scary undertaking for even the most confident returned missionary. It takes a lot of courage for a fledgling R.M. (returned missionary) who has just been kicked out of the safety of the do-not-date-nest, to spreading his wings and learning to fly with confidence, as he starts to immerse himself in the dating-someone-to-marry mode.

Before his mission, if the young man chose to follow the counsel of our Church leaders, he had the safety of the counsel of our Church leaders to avoid serious dating, and to go on group dates whenever possible. Making the transition from maintaining arms distance, to asking a young woman on a date where they will be alone, is new territory for the fledgling R.M. because it has the potential to destroy his confidence.

Some young men transition into the "serious" dating mode with grace and ease, whereas others may go months and even years before getting up enough nerve to approach a young woman and manage to get out those terrifying words, "Would you like to go on a date with me?"

Our Church leaders have said that a woman will not be held accountable if she does not marry in this life (through no fault of her own). However, the men will be held accountable if they do not make the effort to marry and start their own family while in this life.

With the responsibility being placed on the man to initiate dating, as well as the marriage proposal, it would make his job much less stressful if the woman would make the process less painful and more enjoyable for him. Far too many single women give little consideration to the consequences of their thoughtless or unkind rejections when they choose to turn down a date.

You single young women, be kind if you MUST turn down a date. Do not make the guy feel like he just stepped out of a leper colony. Besides, you do not want to be responsible for causing the young man to be too scared to ask anyone else out, including his future eternal companion, do you?

Remember the Golden Rule when someone you do not want to go out with asks you on a date, as you may be the one on the receiving end someday, and you will want that person to treat you with kindness and consideration for your feelings. It is amazing how often what we do unto others come back to either haunt us, or bless us. I speak from experience of having been on both sides of the fence!

Dating 101

When I was a young adult, it seemed that getting married and having a family was the goal of most of my peers. However, now with more single women pursuing professional careers and putting off marriage and family…and more and more men who seem to shy away from the marriage commitment…we are seeing an increase of singles waiting until they are well into their late twenties and mid thirties before getting serious about marriage.

In his article in *Time Magazine*, Les Grossman wrote, "The years from 18 until 25 and even beyond have become a distinct and separate life stage, a strange, transitional never-never land between adolescence and adulthood in which people stall for a few extra years, putting off the iron cage of adult responsibility that constantly threatens to crash down on them…What are they waiting for? Who are these permanent adolescents, these twenty-something Peter Pans? And why can't they grow up?" [1]

Our Church leaders counsel the 16-18 year olds to avoid pairing off, choosing instead the safety of group dates. However, when a young man returns from his mission, he is encouraged by our church leaders to be marriage-minded in how and whom he dates.

Along with making it easy for the young men to ask them on dates, the young women are encouraged not to expect the young men to spend unreasonable amounts of money on them that would hinder the young man from being able to provide for his living expenses and schooling.

With that in mind, I came up with some ideas for inexpensive dates that can be used by singles, as well as married couples:

1. Do family research together. New.FamilySearch.org and FamilySearch.org are great places to start and they do not cost anything to use. There are sites like Ancestry.com that offer free searches for some of what they offer, but if you want to search Census and military records, you need a paid subscription. The LDS Family History Centers now have access to the more popular paid subscription sites at no charge to the patron. Plus,

the patron will have access to microfilm and microfiche that can be ordered from the Salt Lake Family History Library and will have the help from volunteers at the Center that can aid in their research, at no charge.

2. If there is a temple close by, take names you have prepared and do baptisms for the dead. Or, if each of you is endowed, do other temple ordinances. Or, if there is a visitor's center on the temple grounds, watch Church movies. Or, the couple could walk around the temple grounds and discuss what the temple means to them.

3. Adopt a Grandparent at a nursing home. Pick a few days a month to visit them. Ask questions about their life, family, and interests, and let them do the talking. Remember and do something special for the person's birthday and other special days. However, remember to find out if they have dietary restrictions. The couple could do a sing-a-long or talent show; or play games that would include anyone in the nursing home that wants to participate.

4. Make cookies and thank-you cards for hospitalized veterans on Veterans Day. Check with the VA hospital first, to make sure they allow you to take cookies to their patients, as some may have dietary restrictions. Take the cards (and cookies if allowed) to each room and thank each veteran personally for their contributions and sacrifice for our country. Make sure to ask what war(s) they served in and ask them to share their stories. The most important part is to verbally thank them for their service in defending our freedoms and country.

5. Lay a large thick sheet of plastic on the grass, turn on a garden hose and run water on it while you run and slide on it. Or, set up a sprinkler in a grassy area and run through it.

6. Visit a pet store and play with the pets that the store allows you to play with.

7. Offer to watch a couple's children so they can go on a date, or so they can go to the temple. This will help you get a better idea how your date deals with children and stressful situations as it is hard to watch children without stressful situations coming up.

8. Teach each other skills such as how to do laundry, clothing repairs, sewing, ironing, cooking, gardening, car repairs, the use of tools and kitchen appliances, or computer skills, etc.

9. Take dance lessons or other classes through the parks and recreation center or extension departments.

10. Go to the beach and watch the sunset while talking over your career and/or schooling goals. Or, lie on the grass or blanket outside and see what shapes you can see in the clouds.

11. Repair and/or refinish a piece of furniture together.

12. Check out movies from the library and watch them together or go to the library together to study.

13. Service Scavenger Hunt: Go around your neighborhood and ask neighbors if there is something you can do for them, such as yard work, dishes, reading to kids, etc. If they say, "No", offer to sing a Primary song for them. "I am a Child of God" is always a good choice. Do not go into a home that you do not feel comfortable doing so.

14. Make up additional or new words to Primary Songs and sing them together. Sing songs to or with each other karaoke style. You can sing or lip sink along with the artists if you are not comfortable singing a solo.

15. Go through your photographs and share your memories with each other. This would be a good time to make sure the photos have descriptions on them. Make scrapbooks or photo journals from your mission, high school, or other photos.

16. Go visit each other's parents or other family members. It would help you to see what each other's family is like.

17. Learn the alphabet and some simple signs from sign language, and try to have a conversation with each other using them.

18. If one or both of you knows a foreign language, teach the other some simple phrases used in conversations.

19. Go through recipes together and come up with some inexpensive dinners for the week. Go shopping together for ingredients you do not have. Then cook and eat the dinners together.

20. Play board and card games together or make up your own games.

21. Go walking, running, rollerblading, bicycling, playing in the snow, or swimming together.

22. Go to the zoo, museum or art museum together.

23. Play with matchbox cars together. You could draw or paint your own streets and buildings on an inexpensive tablecloth.

24. Watch a children's movie on your computer or TV. Make some popcorn and root beer floats to enjoy.

25. Clean up trash along the road together.

26. Offer to do yard work, clean house or go shopping for or with an elderly or sick person.

27. Use large pieces of cardboard and slide down a grassy or sandy hill.

28. Make your own video or music video together.

29. Plan a surprise dinner and make up a clever way to invite the other person, or have a theme dinner. You could go to a second hand store and buy costumes. The evening could end by having a fun activity and/or dancing to music from the time-period or theme you chose. Or you could plan a mystery dinner where numbers coincide with different

foods, utensils and dishes, or plan a meal where you feed each other using odd kitchen utensils and dishes.

30. Read and discuss an article in the *Ensign* or a General Conference talk found on LDS.org once a week, and/or read good books together. You could even write a book together.

31. Make bread, or a cake or cookies together, and decorate the cake or cookies. Take them to neighbors or friends.

32. Make a duct tape book cover or wallet; or make clothes from duct tape and wear them on a date in public. However, first make sure they will not come apart with movement. There are contests that pay good money for duct tape clothing and creations. (You can go to places like: avonducttapefestival.com and houston.com/education/19834261/detail.html or type in "duct tape clothes" on a Google search to get ideas)

33. Make homemade cards for family and friends.

34. Cardboard Drive-in Movie: Get cardboard boxes that comfortably fit around each of you in a sitting position. Then each of you designs a car. They can be as elaborate or as simple as you wish. Cook some popcorn and get some drinks and sit in your cars on the living room floor while you watch a movie together.

35. Choose a country to study together. Learn about the history, clothing, culture and foods. Then look for recipes and create a menu from foods from that country. Have a dinner and make sure to dress the part. If you are able, include music and decorations to go along with the theme. To make it more fun, choose names from that country for each of you to use for the evening and make sure to speak with accents. Take pictures or a video that you could watch at a cardboard car drive-in movie night (see #34).

36. Paint t-shirts with fabric paints or permanent markers. Wear them when you go into public (i.e.: "I am with him" with an arrow pointing off to the side and "I am with her" with an arrow pointing the opposite direction; or "I found my stripling warrior" for her, and "I found my 8 cow girlfriend/wife" for him).

37. Get two Rubix Cubes® and scramble them and see who can finish it first. Google "Rubix Cube" to find helps and instructions.

38. Work a crossword puzzle, Sudoku or play Tick Tack Toe together. There are free sites on the Internet where you can make up your own puzzles.

39. Buy a cheap pair of sunglasses for each of you at a dollar store. Then buy or cut out shapes and designs from colored cardstock or colored foam to glue to the frames. Use craft glue, a hot glue gun or sticky tabs used in scrapbooking to secure them. If you are

bold, wear them to the mall while window shopping, or while taking a walk on the beach or in the park.

40. Go through old Church magazines (*Friend, New Era, and Ensign*), cut out pictures and make a collage of things that represent your goals and who you are.

41. Go to a doctor's office and ask if they have any outdated magazines that you can have. Go through them and make collages of places you would like to visit or types of furniture, decorating or landscaping ideas you like.

42. The guy could polish the girl's finger and toe nails and then the girl could clip and file the man's nails.

43. Write and share poems and/or songs about each other. Or you could find poems and/or songs that express what you feel for each other…however, coming up with one on your own will have more of an impact on the recipient.

44. Write a children's book together - complete with illustrations, and either save it for your future children, or read it and/or give it to a child that you know.

45. Make up a recipe, cook it and eat it together. Make sure to write down the ingredients and directions if it turns out good.

46. Make your favorite collection of recipes. You could make your own cookbook out of the ones you collect. You could also put them on a DVD to share with others.

47. Make shadow puppets on the wall.

48. Sit across from each other and then while looking into each other's eyes, take turns telling a few of your hopes and dreams. Then sit for 5 minutes staring into each other's eyes without saying anything to each other. This may feel silly or be awkward at first, but hang in there. I have read where strangers who have done this as an assigned activity have ended up getting married to each other.

49. Tell a story together. It can be about a real event or a made up one. One person starts and after a minute (it would help to use a timer), the other person picks up where the first person let off, and then go back and forth until the story is complete. You can record it if you wish so you do not forget it and can listen to it later. If you video tape it, you can watch it at a cardboard car drive-in movie night (see #34).

50. Make sand castles or sand creations together at the beach. If you do not live near a beach, then bring it to you. Put some sand in a hard plastic kiddy pool or sand box in the backyard and pour enough water over it to get it wet enough to stick together, and then have fun making your creations together.

51. Watch a familiar movie with the volume off, then each of you take different parts. You can make up lines to make it funnier if you wish. "Princess Bride" is a great one to do this with.

52. Color in coloring books together. You can also upload photographs into a coloring book page on the Crayola.com site. However, you will need a code from a box of Crayola Crayons ® to print them, and make sure the box has a sign saying it has the code inside of the box before buying it. You can also look on the Internet for sites where you can upload a picture to turn into a coloring page.

53. Make origami together (you can find instructions on the Internet).

54. Watch favorite chick flicks and guy movies together. Discuss with each other what you like or dislike about them. Warning! Be sensitive with each others feelings with this one.

55. Watch a movie or TV show and when the commercials come on, mute the volume and ask each other a question. Write the questions before hand (i.e.: "What is your favorite pastime?", "What are your favorite books or movies and why?", "What do you want to do with your life?", "If you were given a million dollars and told you could do anything you want with it, what would that be?"). Or, you can say one thing you admire about each other.

56. Build something together with Lego's ®.

57. Make a creation together out of Popsicle ® sticks.

58. Read "The Family: A Proclamation to the World" and discuss what it means to you.

59. Together, read "Between Husband and Wife" by Lamb and Brinley (set aside time that works best for you until the book is completed). Make sure to discuss the different parts of the book with each other.

60. Read "the Divine Center" by Stephen Covey, and discuss with each other what you learned from it.

(These dating ideas were designed to help couples to improve and blend their spiritual, emotional, psychological and even physical aspects of their relationship.)

In his May 1, 2005 CES address to the young adults of the Church, Elder Dallin H. Oaks expressed his concern that too many marriage-aged young adults are choosing to "hang out" rather than date for the purpose of marriage. After hearing that inspired and enlightening talk by Elder Oaks, my husband and the other members of the Bishopric (in the singles Ward he served in) decided it was time to provide the opportunity for the young adults in the Ward to hear the message again. When it was my husband's turn to put on the Family Home Evening lesson, he chose to implement Elder Oaks talk. The following is his account of the events of that evening:

"I girded my loins, said a prayer of faith that it would go well and of repentance if it did not, and planned the evening's event. The women would go to one room and the men to another in order to make a list of things that each wished the other would know/recognize/acknowledge/avoid/etc. If you ever decide to do this, make sure your seat belt is fastened. It was sort of like riding a roller coaster. The men went first and were, almost without exception, gentle and almost apologetic about what they said. I will omit the gory details about how some of the sisters acted, but I will admit to having neglected to foresee the need of setting up a first-aid station.

"Actually, for the most part it was pretty good. Admittedly, the most vocal females (as of this writing, some four years later) are still single. And most of the girls were not all that vicious. The interesting part of the whole experience was that the rate of dating increased and several young men, many of whom had been either wallflowers or 'afraid of commitment', started dating and many of them married and are now serving in many of the local wards."

It was encouraging to see so many of the young adults take seriously the inspired counsel of Elder Oaks as well as their Ward leaders.

As important as it is for young adults (and sometimes the not so young adults) to be anxiously engaged in finding their eternal companions, I fear that too many either rush blindly into marriage without paying much attention to whether or not they are equally yoked with the person they are considering spending eternity with, or they are so afraid of the outcome if they do get married that they become overly concerned that they will add to the statistics of those whose marriages never made it much past the starting gates, or in this case, the gates of the temple. Thus, far too many of these overly cautious singles either lose hope that they will ever marry, or become so set in their ways or are cynical, or critical of the opposite sex that the potential mates dare not come within verbal battering range out of fear of becoming a casualty of war.

Either way, it would be wise for those who feel like the prospect for marriage is passing them by to remember that is it easier to catch flies with honey rather than with vinegar…not that the potential mate should be compared to a fly.

Are You Someone You Would Consider Marrying?

To the one who desires marriage, but pursuers seem to be too few and far between, there are numerous articles written where the authors suggest that the wise single (whether young or old) might consider taking a careful inventory of the following items. Let me first point out that these suggestions are not meant to offend, but to enlighten; and are given in a spirit of love, not criticism. In addition, let me point out that these are excellent suggestions for anyone who desires to take a personal inventory, including long time spouses who desire to become more refined:

1. Grooming habits:
   - Is your hair clean and neatly styled? If you are a guy, do you need a hair cut?
   - Is your hairstyle outdated? Is it flattering to your facial features?
   - If you are a girl, are you in the habit of pulling your hair back into a ponytail, or do you take the time to make sure your hair is attractive *most* days? Do you have extreme hairstyles or haircuts; and/or do you put extreme colors in your hair?
   - If you are a female, do you wear makeup daily? If you do wear makeup, is it too much or too little? Is it appropriate for the occasion?
   - If you wear jewelry, is it too gaudy, or do you wear too much jewelry? If you are a female and have pierced ears, do you follow the prophetic counsel about wearing only one pair of earrings? If you are a male, pierced ears are not appropriate for priesthood holders. Do you have piercings anywhere else on your body? Read what our Church leaders have said about body piercings and tattoos on LDS.org. Once there, click on *Menu* and then on *Youth* under the heading *Family;* then click on *For the Strength of Youth;* then click on *Dress and Appearance.* In 1 Corinthians 3:16-17 it says, "Know ye not that ye are the temple of God, and that the Spirit of God dwelleth in you? If any man defile the temple of God, him shall God destroy; for the temple of God is holy, which temple ye are."
   - Do you brush and floss your teeth daily? Do you need to whiten your teeth? Do you see a dentist for regular cleanings, and to check for cavities? Do you use breath mints or mouthwash if you have bad breath?
   - Do you shower and use deodorant daily? Do you use deodorant that has a strong offensive smell? Do you use lotion or moisturizer if you have dry hands or skin?
   - Are your fingernails and toenails clean and trimmed? If you are a female and wear nail polish, is it chipped and in need of repainting? Do you use extreme colors?
   - Are your clothes clean and neatly pressed, and/or do they need to be repaired? Do your clothes match, and are your shoes clean and/or polished?
   - Do you dress appropriately for the occasion? Are your dresses or shorts too short or too revealing? If you are endowed, do you let your religion show? Hopefully there is no need for explanation.

2. Conversing with others:
   - Are you upbeat and happy, or depressed and moody? Do you smile or scowl?

- Are you loud? Do you dominate a conversation? Do you draw attention to yourself? Do you ask others about themselves?
- Are you a good listener, or do others have trouble getting a word into the conversation?
- Do you give others the benefit of the doubt, or do you accuse and find fault without hearing the other person's side of things?
- Are you respectful, and do you keep confidences?
- Do you gossip or speak ill of others?
- Do you use foul language or tell vulgar or off color jokes?
- Do your conversations make others want to lift their standards and sights?
- Do you repeat the same stories and jokes over and over again?
- Are you a judge or a light in what you say and how you act?
- Are you bossy? Do you order people around?
- Do you look people in the eye or do you divert your attention from any and all eye contact?
- Do you have to be right all the time? Are you arrogant or boastful? Do you come across as your opinion in is the only opinion?

3. Habits or eccentricities:
   - Do others shy away from you? If you are not sure, start paying attention to when others seem to back off when you are around. Also, if this is happening, pay attention to what it is about your behavior or comments that seems to trigger others seeking an exit.
   - Do your tastes in movies, music, or T.V. programs offend or turn people off?
   - Do you bite your fingernails? Do you have habits like chewing on pencils or pens? Do you tap your fingers repeatedly?
   - Do you interrupt others on a regular basis?
   - Do you have addictions that would cause people with high standards to shy away? If so, have you seen your priesthood leader and if needed, a professional counselor for help? If not, why not?

4. Health and appearance:
   - Do you practice good health habits?
   - Do you eat healthy foods or do you have a steady diet of junk food?

- Are you heavier or slimmer than is healthy? If so, is there anything that you can do about it? If you have tried and have trouble with either taking off or putting on weight, then make sure to wear clothing that is flattering, that does not accentuate your size. Hint: Black is very slimming; horizontal stripes tend to accentuate a wider waistline, where as, for the slimmer person, it can be more flattering. Study styles and designs in material or clothing that are more flattering for your body shape.
- Do you exercise on a regular basis, or are you a couch potato?
- Do you stand straight, holding your shoulders back? Do you sit up straight, or do you slouch when sitting in a chair?
- Do you get at least 6-8 hours of sleep each night, or do you go to bed late and wake up when you feel like it?

5. Education and responsibility:
   - Are you improving your life through education and/or are you gainfully employed?
   - Are you responsible with your finances? Do you keep a budget, or do you spend your money as quickly as it comes into your possession?
   - Can others count on you to keep your word?
   - Are you satisfied with mediocrity, or are you focused on becoming your best self?
   - Are you a good team player or do you try to accomplish things on your own without seeking advice or help from others? Jethro, Moses' father-in-law, reminded Moses that he could not do and be all things to others; that he needed to delegate his responsibilities and seek for help when his load became too heavy to bear alone (Exodus 18:13-26).

6. Pay attention to others who are well liked and respected:
   - What do you like about them? What do others like about them?
   - Are there traits about them that you could incorporate?
   - How do they treat others? How do they treat those who are less popular? How do they handle stress? How do they act when driving in rush hour traffic?

7. Modesty and Spirituality:
   - Do you read and study your scriptures and pray daily?
   - Do you attend *all* your church meetings and magnify your callings?
   - Do you ward hop or look for excuses to miss or leave church early or not go at all?

- Do you magnify your callings, or do you find reasons for not accepting, or fulfilling your callings?
- Are you modest in your dress and appearance?
- Would you feel comfortable with your movies and forms of entertainment and music if the prophet or Savior were in the room with you?
- Are you temple worthy? If not, are you working with your priesthood leaders to become temple worthy?
- If you are temple worthy, do you attend often?

8. Manners and Etiquette:
   - Do you use proper manners?
   - If you are a guy, do you open and hold doors for females? If you are a female, do you let the young man open and hold doors for you?
   - Do you thank people for things they do for you?
   - Do you compliment others, especially your date or spouse?
   - Guys, do you hold chairs for the ladies?
   - Guys, do you stand when a lady enters the room?
   - Guys, do you offer your chair to the ladies?
   - Do you intentionally make offensive noises in public? If it happens by accident, do you say "Excuse me"?
   - Do you offer to share what you are eating with others in the room?
   - If you get something for yourself to eat or drink, do you offer to get some for your date or spouse?
   - When invited to dinner, do you offer to help prepare it, clean off the table, and to help with the dishes?

Something to consider after careful evaluation of the items above is if you are single, do you feel you fit the profile of someone you would be interested in dating and/or marrying? If you are already married, then ask yourself if you are the kind of spouse you would want to be married to.

No matter what your answer is, and no matter whether or not you are married or single, it would be a good idea to review the items on the list from time to time to see if there are areas in your life that need some attention or course corrections.

One of the best ways to show your spouse or potential spouse that you love them is to give them your best self!

Hint to the single person: Do not expect a potential suitor to accept you the way you are if you possess traits or habits that would cause you to lose interest in someone who possessed them.

If you want to read some of the counsel and suggestions from our Church leaders on this subject, then go to LDS.org; then type in *A Parent's Guide* in the search box; and then click on A Parent's Guide on the right side bar; and click on *Chapter Six: Mature Intimacy: Courtship and Marriage.*

"I learned to love him more than I have ever loved before or after." - Maria Von Trapp

Many years ago after seeing the movie "Sound of Music" with a friend, she made the comment: "It better happen just like that for me or I am not going to get married!"

I knew she was joking at the time…at least I think she was…and I remember being amused over her comment. However, I cannot help but wonder if some of the young adults (and not so young adults) are expecting something that is unrealistic in a spouse, and it is keeping them from recognizing the person the Lord would be pleased for them to marry.

A little side note: When I read the real account of Maria von Trapp in her book: "The Story of the von Trapp Family Singers" (published in 1949), I found out that the movie version was very different from the real life account between Maria and Captain Georg von Trapp. In her account, she told how she did not marry the Captain because of being in love with him. In her own words, she explained: "I really and truly was not in love. I liked him but did not love him. However, I loved the children, so in a way I really married the children…[B]y and *by I learned to love him more than I have ever loved before or after.*" (Italics added) [2]

In fact, the real account of how Maria and Georg fell in love and married was much more of a true-to-life love story than the one portrayed in the movie. It is a story that bears repeating over and over again, for that very reason.

Notes:
1. "Grow Up? Not So Fast", *Time,* Jan. 24, 2005, 44, 42
2. *Movie vs. Reality: The Real Story of the von Trapp Family,*
   By Joan Gearin, Winter 2005, Vol. 37, No. 4 (page 42)

Chapter Five

Marriage is a Partnership with God - So Choose Wisely

There is only one thing more beautiful and endearing than "young love", and that is "love" that has endured the test of time, that has been tempered and strengthened in the furnace of adversity and affliction. The tell-tale signs of such *love* can be seen in the radiant glow of faces that have long sense lost their youthful beauty—in hands, though gnarled, are tightly clasped—in bodies, though bowed with age and slow of gait, still exude the energy of youthful vigor when in the presence of their beloved—and whose hearts, though battle scared and weary, still burn bright with loving devotion one for another.

This type of "love" is not found so much in gazing *at* each other, as in gazing forward in the same eternal direction. Such a relationship is evidence of God's handiwork...a hallmark of the beauty and majesty of celestial love.

The perfect wedding picture has not been captured on film...at least no film that I know of...and not by the mortal eye. For the "ideal portrait" would show the newlywed couple wrapped in Christ's loving embrace. Imagine the potential of a couple if such a portrait could be displayed in a prominent place in their home, acting as a constant reminder of "Who" should be an integral part of their marriage, family life, and home. For it is when God is allowed to be the Architect of such a relationship, that nothing less than a "celestial masterpiece" should be expected.

Grounds for a Celestial Marriage

A lasting and happy marriage is the result of a husband and wife falling in love over and over again...even though there are times when weaknesses and diversities cloud their eternal perspective of each other. Billy Graham said the secret to his lasting marriage, is that he and his wife are "happily incompatible". It is when husbands and wives learn to accept and blend their incompatibilities that love and happiness is able to flourish in their relationship.

Robert Browning said, "Grow old along with me. The best is yet to be - the last of life for which the first was made."

As eloquent as Mr. Browning's words were, I would like to add an eternal perspective to them: "The best is yet to be – together beyond the veil for which the first was made."

Learning to keep an eternal perspective when the going gets tough and the way seems impossible will ensure safer passage towards eternal goals. Truth be told, every marriage that is more than a week old, has the grounds for an annulment or a divorce. Therefore, it is a wise and vigilant couple who, instead of looking for grounds for a divorce, is constantly planting and nurturing seeds for a Celestial marriage.

As beautiful and exhilarating as young love is to behold and experience, such feelings can fade quickly if they are not nurtured and safeguarded on a daily basis. After all, it is not enough to marry the one you love...the magic happens when you continue to love the one you married.

Learning to turn "I dos" into, "We dos" can add beauty and depth to a budding relationship between newly weds...for it is in such a bond that the necessary elements of celestial love are enhanced and reinforced with each passing day.

Paul told the Corinthians, "Love never gives up, never loses faith, is always hopeful, and endures through every circumstance" (1 Corinthians 13:7). This should be a *creed* that every husband and wife would do well to incorporate into their "I dos"

It Is Important To Be Mr. or Mrs. Right

Why would anyone who is contemplating marriage, make the decision lightly? After all, *who* to marry is one of the greatest decisions men and women will make in this life. Consider if you will, the rippling effect from that solitary decision, as it can affect the eternal destiny of not only the husband and wife, but countless generations that have the potential to come from their union. After all, all it takes to lose countless generations is for one generation of parents to fall short in leading by example, lacking the courage to hold fast to the Iron Rod, and in failing to teach their children correct doctrines and principles.

A tragic example of this is Laman and Lemuel, whose poor choices brought about the lack of Gospel blessings not only in their own lives, but the lives of their descendents...including generations that are on the earth today.

Why is it that some singles are very confident in their decision about whom to marry, when others struggle with uncertainty or fear that they will make a wrong choice? Then there are those singles who believe that there is only "one true love" or "soul mate" for them. Such thinking makes it is nearly impossible for them to recognize a prospective mate, because no one that they meet seems to be a perfect match for them.

For those singles who struggle with recognizing "Mr. or Mrs. Right", Zig Ziglar (a popular motivational speaker) said: "I have no way of knowing whether or not you married the wrong person, but I do know that many people have a lot of wrong ideas about marriage and what it takes to make that marriage happy and successful. I'll be the first to admit that it's possible that you did marry the wrong person. However, if you treat the wrong person like the right person, you could well end up having married the right person after all. On the other hand, if you marry the right person, and treat that person wrong, you certainly will have ended up marrying the wrong person. I also know that it is far more important to be the right kind of person than it is to marry the right person. In short, whether you married the right or wrong person is primarily up to you."

Mr. Ziglar's quote caught my attention as it so closely aligns with what President Spencer W. Kimball said about any good husband or wife being able to make a marriage work if they are willing to pay the price. [1]

Many people seem to think that they have to feel romantic love for the person they marry. However, it is not romantic love that binds hearts and holds marriages together, for there are far too many divorced men and women who are still deeply in-love with their former spouse. Therefore, the love that has staying power comes from the consistent and daily efforts of husbands and wives in loving and forgiving each other. *Love* is a verb as well as a noun. Therefore, "like" can quickly turn into "love" when selflessness, service and tenderness become each husband and wife's individual as well as collective clarion call.

However, in regards to "soul mates" (as President Spencer W. Kimball referred to in his "Oneness in Marriage" talk [1]), I believe that any couple, no matter how diverse, who will cultivate Christ-like traits in their marriage, will in time, find that they have become compatible with each other in disposition, point of view, and sensitivity…which *is* the definition of "soul mates".

As desirable as it is to be on the same page with each other, it would be good for the couple to remember that becoming "one" in disposition, point of view, and sensitivity, cannot be forced or coerced. Such a relationship will eventually get to a point when getting along is no longer on the couple's list of "to-dos", but will be a natural outcome of their Christ-like attitudes and efforts.

The formula to finding Mr. or Mrs. Right quite simply is to *persist in becoming* Mr. or Mrs. Right, even and especially after years of being married.

Flesh of My Flesh, Bone of My Bone

It is very common when bitten by the "love bug", for couples to view each other's differences as no more than harmless annoyances—and in such a euphoric state, there is no more beautiful sight than of the one who has captured his or her heart. However, the frustration comes into play when their diversities and the realities of married life start to cloud the couple's vision. Furthermore, it is when this unavoidable metamorphosis takes place that recalling what it was that first attracted them to each other, can be a daunting task. However, going through this *marital refiner's fire*, is a necessary step for their relationship to be able to blossom into one that is suited for the Celestial Kingdom.

When a couple goes through these growing pains, it is common for one or both to invite and even nurture thoughts of abandoning their eternal hopes and dreams with each other. When tempers are flaring and good judgment has been replaced with selfishness, pettiness, shortsightedness, bitterness and hurt feelings, it would be wise for the husband and wife to remember that much more can be accomplished by quickly approaching Heaven's door rather than looking for ways to exit their front door.

Even the most battle weary and thread-bear relationship can come to experience the depths of the emotions that filled Adam's heart when he beheld for the first time, his beloved Eve in all her radiant beauty and splendor, where he exclaimed from the depths of his soul, "This [Eve] *is* now bone of my bones, and flesh of my flesh: she shall be called Woman, because she was taken out of Man."

The imagery and symbolism found in that simple yet eloquent phrase, gives a perfect pattern for every couple to embrace and cultivate. For it is only when a husband and wife have learned to become "one" in heart, mind, purpose, body and soul that they can come to imbue the pure testimony that was borne to Adam's heart and mind of the divine roles and purposes of Celestial bound husbands and wives.

Such a relationship is not only deliciously desirable, but also possible with the mind expanding and strengthening that comes through impressions and tutoring of the Spirit. For it is only through His guidance and tutoring that the diligent husband and wife are able to fulfill not only their individual, but also their collective missions in this life as well as in the eternities.

The downside of not working towards "oneness" in marriage, is that the alternative can lead to "parallel lives", which in and of itself can lead to a marriage that would be more akin to a couple of remaining strands of a rope that is being used to tether a ship to a dock, while being battered by hurricane force winds. In such a relationship, the husband and wife can live in the same house, but have little in common—rarely speaking or connecting emotionally, spiritually, or physically. The dangers in allowing such a relationship to go unchecked or unaltered, can lead to "marital suicide".

Capturing the essence of "love-gone-right" is not an easy task. However, it is a noble and worthy one that not only can bring some of our Father's sweetest joys and blessings, but also has the power to bless future generations who will be able to see firsthand, what a covenant marriage should be like.

Wouldn't it then, make sense for each husband and wife to commit daily to cultivating their "at-one-ment" with each other, as well as with the Lord? For it is only when they make those courageous and sterling efforts, that they can come to experience the euphoria of knowing what Adam felt when he exclaimed, "This [Eve] *is* now bone of my bones, and flesh of my flesh".

The Lord's Way, Or No Way!

So, if marriage is to be a partnership with God, wouldn't it make sense to include Him in the decision process? In addition, even if any good man or woman can make a marriage work, wouldn't it be much better and wiser for the man and woman to start out on more solid footing, by seeking first the mind and will of the Lord about their decision to marry?

I once heard a Bishop tell how when couples would come to him with their marital problems, he would first ask them to remember the answer they got when they prayed to know if they should marry each other. He said he was alarmed and frustrated when time and time again the couples would give him a look of confusion as they said they never considered praying to know if they should marry each other. Upon hearing such disappointing confessions, he would then ask them why they would not ask for the Lord's approval when making the most important decision of their lives.

Preparing for Life's Most Important Journey

Once the Lord has given His approval of a couple's decision to marry, then, the natural outcome would be for them to become engaged to be married. Some of you may be wondering what the need is for an engagement period. After all, it is hard to understand why anyone would want to be involved in family feuds and financial hardships for themselves, as well as for their parents that are the result of most, if not all weddings and wedding receptions. So, why do it? To answer that question, I will first give a brief history and explanation of this long-standing ritual.

First of all, the engagement is an agreement between a man and woman who has decided to become husband and wife, and to start a family of their own. In Biblical times, it was customary for couples to become betrothed before getting married. Those betrothals usually lasted a year.

At the betrothal ceremony, it was customary for the groom to give money to the bride so she could purchase linens and items for the home that he was supposed to build for them.

After the betrothal ceremony, the bride and groom became husband and wife, however, they did not live together, nor did they consummate their marriage until the formal ceremony took place, usually at the end of a year. Nevertheless, if for any reason during the betrothal, one or the other did something to break the marriage contract, the couple would have the option of going through a legal divorce.

On the evening the bride and groom were to finalize their marriage, there was a ceremony where the groom would go to each home of their friends and family looking for his bride. Each time he would stop at a home, the inhabitants of the house would say the bride was not there. Then the people of the house would join the groom in helping him look for his bride.

This continued until the groom arrived at the home where his bride was waiting for him—which was usually her parent's home. The bride and groom, along with all their wedding guests, would then go to the place where the wedding ceremony was to take place.

However, in modern Western culture, the betrothal has evolved into a less formal practice referred to as "the engagement". It is customary in some cultures, for the man to give the woman an engagement ring. In some countries, it is customary for the engaged man to wear his wedding band on his right ring finger until he is married, then he changes it to his left ring finger. I like that custom, as it lets other single women know that he has been removed from their potential-mate-list.

It is less common now, but it used to be set in stone, that unless the single woman's father gave his approval for the man to marry his daughter, the marriage did not take place.

Getting engaged seems to be losing the more formal approach, as it is more and more common for a single man or woman to simply *ask* the other to marry them. There are some couples, who get married without a proposal or an engagement period. I have known couples, who decided they wanted to marry each other; so they went to the justice of the peace and got married without telling anyone until after they had become husband and wife.

Recently, I read an account of a widowed ancestor of mine who became very close to her deceased husband's financial advisor, who subsequently became her financial advisor. One evening while she was mending some clothes, the financial advisor showed up at her home with a minister and announced, "I think it is time for us to get married, so why wait?"

According to the account, I do not believe he waited for an answer from her, as it was reported that she put her mending down on a table beside the chair she was sitting in, and stood in front of the minister, and the ceremony commenced.

A little hint: I would NOT recommend that way of getting married, especially with Temple weddings, as couples cannot elope to the temple because they need an interview with their Bishop and Stake President to be able to get a recommend to be married in the temple. However, my husband has said numerous times that it would be so much easier for the couple if they could elope to the temple, then all the drama and expense that is associated with most weddings could be avoided. However, I say it would only postpone much worse and longer lasting drama that would pretty much be assured, after it comes to the attention of the parents and family members, that their beloved family member got married without letting them be a part of the wedding plans and ceremony.

Sometimes the parents of either the man or the woman choose to announce the couple's engagement to friends and family at a formal gathering. However, finding newer and more cleaver ways of letting family and friends know of the couple's decision to marry, have evolved into anything from sending out e-mails to text messages, and even placing the announcement on *facebook*. I like the latter, as the couple's engagement story and pictures usually accompany it. Let's face it, wedding announcements alone, do not give anyone any idea of how the couple met, fell in love, and made the decision to marry. If you are a hopeless romantic like I am, you love hearing the romantic and heartwarming stories about how a couple met, fell in love, and got engaged, rather than just being told when and where the wedding and wedding reception will take place.

The engagement period should be a time used for the couple to get to know each other better, as well as to prepare them for when they will become a family unit. Imagine the outcome, if more couples during the engagement period, would put in as much (or more) focus and effort into planning the next 50-70 years (as well as eternity) together as husband and wife as they do with planning their "perfect wedding".

Sadly, as exciting as their falling in-love story and the engagement and wedding day are, it seems what happens after the wedding day, lacks the luster and excitement to keep the couple's family and friends interest for very long. What is wrong with a society that places more focus on the joining of couples, rather than helping them learn how to stay together before they say their "I dos"?

All too often, too little mentoring is done, and too few good examples are given for youth, young adults, and young marrieds' to follow. We can turn the tide, and turn we must! After all, in the rising generation is some of our Father in Heaven's choicest spirits who have been reserved to be the standard-bearers that will usher in the Second Coming. Then shouldn't we as their parents, aunts, uncles, grandparents, teachers, church leaders, and even friends, gird up our loins, take fresh courage, and seek for Divine guidance and insight into how we can become more sterling examples and mentors in teaching and training these children of a noble birthright, in their duties, and divine missions in life … even, and especially in their most important roles of being spouses and parents?

There is so much misinformation, as well as down right lies that are being spoon-fed to these choice spirit children of our Father in Heaven, which is causing many of them to loose sight of, and to in too many cases, abandon their divine missions altogether.

It used to be that parents taught their children homemaking skills, work ethic, and the skills of what it takes to be good husbands and wives, and fathers and mothers before they stepped over the threshold. Sadly and tragically, too many of the should-be-mentors, falsely believe that any effort to teach or train youth, young adults, and even young marrieds, in these skills, would be considered meddling, or taking away from their agency, when in fact, it is just the opposite. For, it is the Lord that has given parents, teachers, and leaders the charge to raise and *train* their children in the paths of righteousness (D&C 121:34-46) … not to stand idly by while watching newlyweds try to reinvent the matrimonial wheel. For it is in moments of frustration and doubt, when uneducated and un-mentored couples often choose to abandon the broken pieces of their marital relationship, tossing them by the wayside because they lack the skills or knowledge to know how to mend them before they are beyond repair.

Too often, the poor example of the "should-be mentors", sets the pattern for the fledgling newlyweds to follow. How are these young men and women to know how to build and strengthen their marriages when so many in their area of influence have chosen to treat their spouse's and children with a lack of commitment and love; or have chosen to break their marriage vows and covenants; and/or have abandoned home and family? After all, actions speak louder than words.

Parents and older family members can put in many hours tutoring and training these youth and young adults, but if those words have lost their impact because of the poor examples of those who impart them, what can we expect of the young bride and groom when they hit the rough open seas and storms that every marriage and family will go through?

In 2001, Pope John Paul II went as far as to suggest that parents and church leaders should give "…great care to the preparation of engaged couples and be close to young married couples, so that they will be for their children and the whole community an eloquent testimony of God's love." (Emphasis added)

It is for this very reason that I decided to write the "Pre-Wedding Study Guide for Latter-day Saint Couples" (which is included later in Chapter Six). Even though it is a study guide intended for engaged couples to read and study individually, as well as together, BEFORE and AFTER they become husband and wife, singles or couples (no matter how long they have been married), would benefit greatly from reviewing it periodically.

It would be wise for men and women to keep their eyes wide open before the wedding day, and then after they become husband and wife, to put on blinders and make sure to keep them firmly in place, unless of course there are real concerns for theirs or their children's' safety, physically, emotionally, and/or spiritually. In those cases, the spouse should seek their priesthood leader(s) and the Lord's guidance before making hasty and permanent decisions.

During the engagement, the bride and groom should pay close attention to each other's likes, dislikes, attitudes, quirks, and how the other treats those in their sphere of influence - especially family members…or soon-to-be family members.

However, after the couple has tied the knot, they would be wise to hone the skills of learning to overlook and forgive each other's faults, failings and sins…as well as learning to blend and celebrate each other's diversities. The same philosophy should be applied when dealing with each other's families. It is in developing these skills that some of the most endearing and wonderful relationships are kindled. Imagine eternity with family members that you have built celestial relationships with during this life, instead of living with heartache and regrets over broken or injured relationships that could have been avoided had Christ-like attitudes and forgiveness been applied … especially at times when it is the hardest and most challenging to do so.

Thy will, not mine be done…NO MATTER WHAT!

When the spiritual promptings are strong in whether to marry or not to marry, then the single man and/or woman should have the courage and conviction to follow those promptings…no matter how hard it may be…even if it means their fiancé or family and friends strongly oppose them. The Lord never said it would be easy, He only said it would be worth it…even in regards with whom, when, and where to marry. Therefore, learning to trust and follow the promptings of the Spirit, even with the "marriage decision", will bring blessings beyond comprehension…even though it may take some time before those blessings may be realized.

Choosing to disobey or to ignore the promptings of the Spirit…or choosing to get married without seeking the guidance of the Spirit, can lead to much misery, and in some cases, the outcome can be very tragic. However, not all disobedience to spiritual promptings turns out as tragic as the following story. My reason for sharing this very sad but true story is to act as a reminder of what can and has happened when people choose to ignore the promptings of the Spirit:

A number of years ago on her wedding day, Cynthia (not her real name) told her family that she had had a dream the night before that she should not marry her fiancé. She then told how she had been having strong impressions for some time, that she should not marry him. Her family reassured her that she was experiencing pre-wedding jitters and not to worry about it.

Therefore, trusting her family, the young bride went through with her temple wedding. A number of years went by and children came to their union. Then one tragic day, her husband contacted family members to say his wife had been missing since the day before. After a couple of frantic days of searching, they found her dead from a gunshot wound.

After some in-depth investigation by the police, it was discovered that her husband, with the aid of his mistress, had murdered his wife. The police later told the family that they had found strong evidence that the husband had been living a secret life for a number of years… which included deception and serious criminal activity.

To make it even more tragic, the week before her death, Cynthia called a family member to tell how an older couple from church alarmed her when they insisted that she should immediately get away from her husband. Neither she nor the couple knew what to make of their comment, so she chose to stay, and tragically the reason for the urgency of their warning to her played itself out before the next Sunday.

I have wondered many times what would have happened if that woman had heeded the promptings of the Spirit on both occasions in regards to her husband.

Obedience...The First Law of Heaven

Fortunately, not all choices to ignore or disobey spiritual promptings, ends as tragically as this woman's did. However, the danger of getting married to each other when a man and/or woman feels they should not, can place theirs and their posterity's future on very shaky grounds.

Another challenge some couples face, is when they have received confirmation from the Lord, that He approves of their decision to marry someone, and their family and/or friends strongly oppose their decision. In such a situation, the wise couple should at least hear and consider the reasons for the objections. Nevertheless, in the end, the couple should trust in the Lord, not in the arm of flesh (2 Nephi 4:35)...even if it is extremely difficult to do so. This is easier said than done...and sometimes it can be down right gut wrenching, lonely, as well as heartbreaking. I speak from personal experience!

Therefore, since the Lord knows hearts and intents, it would be wise for the couple to seek His wisdom, guidance and strength in how to help family members and friends to feel the joy of the wedding day ... especially if any of them will not be able, for whatever reason, to go into the temple to witness the marriage. It helps in such circumstances, to remember to exercise patience, tolerance, Christ-like love and consideration for their feelings, and not let comments and behavior from the hurt and/or disgruntled family members, ruin the otherwise beautiful and happy occasion.

I have gained a strong testimony of following the promptings from the Lord in regards to marrying the right person, at the right time, in the right place...from going through not one, but four different engagements in a year and a half's time! You read that right! That was not a typo! However, before you think I suffered from the "Runaway-Bride-Syndrome", or wonder if my engagements only had to do with my being "in-love" with the idea of getting married and nothing more, I want to make it clear that I have firm convictions that the Lord meant for me to go through each of those engagements, along with the experiences and tutoring that were associated with each. The reason for saying this will come out as I share my journey...

My first proposal of marriage took place while on a date with Landon (not his real name). I gave little thought to why one night when driving me home after a date, that he parked his car and told me that he was going to step away from the car because he had something he wanted to pray about. I thought it was odd, but since he was a recent returned missionary, I figured he was being prompted to pray and was committed to immediately following those promptings.

While he was away, the thought come to my mind three different times, and with perfect clarity, that he was going to ask me to marry him. Then, within minutes, he returned to the car and did exactly what I had been told he was going to do.

I was on Cloud Nine because Landon represented everything I desired in an eternal companion, and I was sure that ours was a match made in Heaven. However, one evening after letting him read an entry in my journal about our engagement, he shocked me when he said, "I wonder what your future children will think someday when they read that entry and wonder why you would say that about someone who is not their father?"

Not knowing what to make of his comment, I quickly blurted out, "Why did you say that?"

He looked equally shocked as he said, "I don't know."

However, his question stirred something inside of me, as I could not shake the feeling that what he had said was prophetic!

Then, to add fuel to the already growing flames of doubt, a friend shared her doubts about her upcoming wedding, and I decided to confide in her about what I was going through. However, her reply startled me as she said, "I wonder if someone else needs you more than Landon?"

I wanted to tell her to take back what she said! Nevertheless, it would not have made any difference, because deep down inside of me I knew that it was not *what* she and Landon had said that was troubling me so much as the fact that something "rang true" about *what* they said.

Yet, in spite of the doubts, I continued to rationalize that if what I was feeling was from the Lord, then surely Landon would be feeling it also. Therefore, since he had not shared any such feelings with me, I figured the doubts would leave as we moved forward with our wedding plans.

Then one day while talking with our Stake President, he took Landon's and my hands in his, and with conviction in his eyes and voice, said not once, but *twice*, "I know it is right that you two get married!"

Who wouldn't have taken that as a confirmation that our decision to marry was right? So naturally, I chose to ignore the mounting doubts that told me otherwise.

The long awaited day finally arrived for us to quit our jobs and move to Provo, Utah, where we were going to get married and go to school. It did not take long for us to find an apartment, and since our wedding was only a few weeks away, Landon moved into the apartment while I stayed with friends. However, all my efforts to move forward with our wedding plans, felt awkward and forced. In fact, it got so bad that I could no longer keep up the façade. Therefore, I girded up my loins and mustered the courage to share what I was going through with Landon.

Fortunately, when I told him what I was going through, he suggested that we pray to know the mind and will of the Lord concerning our decision to marry. It was a huge relief that instead of being upset with me, he treated me with kindness and understanding. However, as much I wanted our answer to be "Yes", I could no longer deny the unmistakable clarity that our becoming husband and wife, was not meant to be.

Then, the next day when Landon informed me that he had received the same answer, we decided there was no point in continuing with our wedding plans. Therefore, we immediately broke off our engagement and purchased a ticket for me to fly home the following day.

There are no words to describe the overwhelming heartache and sadness that consumed me as we said our final goodbyes. Yet, in spite of not knowing how I was going to get through the upcoming days and weeks, I had faith that our decision was the will of the Lord, and somehow He would help me get through it.

I was not home for long when an opportunity opened up for me to go stay with friends in a neighboring state. However, what I had hoped would be a respite, proved otherwise, as no matter how hard I tried to move on with my life, I continued to grieve, and found myself hoping that somehow Landon and I would get back together.

Then one day, it came to my mind (once again with perfect clarity), to let go of my feelings for Landon, and to put all thoughts of him out of my mind. After making the immediate mental effort to follow those promptings, it was as if a clear mountain breeze swept through my mind and heart, and all the feelings I had for Landon were gone and were replaced with peace and pure joy.

It was not long after that that the Lord sent yet another R.R.M. (recently returned missionary) into my life. Our friendship quickly blossomed and before long, he too asked me to marry him. However, the joy of thinking I had finally met the man I was to marry, did not last long, as those all too familiar persistent doubts that I had had with the first engagement, started to return. Only this time, I decided early on, to share what I was going through with my Bishop to see what advice he had to offer me.

However, after listening to what I was going through, he tried to reassure me that he felt my feelings were borne out of fear because of my previous failed engagement. Therefore, since I knew him to be a humble, righteous priesthood leader, I put my trust in his counsel.

Nevertheless, no amount of forcing myself to feel good about marrying Jacob (not his real name), could make me feel it was right. Therefore, after struggling with doubts and not finding any peace of mind, I finally got up the courage to tell Jacob about what I was going through.

I suppose that somewhere inside of me, I hoped that somehow he would help me put my doubts to rest. However, even though he suggested, like my Bishop, that what I was feeling might be from my previous failed engagement, I could not shake the feeling that something did not feel right.

Yet, in spite of the rising doubts, there were moments when I felt more confident about our upcoming wedding. However, the more I submersed myself into the scriptures and poured my heart out to the Lord to know His mind and will, the doubts started to return…first in small nudges, and as time went on, the impressions were unmistakable, and would not leave.

As painful as it was to think about, I could have accepted that it was not right to marry Jacob, yet my struggle had more to do with not being able to understand why once again I seemed to be the only one having the doubts.

I found out later, that Jacob was dealing with his own doubts about getting married, and like what happened with me, his family and Bishop tried to convince him that his decision to marry me was right. Therefore, he too moved forward, all the while growing increasingly unsure about our decision to marry. Unfortunately, he did not reveal to me what he was going through until the night we broke off our engagement.

In an effort to get past the uncertainty of our getting married, I tried to convince myself that once Jacob and I were married, the doubts and uneasiness would go away. Yet, something kept coming back to my memory…something that had taken place a few summers before…

It happened late one night while waiting for the technician to fix the very large mainframe computer at the bank where I worked. Since I could not go home until the checks had been processed, I had to wait until the computer was fixed. Minutes turned into hours as I waited with nothing to do. To make matters worse, it had been about 9 hours since I had eaten lunch, so naturally I started to get hungry. Therefore, in an effort to stave off hunger until I could get some dinner, I decided to go to the break room to buy a pack of cookies from the vending machine. However, I no sooner started to put the dime into the machine when a strong impression came to my mind telling me not to do so. Since I could not see what harm spending one measly dime would be, I shoved the feelings aside and quickly put the coin into the machine and turned the handle. However, I was surprised when the sense of urgency increased. Yet, still being unconvinced that eating the small pack of cookies could do me harm, I tore open the wrapper and quickly consumed them.

I did not have to wait long to discover why I had had that warning, as within 10-15 minutes the room started to spin and I became violently ill. As the pains in my stomach intensified and other symptoms that accompany food poisoning continued to increase, I found myself wishing I had trusted and heeded the unmistakable spiritual warnings I had received earlier.

That experience left an indelible mark in my mind and heart, which has saved me from making some choices that would have put me in serious physical and/or spiritual danger. One such occurrence took place not long after breaking off my first engagement. After going home for a short while, I made the decision to go back to my previous plans of attending BYU in Provo, Utah. However, the evening before my ride was to come for me, I did not get any sleep, because I kept having the feeling that if I followed through with my plans, it would be spiritual food poisoning for me.

As I wrestled with my decision, I knew it was not attending BYU that was the problem. I later figured out it had to do with following the Lord's timetable and plan for me. So, as hard as it was when my ride came to pick me up the next morning, I simply told the driver that I had changed my plans. And as difficult as it was to make that decision, I knew that I had done what the Lord wanted me to do, and that somehow He would make things work for my good if I continued to prove faithful and trust in His guidance (Mosiah 7:33; Proverbs 3:5; 141:8; Isaiah 12:2).

Now I will resume where I left off with Jacob's and my saga…

Trying To Swim Up the Wrong Stream

The best way I can come up with to explain what I struggled with leading up to the day I was to marry Jacob, was akin to the resistance a salmon goes through as he swims upstream, while fighting against very strong currents and rapids. Only in my case, it felt like I was trying to swim up the *wrong* stream. Yet, since no one else seemed to share what I was feeling, I decided once again, to move forward with our wedding plans.

Therefore, once again as the wedding day approached, I quit my job and went to stay with Jacob's sister who lived near him. The plan was for me to stay there until Jacob and I were to leave a few days later, to travel to the temple where we were to be married.

However, even though Jacob and his family treated me like gold, each day I was there, felt like an eternity, because I kept hoping the red light would magically turn green and I could finally be at peace about going through with the wedding. Nevertheless, as much as I wanted our getting married to be right, my commitment to make sure we were doing the will of the Lord, was stronger. Therefore, I intensified my prayers, telling Him that I had to do His will no matter what. The thing that helped me to keep seeking to do His will was in knowing that the only way to lasting happiness, is to surrender my will to His.

The turning point took place one evening after attending a dance at the Institute. The dance had been almost too much for me to endure, as I could not have faced another person as they offered their congratulations for our upcoming wedding without running from the room to avoid their faces.

Finally, while driving me to his sister's home, Jacob confided that he had also been feeling that our decision to marry was not right. However, even though it was a huge relief that I was no longer alone in what I had been feeling, I was not prepared for the flood of emotions and questions that started to fill my weary mind and heart.

Fortunately, going back home to face family and friends was not as painful and humiliating as I thought it would be. Yet, dealing with the heartache and embarrassment of yet another broken engagement, as well as the uncertainties of what lay ahead for me, weighed heavily upon my mind and heart.

Then one day when struggling to find peace of mind and answers to my many prayers, my dad came to my room to see how I was doing. After letting me pour my heart out to him, he offered to give me a father's blessing. I was relieved when I heard him bless me with comfort and peace, as both seemed foreign to me at that time. I was surprised when I heard him say that the Lord wanted me to go through the previous engagements so I could help others as well as my own children some day.

I had mixed feelings as I realized first that the Lord had meant for me to go through those engagements, and second that someone else...including children that I would have in the future, might have to go through similar trials. The only words I could come up with as I pondered that possibility was..."Those poor children!"

Doomed To Be the Eternal Fiancée

I know a young woman who claims she is the "eternal bridesmaid" because she has been a bridesmaid or helped with more weddings than she has fingers; and yet, she has never been engaged or married. However, in my case, I felt like I was doomed to be the "eternal fiancée"...but never the bride.

About the time I received that priesthood blessing, I was ready for things to improve in my life. However, I am either a slow learner, or the Lord had more for me to experience and learn, as I was about to go through yet another practice run before meeting the man I was to marry.

I hadn't been home long, when yet another young man returned home from his mission. We started hanging out together; only this time, it was someone I had known from before his mission. I was surprised when my feelings for him started to blossom into more than just the feelings of friendship that I had felt for him before his mission. Then one Sunday, I had a number of strong impressions come to my mind that he was going to ask me to marry him. However, when he asked if I would consider marrying him, I told him that I would need to pray about it before giving him an answer. I felt sure that I would never again let anyone convince me to ignore the impressions and answers I received through prayers.

Yet, even though I thought my resolve was firm, I was not as prepared or sure-footed as I thought I was, for upon returning home and telling my parents what had happened, my dad got a radiant glow in his countenance as he said, "You will get an answer!"

He said it with so much conviction, that I had no doubt that I *would* get an answer. That was a comfort, as I did not want to go through the humiliation and heartbreak of yet another failed engagement. However, in spite of thinking I had time to ponder and pray about the answer, friends started congratulating me for my engagement. I had not told anyone other than my parents, and I had also not replied to Franklin's (not his real name) proposal, yet people were still congratulating me.

Then to complicate matters, from the moment my dad told me I would get my answer, the excitement of possibly finding the person the Lord wanted me to marry, quickly went away and was replaced with a dense fog. Then, those all-too-familiar-feelings that my decision was not right started to return. I got my answer all right, but it was not the answer I had expected…nor was it the answer my parents were hoping and praying for.

I was frustrated, as I actually wanted to have at least one engagement work out. I spent long hours on my knees pleading for help to know what to do. Therefore, once again, I decided to go see my Bishop (a different one from the last time). However, he, my parents and Franklin, all tried to assure me that what I was feeling was fear because of my previously failed engagements.

I felt defeated. First of all, I did not understand why once again, I had to be the only one who was dealing with doubts. Another complication was something I had not had to deal with before, which was having my parents being part of the opposing side. It might have been easier for me to stand firm in what I was feeling if they had given any glimmer that they too had their doubts. After all, I knew my parents to be spiritually-minded, as I had seen them on many occasions, go to great lengths to pray and fast for answers to their concerns. They had set the perfect example of walking by faith most days of their trial-ridden lives. So I had a very hard time believing that they could be wrong in their feelings about my marrying Franklin.

Secondly, Franklin had proven over the years that he was committed to seeking for and following the will of the Lord. Yet, I could not deny what I felt after praying and fasting for answers, which was the opposite of Franklin's views.

Another thing that kept coming to my mind was a part of my Patriarchal Blessing that said: "Remember that when the time comes for you to take unto yourself a helpmate, by living the gospel and being faithful and true unto your covenants, there will *come into your life* one of God's chosen sons."

Franklin had been in my life for a number of years, and therefore, he did not fit that part of my Patriarchal Blessing. Therefore, within a week of Franklin's proposal, I mustered the courage I needed, and as gently as I knew how, I let Franklin know that I could not feel right about marrying him.

However, as relieved as I was that I had finally found the courage to stand up for what I knew to be right, I was not prepared for the flood of people who came forward and told me how wonderful Franklin was, and that I was making a big mistake in not marrying him. I knew they were right about the first part, but with the second part, I was not convinced.

Nevertheless, I reasoned that so many people could not be wrong, so I told Franklin that since everyone else felt we should get married, then I must be wrong, and I agreed to marry him. However, my words felt forced and mechanical, and there was no peace or spiritual confirmation about my decision. But by this time, I was so beaten down with self-doubt, and feeling so alone with what I was going through, that I ignored what I could no longer deny, so I moved forward with plans to marry Franklin. Yet, the more I stepped out in faith with the wedding plans, the denser the fog became, and the stronger the impressions came that I should not marry him.

The peace of mind that I craved eluded me. In addition, no amount of prayer and fasting would bring those feelings to my heart or mind. I was deeply troubled, yet each time I tried to convey my feelings to my parents and Franklin, they each continued to reassure me that I was just scared and was allowing Satan to influence me.

Then one day, a friend of mine returned from college for a brief visit. When she found out that I was engaged to be married, she asked about my wedding plans. I quickly rattled off the date and temple we were planning on getting married in…all the while avoiding her gaze to try and hide my true feelings. She then looked me in the eyes and asked, "Have you gotten an answer that it is right?"

I quickly blurted out, "No, but everyone else says its right, so I must be wrong!"

She then told me she was not leaving until I promised her that I would not marry Franklin until I got an answer that it was right. When I half-heartedly agreed, she turned my face to hers, and like a mother who is scolding her child, made me promise and say it like I meant it. I will be forever grateful to her for having the courage to say what I needed to hear, and for helping me to get my feet back on the correct path when I lacked the strength and conviction to do so on my own.

Shortly after that, Franklin and I rode with friends to Utah. I stayed with a friend in Salt Lake while Franklin went with our friends to Provo. After hearing my plight, the friend I was staying with suggested I go talk with the High Councilman over her Young Adult group in her Stake. Then, after making sure he understood why I wanted a priesthood blessing, he then laid his hands on my head and proceeded with the blessing.

As he placed his hands on my head, I made sure that my mind and heart were open to *anything* the Lord wanted me to know and do. I was determined to do His will no matter what He required me to do. Tears flowed from my eyes, and gratitude filed my heart as I heard him say that *I would soon meet the man I was to marry*, and that I would rejoice that I had not married anyone else.

It was not that I was glad that I was not supposed to marry Franklin. He would have been a great husband and father, and he honored his priesthood and was committed to living the Gospel. Yet, after being told that I would soon meet the man I was to marry, there was no doubt about what I was supposed to do. Therefore, as hard as it was, I mustered all my courage to let Franklin know of my decision.

Since I already had an apartment and a job lined up in Provo, I decided not to return home. That proved to be a good thing for me, as I do not think I could have faced my family and friends back at home and still remained committed to my convictions about not marrying Franklin.

Because of what I had been through, I was more determined than ever to get my education and serve a mission before giving *any* thought to getting married. However, once again the Lord had other plans for me, as it was only a few days later, that I met Eric (his real name), the man I was to marry. Sometimes when the Lord says, "Soon", He means *SOON*!

While visiting with each other at an opening social for our BYU Branch, I learned that Eric had returned home from his mission two weeks before (which made him a R.R.M.), and was planning on attending BYU. As we talked, I learned that he was going to Ogden, Utah the next day to see his Aunt Mary, who was in the hospital. I saw it as an opportunity to pick up my things that I had left with my friend in Salt Lake. I therefore asked Eric if he would mind dropping me off at my friend's apartment, and then pick me up on his way back to Provo. However, my friend was not at home, so I ended up going to Ogden with him.

After picking up Eric's grandmother, a funny thing happened as her neighbor (who had known Eric from before his mission) saw us and asked if I was his wife. Eric told her that I was just a friend…to which she replied, "Well, you have to start somewhere."

I do not think either of us thought anything about her comment, except to feel a little embarrassed. However, the next time we saw her, we were engaged!

While his aunt and I hit it off like old friends catching up on what had happened since we last saw each other (probably in the Pre-existence), Eric sat across the room contributing very little to the conversation.

On the way home from Ogden, I bore the tale of my broken engagements. After reaching a point of not wanting to hear me complain about wanting to avoid all newly returned missionaries, and how I wanted to serve a mission and get my schooling before getting married, Eric very calmly said, "If you weren't LDS, I would suggest that you become a nun".

I then blurted out, "If I were not LDS, I might take you up on your suggestion!"

I reasoned instead, that my going on a year and a half on a mission, would have to do. Yet, try as I might, I never got the chance to pursue that avenue. In spite of our awkward start, Eric and I became instant friends, and it was not long before our friendship turned into something deeper and more endearing. Over the next few months, Eric and I spent long hours talking on the phone about anything and everything. However, there was no thought in my mind that anything more than a friendship would come of it (remember my determination to finish my schooling and serve a mission *before* getting married?). Yet, as much as I tried to keep our relationship at an arm's distance, each time we spent any time together, or talked on the phone, my resolve to keep pushing him away, started to weaken, until I found myself deeply in love with him.

Then one night, I needed someone to talk to about a weighty decision I had to make, and Eric offered to come over. As we sat on a long couch (him at one end, and me at the other), we talked over my dilemma…which had to do with my having a strong impression to move out of my apartment and in with a single woman from our Branch. I had a job and a car that came with the apartment that I lived in, so if I moved, I would no longer have a way to get to school or a job to pay for my living expenses.

After discussing my dilemma, Eric stood to leave. However, before going, he gave me a gentle hug and assured me that he knew I would make the right decision in the matter. However, as he wrapped his arms around me, a feeling of coming home enveloped me. Then, as I looked into his eyes, it was as though I saw the vastness of eternity. Eric then told me that he did not know what it was, but there was something very special between us. I agreed, but did not give any thought to what it was.

A few days later, while on a date with him, I concluded that I would quit fighting the feelings I had for him. Yet, the challenges did not stop, as a couple of days later, he showed up to church with a young woman I had never seen before…and it was obvious that they were MORE than just friends. Think of how a cat looks when he is being held against his will, and you have the picture of what Eric looked like. However, he was making no effort to get away from her iron grip.

I could not bring myself to look at them because of the pain it caused me. However, every time I closed my eyes to try to erase from my mind the image of him with her, a picture of the two of us walking hand in hand from the Provo Temple, kept flashing into my mind, along with the calm, reassuring words, "Don't worry, it is what you think, but it will be okay".

This happened three times in a row. However, because of the previous experiences with engagements, I shoved the impressions aside. I have no doubt the Lord was trying to reassure me, but, I did not feel reassured each time I opened my eyes and would see her tightly holding onto the man I was in love with.

The next couple of days were difficult to get through. Confusion and heartache were pounding away at my battle weary mind and heart. Then as I pondered what was in my heart, I told the Lord that I loved Eric, and to my surprise, a peaceful assurance washed over me like a warm ocean wave.

I was so used to being told, "No", that I did not know what to do with a "Yes" answer…especially since it seemed like there was no way things would work out between us. Therefore, just to make sure I had not imagined it, I once again told the Lord how much I loved Eric, and once again the ocean wave of peace washed over me till it literally filled every fiber of my being.

However, as it usually works for me, I had to test the waters one more time just to make sure I had not imagined it. Only the third time, it was unmistakable! There was no doubt about the source of my answer. The Lord wasted no time in giving me proof of His assurance, when within a few days, Eric told me how he had let the other girl know he was not interested in her, and then he tenderly looked me in the eyes and asked if I would marry him.

Under normal circumstances, I would have quickly answered "Yes!" However, I told him I did not want to get engaged unless I was sure it was right. Therefore, he agreed to give me some more time. Then a day or two later, after some discussion, we both came to the same conclusion that we loved each other and felt we should get married, yet, neither of us felt ready. Therefore, we decided to seek counsel from our Branch President. However, he did not react as we had anticipated. He was elated, telling us he knew we were going to get married. That did not make it any easier because of my previous priesthood leaders telling me the same thing with my previous fiancés.

Unsure of what else to do, Eric and I went back to my apartment, where we decided to have prayer together. As we knelt to pray, it felt like a warm blanket had wrapped around us. Then as Eric stood to leave, the Spirit prompted him to ask me to marry him…to which he promptly asked if he could wait. The Spirit wasted no time in responding with a firm and unmistakable, "No. Ask her."

Eric then stated he was not ready to get married and asked if he could wait. However, after the third time being told not to wait, and to ask me to marry him, he decided to obey.

I was surprised as I heard myself calmly answering, "Yes".

Furthermore, as I did so, a quiet assurance and peace washed over me.

Then the next night, the two of us went through the VERY unpleasant task of telling our parents. As Eric listened over the phone to his mother's very loud and angry protests, I was dreading having to break the news to my parents. After all, they were still holding out that I would marry the man of their choice (which was Franklin), plus they did not even know that Eric existed!

As I raced through my mind with how they would react, I had the peaceful reassurance that they would react as I thought they would, but that it would be okay, that I was making the right decision. So, as painful as it was that none of Eric's or my family supported our decision, Eric and I had the peaceful reassurance that we were marrying the right person, in the right place, at the right time, and that it was the Lord's will, and that is all either of us needed to know.

What the complete reason is that the Lord wanted Landon, Jacob, Franklin and me to go through those practice-run engagements before we met and married our spouses, is known only to Him. However, I believe it had in part to do with that priesthood blessing, where I was told that I would be able to help others because of those experiences. It is for that reason, plus the feeling that I should do so, that I have included these very personal experiences in this book.

I will be forever grateful for the caliber of young men the Lord placed in my life to provide learning experiences that I would not have gained in any other way. I hope if any of them read this, that they will know that I have the utmost gratitude and respect for each of them. Each can be proud of the examples they set for me, as each of them were righteous sons of God who honored their priesthood, and were perfect gentlemen every minute we spent together. They also made it easy for me to keep my standards high and to stay true and faithful to my covenants.

I will also be forever grateful for the lessons learned on bended knee through each of those experiences, where I learned, that with God, nothing is impossible, even in helping us find the eternal companion He approves of.

True love

As hard as it is for some to believe, there are singles who allow anything from differing tastes in movies, entertainment, music and even foods, to keep them from marrying someone. I have even heard some singles who are in their late twenties and thirties, use the reasoning that they are not ready to get married; or that even though they love the person they have been dating, it is not enough for them to want to marry them.

Whenever I have heard that last excuse, I cannot help but wonder (as I mentioned at the beginning of this book) if Hollywood, fairytales, and romance novels have played a role in making it difficult for singles, and even people who are already married, to know what "real love" is.

When parents used to arrange marriages for their children, "love" was rarely a part of the decision process. In the movie, "Fiddler on the Roof", Tevia (a Jew who lived in a tiny, remote village in Russia), became enraged when his oldest daughter Tzeitel, announced that she and Motel (the tailor) decided to get married.

In their village, it was unheard of for a girl to arrange her own marriage, as it was tradition for a matchmaker to find brides for the men or boys. In addition, the agreement was usually between the father of the potential bride and the parents of the potential groom. However, in the case where the potential groom was older, the agreement was usually made between the man and the girl's father.

Tevia's unyielding commitment to the centuries-old tradition of using a matchmaker, was softened as Motel asked, "Shouldn't a poor tailor be entitled to some happiness?"

As Tevia looked into Tzietel and Motel's eyes, he could see that they really loved each other. How could he refuse them the happiness that they deeply desired? Therefore, out of love for his daughter, he agreed to give them his blessing to marry. However, he no sooner did so, when he remembered that he had made an agreement the evening before with Lazar Wolf (the much older, widowed butcher), to give him Tzeitel's hand in marriage.

In an attempt to divert the train wreck that would surely come from breaking the marriage agreement with Lazar Wolf, and with getting Golda (his wife) to agree to let Tzeitel and Motel marry, he concocted a story in which he told his wife that he had a dream where there was a huge celebration in the graveyard. While he was wandering around trying to figure out what was being celebrated, Grandma Tzeitel (whom his daughter was named after), came back from the grave to congratulate him for Tzeitel's betrothal to Motel.

Alarmed, Golda said that Grandma Tzeitel was mistaken because Tzeitel was to marry Lazar Wolf. Tevia then told her how he tried to tell Grandma Tzeitel that she was mistaken. However, Grandma Tzeitel insisted that Tzeitel was to marry Motel.

As the dead ancestors rejoiced over such glorious news, Fruma Sarah (Lazar Wolf's deceased wife) appeared on the scene and told Tevia that if Tzeitel marries Lazar Wolf that she would give him and her three weeks, and then she would come in the night and strangle Tzeitel while she slept.

Golda was so troubled by Tevia's dream that she insisted, since Grandma Tzeitel had come back from the grave to give him that message, then they should heed her counsel.

Not long after that, Hodel (his second daughter) announced that she and Perchik (who tutored Tevia's daughters in trade for room and board) loved each other and wanted to get married. When Tevia realized that his protests about not breaking tradition had little effect on changing his daughter's mind, he gave into her request.

Marrying for love was something Tevia had not considered before. These new ideas were hard for him to digest. Yet, as he thought more on the idea of "marrying for love", he decided to ask Golda if she loved him. Being annoyed by his question, Golda growled back, "Do I what?"

Tevia persisted in asking if she loved him. By this time, Golda was starting to give some thought to what Tevia was asking her. However, this was a new idea for her as well, because she had never considered that love had anything to do with why a man and woman got married.

By this time, Tevia was becoming impatient with Golda's reluctance to answer his simple question. Therefore, to put him off, Golda told him she had a lot on her mind with their daughter getting married and all the political trouble in the town. Then she pointed out that she was upset and insisted that Tevia must be tired or ill, and suggested that he go lie down.

By this time, Tevia's patience had worn thin as he let Golda know that his question had nothing to do with any of those things…that he simply wanted to know if she loved him. Golda's patience had also reached its limit as she told him he was a fool for asking such things. However, even though Tevia realized Golda was probably right, he continued to try and get an answer to his question.

Realizing Tevia was not going to drop it until she gave him an answer; Golda asked, "Do I love him?"

Tevia then blurted out, "Well?"

Golda, still not willing to give into what she viewed as foolishness, she bemoaned about how for 25 years she had done his laundry, made his meals, cleaned his house, given birth to his children, and even milked his cows, and she wanted to know why after 25 years, he wanted to know if she loves him.

Then in a more gentle and submissive tone, Tevia recounted how the first time they met, was on their wedding day, and how he was scared and nervous. Golda then echoed his words.

Tevia told how his mother and father told him that he and Golda would *learn to love each other*, and he wanted to know if their predictions were true.

Exasperated, Golda blurted out, "I am your wife!"

However, Tevia did not let Golda's annoyance keep him from getting the answer to his question. Only this time, his question was more of a gentle pleading.

Still not wanting to give in to what she viewed as a foolish question, Golda recounted that for 25 years they lived together, fought with each other, starved together, and slept in the same bed. Only this time, as she wound down from her rant, she gently pondered aloud, "If that's not love, what is?"

Tevia, realizing that may be the closest his wife would come to admitting that she loved him, quickly replied, "Then you love me!"

Golda, looking a bit surprised and worn down, simply stated, "I suppose I do".

Tevia, reacting like a newly engaged man, announced enthusiastically, "I suppose I love you too".

Then both Tevia and Golda chimed in, "It doesn't change a thing, but after 25 years, it's nice to know."

It is interesting to note that arranged marriages rarely ended in divorce. In addition, it is interesting that many couples in arranged marriages *grew to love each other.*

It seems couples today could learn a lot from what helped their ancestors' marriages stand the test of time. It is a shame that the ones whose marriages were arranged by their parents are probably no longer alive; else, they could share the secrets of their successful marriages with their descendents. However, if I could borrow Golda's observations about what she and Tevia had accomplished together over 25 years, I would point out that it was service to each other, along with commitment, sacrifice and similar goals that made the difference. In addition, there was an element that many of these arranged marriages shared, and that was a love for God (or some supreme being), along with their combined devotion to Him.

As annoying as diversities could be in those marriages, it was rare for the couple to allow them to become brick walls that would cause them to abandon their commitment to each other and/or their marriage, family and God.

If more children would be taught from birth, the importance of commitment to God, country and family, and what true love is between a husband and wife, we would see many of the ills in the world, healed.

Notes:
1. President Spencer W. Kimball, First Presidency Message, "Oneness in Marriage", *Ensign*, March 1977
2. Dictionary.com

Chapter Six

We Don't Plan to Fail…We Fail to Plan

We are told if we are prepared, we shall not fear…*even in marriage* (D&C 38:30). Dr. Ed Wheat (a now deceased family physician and author) considered pre-marriage counseling, an essential part of his responsibility as a family doctor. He wrote, "It is not only a preventative measure, protecting against family breakups, but it can also trigger a positive course of action that will bring pleasure and joy as the young couple learn to love in an enduring relationship" [1]

When an engaged couple would go to him for their pre-marriage physical, Dr. Wheat would strongly suggest that they go through pre-marriage counseling either with him, or their pastor. If they chose to go through it with him, he would ask them as individuals, to read some books and to listen to some tapes that he co-authored, for the purpose of helping engaged couples prepare for the wedding night, and to keep the home fires burning long after the honeymoon. Then in each subsequent visit, he would discuss and answer any questions and concerns that the couple might have about what they had studied.

Dr. Wheat believed, if any couple (Christian or not) would apply the scriptural principles he taught in his books and tapes, then they would be better able to enjoy a long, happy and loving marriage. It makes sense that laying a firm foundation before entering into marriage, is not only smart, but could make the difference in the couple "living happily ever after", or ending up in a loveless and unhappy marriage, or eventually joining the endless procession found in the divorce courts.

After I read Dr. Wheat's pre-marriage outline from his book "Intended for Pleasure", and on his CDs/tapes, titled, "Before the Wedding Night: Pre-Marriage Counsel by Ed Wheat, M.D.", I thought it might be helpful to design a pre-marriage study guide with an LDS perspective for engaged couples. However, even though my study guide is designed for engaged couples, I believe anyone, single or married, would benefit from what is contained in it…no matter how many years they have been married.

FYI: Anyone who is interested in ordering any of Dr. Wheat's books, and/or CDs, and tapes, you can contact me at 2HeartsOneDream@gmail.com to find out how to order them, as the bookstore that carries them is not online at the writing of this book.

Notes:

1. Ed Wheat, MD, "Intended for Pleasure"

Pre-Wedding Study Guide for Latter-day Saint Couples

By Terry Hardy Olsen

For the couple who has decided to get married, you may be wondering what to do next. That is not an easy question to answer, as there are so many things to consider when planning a wedding. However, there is no need to reinvent the wheel, as there are some key elements that can make the experience memorable and enjoyable for everyone involved. But the sooner you get started, the better:

1. First, start with a plan.
2. Make sure there is open and clear communication between everyone involved in planning the wedding.
3. Remember, this is the groom's wedding as well; he should have a say-so in what takes place.
4. Organization and follow through are keys to a successful wedding and reception.
5. Remember patience is a virtue and to practice the Golden Rule…even when you feel justifiably upset, hurt, angry, neglected, ignored, left out, humiliated and ridiculed…did I leave out any expletives?

Get to "Know Each Other Better" Before Getting to "Know" Each Other

Since our decisions determine our destiny, I strongly recommend that the couple take the time to get to know each other's likes, dislikes, core beliefs and attitudes on many subjects that play a part of married life. The couple does not have to see eye to eye on everything, nor even share an interest in the same types of movies, TV shows, music, games, etc. Nevertheless, it would be helpful before the wedding to know what is important to the person they are going to be spending time and eternity with. In addition, it would be highly recommended to marry someone who shares the same religious views.

The couple can have VERY different attitudes in all these areas, but if they both have as their primary goal, to reach the Celestial Kingdom, and are committed to loving and cherishing each other, as well as being committed to blending their diversities, then they will be better able to find great joy in their journey together.

My guess is, every spouse desires to have a marriage where there are few arguments, and where both the husband and the wife feel like their views and interests are important to each other. Therefore, it is crucial for them to get to know each other better before they get married. One way to accomplish this is through a series of questions designed to initiate the process. A very good book that is a good bridal shower gift is "300 Questions LDS Couples

Should Ask before Marriage", by Shannon Adler. However, if the couple wants, they could use the following questions; adding ones that are not included in the list. Even though some of the questions would not normally need to be asked by an active LDS couple, I encourage each person to answer them anyway:

GENERAL QUESTIONS A COUPLE COULD ASK EACH OTHER BEFORE THEY GET MARRIED

(Answer on separate pieces of papers)

1. Why do you want to marry me?
2. What is your definition of a happy marriage?
3. Where do you see us in thirty or forty years?
4. List your ten most important goals in order of importance, and describe why.
5. What are your goals for reaching the highest degree of the Celestial Kingdom?
6. What do you feel you and I need to be doing to reach those goals?

Family of Origin Issues:
1. What was your childhood like?
2. Was your family an affectionate one?
3. Whose house will we spend Thanksgiving with? List your reasons.
4. Whose house will we spend Christmas with? List your reasons.
5. What do you consider an ideal way to spend your birthday?
6. How do you feel about surprise birthday parties?
7. What are your family traditions?
8. What family traditions are important for you to keep, and which ones would you rather not continue?
9. What family traditions would you like our family to adopt?
10. What values would you like to bring from your family into our marriage and why?
11. What do you like and dislike about your family?
12. What do you feel are strengths and weaknesses in your parent's marriage?
13. Describe in some detail your idea of an ideal marriage and family.
14. Were your parents sealed in the temple?
15. Were you born in the covenant or were you sealed to your parents?
16. Are your parents still alive?
17. Are your parents divorced? If so, how does it affect you?

18. If your parents are divorced or separated, are both involved in your life?

19. Do you have any concerns about the dynamics of either of our families and how it will affect our marriage?

20. What do you see as a healthy involvement with our parents in our lives?

21. Is there any question or concern about yours or my family that is not addressed in this section?

Self Image Issues:

1. How would you describe yourself?

2. How would others describe you?

3. How do you describe me?

4. How do you think I see you?

5. How do you view others?

6. Am I a jealous person?

7. Are you a jealous person?

8. Do I have trust issues or feel insecure? If so, does it bother you?

9. Do you have trust issues and/or do you feel insecure?

10. Do you need to have the support or approval of others?

11. How do you handle compliments?

12. How do you think I handle compliments?

13. How do you handle criticism, correction, set backs, or failures?

14. How do you think I handle criticism, correction, set backs, or failures?

15. What is your love language?

16. What do you expect me to do to meet your love language?

17. What do you think my love language is?

18. What are you willing to do to fulfill my love language?

19. Do you need compliments, flowers, gifts, or love notes to make you feel loved?

20. Tell me what you do for other peoples birthdays, holidays, mother's and father's days. Rank these events in order of importance to you and your reasons why.

21. What do you feel about each of those special days?

22. If you do not like people making a fuss over you for these holidays, are you willing to make them special for me if I think they are important?

23. If you do not like celebrating holidays, will you allow me or our kids and our extended family to make them special?

Time and Chore Issues:

1. How do you feel about dividing the household chores?
2. Are you willing to clean the toilet?
3. Are you willing to replace the toilet paper if it runs out?
4. Do you prefer the toilet paper to come from the top or bottom of the roll?
5. Are you willing to do dishes?
6. Can you cook? If so, are you willing to cook meals? If not, are you willing to learn how to cook?
7. Do you know how to make up a menu?
8. What is your idea of a balanced meal?
9. What do you consider essential food items to keep at all times?
10. Are you willing to go grocery shopping?
11. What should we do to prepare for emergencies?
12. What should we do to build food storage?
13. Are you willing to vacuum and mop floors?
14. Are you willing to do laundry?
15. Do you fold the clothes and put them away after you empty the dryer, or do you leave them in the basket or dryer until you need them?
16. Do you know how to iron? If not, are you willing to learn?
17. How do you feel about wearing wrinkled clothes?
18. Do you repair clothes that are missing buttons, have holes, or if the hem needs to be fixed; and are you willing to replace irreparable and outdated clothes?
19. Do you know how to use a sewing machine? Can you sew clothes?
20. Are there any craft or homemaking skills that you possess? If so, what are they?
21. How are you with doing repairs to the home, furniture, vehicles or other items that need fixing?
22. Do you fix broken things right away or do you put it off until they fall apart or are past being able to be repaired?
23. Can you change the oil in the car, and/or change tires?
24. Do you know how to put gas in a vehicle?
25. When do you think it is time to fill the gas tank?
26. Do you prefer to do your own auto repairs or pay others to do it?
27. Do you own your own tools? If so, what are they and what are their uses?
28. What are your expectations about how we will spend our free time and/or days off?
29. Do you believe that we should be doing everything together?

30. How do you feel about each of us pursuing our own interests?

31. Do you need or want time alone?

32. How would you feel if I want a night out with my friends now and then? How often is okay or is too much?

33. How will we make sure we have quality time together?

34. How much time do you want to spend with your family?

35. How much time do you want to spend with my family?

36. Will your family expect us to spend every Sunday or another day of the week with them?

37. If they expect us over ever Sunday, and it becomes a problem, how will we deal with it?

38. How do you feel about living with either of our parents? If we did, what would be our reasons and how long would we do it?

39. How do you feel about other people living with us?

40. Are you a morning or evening person?

41. Are you a happy or grouchy morning person? If you are grouchy when you wake up, how bad are you?

42. What time do you like to get up?

43. What time do you go to bed?

Money Issues:

1. Are you comfortable talking about money matters?

2. Are you a saver or spender when it comes to money?

3. Where would you rate your credit score (excellent, good, needs improvement, poor)? If it is not good, why is that?

4. Do you have a checking and/or savings account?

5. Do you balance your checking account when you get the statement each month?

6. Do you check your balance everyday on your checking account to avoid problems?

7. If you have a savings account, and you do not mind saying so, how much money do you have in your savings account?

8. What is your idea of a budget?

9. Explain your unbending rules and the areas you are more lenient in with a budget.

10. Should we have joint or separate checking accounts? What are your reasons?

11. Should we have a separate checking account for household use?

12. How do you think we should plan on seeing to it we have a secure retirement?

13. Who is going to be responsible for making sure that bills are paid on time?

14. Do you want to pay bills online with a check, cash, a money order or cashier's check?

15. Do you keep all your receipts from stores, gasoline purchases, etc?

16. Do you consider going to the movies and having a vacation every year a necessity or a luxury?

17. What is your idea of a vacation (camping, fishing, hunting, going on a cruise, a theme park, visiting historic sites, visiting family or friends, church history sites, church pageants, family research gathering trips, etc.)?

18. If you like to camp, do you like to rough it, take a motor home, a tent, sleep under the stars, take food to eat, or do you prefer to hunt or fish for it, etc.?

19. Which do you prefer for us, a double or single sleeping bag?

20. What do you consider an enjoyable hike?

21. If you like theme parks, which one(s) is your favorite, or which one(s) do you like to go to?

22. Do you prefer to drive or fly to your vacation destination?

23. What is an ideal length of a vacation?

24. What are you willing to spend on a vacation?

25. If you want to drive, do you prefer to stay with family or friends along the way, to stay in hotels, tents, or to sleep in the car at rest stops?

26. If you drive, do you like to stop and see the scenery, historic sites, take photos, take your time, or do you rush to get to your destination?

27. How do you feel about stopping to take a break, to eat or go to the bathroom when you drive long distances?

28. When you travel, do you prefer to take your food (i.e. sandwiches, cut up fruit, etc.), fast food, or to take time to stop and eat at a nice restaurant?

29. How much do you owe in debts and what are your assets?

30. Where does your money go each month?

31. What are your financial goals?

32. Do you want to rent an apartment or house when we get married?

33. What are your plans for buying a home?

34. Where do you want to keep our important papers and financial documents?

35. How should we go about preparing for emergencies?

36. Do you pay alimony or child support each month? If so, how much?

Parenting Issues:

1. Do you want to have children?
2. If we decide we want children, how many children do you want to have?
3. How long should we be married before having children?
4. How do you feel about putting off having children until one or both of us finishes school?
5. Do you think the mother should be in the home or the work place? Explain your reasons.
6. How do you feel about the mother being at home while the kids are still at home?
7. What kind of parent do you think you will be?
8. What kind of parent do you think I will be?
9. What is your idea of an ideal father and mother?
10. What is your parenting philosophy?
11. Are you willing to change a diaper?
12. What are your thoughts about traditional roles of men and women?
13. What type of birth control should we use if we want to postpone or prevent having children?
14. How do you feel about adoption if we are unable to have children?
15. Do you have any children? If so, do you have part or full custody?
16. If you have children, when do they stay with you?
17. If you have custody of your children, when do they see their other parent?
18. If you have children, do any have special needs? If so, what are they?
19. If you have children, what is your relationship with them?
20. If you have children, what is your relationship with their mother(s) or father(s)?
21. If you have children, what role do you want me to play with them?
22. What do you think the following scripture means? "Spare the rod and spoil the child? (Proverbs 13:24); Reproving betimes with sharpness? (D&C 121:43).
23. What is your philosophy on disciplining children?
24. What do you think it means to teach our children correct doctrine?

Spirituality and Religious Issues:

1. How do you like to spend your Sundays?
2. How do you feel about shopping on Sundays?
3. How do you feel about working on Sundays?
4. How do you feel about watching T.V. or movies on Sundays?

5. If you think it is okay to watch T.V. and movies on Sunday, what is your idea of what is appropriate?

6. What order would you place the following? Family, self, God, church, job, friends, callings in church.

7. If you had to choose between an important family event and your home or visiting teaching, which would you choose and why?

8. How do you feel about accepting a church calling even if it is one that you don't like, or you feel is unimportant?

9. How do you feel about accepting a calling that demands a lot of your time?

10. Would you support me if I got a calling that took a lot of my time?

11. If we had family or friends visiting who do not want to go to church, would you go to church anyway or stay with them and do what they want to do?

12. If I did not want to go to church, would you still go?

13. If one of our children did not want to go to church, how would you deal with it?

14. How often do you read and study your scriptures?

15. How do you feel about reading scriptures everyday as an individual and as a family?

16. How often do you pray?

17. How do you feel about having couple prayer every night before we go to bed?

18. How do you feel about having family prayer morning and night?

19. Describe your feelings about marrying in the temple?

20. Do you think regular temple attendance is important (i.e. once a week, once a month, once a quarter, once a year)?

21. How do you feel about paying tithing and fast offerings?

22. How do you feel about giving to other items on the Donation slip (humanitarian aid, education fund, Copies of the book of Mormon, Temples, etc.)?

23. If you are okay with it, how much do you want us to pay for other items on the Donation Slip, and how much to which ones?

24. How much do you want to pay in Fast Offerings each month?

25. Share your testimony about your relationship with God.

26. Share your testimony about the Gospel of Jesus Christ of Latter-day Saints.

27. Share your testimony of the Book of Mormon and Joseph Smith.

28. Share your testimony of the other scriptures.

29. Did you serve a mission? If so, where, and write down the most memorable experiences.

30. Would you like to serve a mission together someday? If so, what would be your idea of an ideal mission(s) for us to fulfill?

Sexual Issues:

1. Should we talk about sex before marriage? If so, when and how much should we discuss?

2. Should we study about sex before marriage? If so, what books would be appropriate, and when should we study the material (i.e. alone, together, in a public place, over the phone, through letters, etc.)?

3. Do you feel sex is dirty?

4. Is it okay to discuss or think about sex? If so, under what circumstances?

5. Do you feel sex is a gift from God that is meant to be enjoyed by husband and wife?

6. How do you think we should differentiate between pornography and wholesome education on sex?

7. How do you feel about viewing pornography? Do you have an addiction to pornography? If so, what are you doing to overcome it?

8. What will we do to protect our marriage and ourselves from pornography?

9. How do you feel about using lingerie? If you are okay with the use of lingerie, where do you feel is okay to purchase it? Are you comfortable going into a store and buying it, or would you prefer to buy it online? Do you want to be the one to pick it out or let me pick it out?

10. Describe your ideal honeymoon.

11. Have you been sexually abused? If so, how does it affect you, and do you think it will affect our being able to have a healthy sexual relationship?

12. Have you ever sexually abused anyone? If so, has it been properly dealt with by your priesthood Leaders or the law?

13. Do you have any sexually transmitted diseases?

14. Are there things you are struggling with about having sex for the first time?

15. If you have had sex before, for whatever reason, are you concerned about how you will deal with having sex after we are married?

16. Are there any unresolved moral issues that you need to take to your priesthood leaders? If so, are you willing to hold off getting married until you work them out?

17. Once we are married, will you be willing to continue to study about how to keep our sexual relations strong and fulfilling for both of us?

Health and mental health issues:

1. Would you consider yourself a healthy person? If not, why not?
2. Do you have any diseases or health concerns that would pose a problem for our being intimate?
3. Do you struggle with phobias or obsessive compulsive behavior? If so, what are they?
4. Does anyone in your family deal with phobias or obsessive compulsive behavior?
5. Have you ever been institutionalized for mental health problems? If so, what were they and are you still dealing with the problem(s)?
6. If so, do you anticipate them causing problems in our marriage, and if they do, would you be willing to seek professional help to resolve them or deal with them?
7. If I have emotional or mental problems, would you be willing to live with them?
8. If you are being treated for mental health problems, what is being done for them?
9. Are there any mental health problems in your family? If there are any, are they hereditary?
10. Is there heart disease, cancer, diabetes or other health problems in your family that can be passed down to children or would affect our marriage?
11. Are you on any medications? If so, what are they, and what do they treat?
12. Do you have health and/or life insurance? If not, why not? If yes, what does the policy cover?
13. If yes, do you pay the premiums or does your employer? If you do, how much are your premiums and how often do you pay them?
14. Do you get regular checkups to make sure you are healthy? If not, why not?
15. Do you have a special diet? If so, what does it consist of and why are you on it?
16. Do you have allergies to any foods or drugs? If so, what are they, and what do you do if you get an allergic reaction? If so, do you show proper precaution to safeguard against coming in contact with the allergens and/or do you carry the medication with you for treating an allergy attack? If so, please explain what I should do for you if you have a life threatening allergic reaction.
17. Do you have a primary care doctor? If we get married, would you be willing to give me their contact information?
18. When did you last see a doctor? What was it for?
19. Do you have emergency contact (ICE) numbers in your cell phone or wallet in the event of a medical emergency? If not, would you be willing to put that information in your phone or wallet?

20. If you do not have one, would you be willing to make a will? If you have one, are you willing to change it to include me? Who do you want to be your beneficiary?

21. If you and I both die after we have children, who do you want to raise our children? What stipulations do you want to include in the will in regards to religion, schooling, missions, etc. for our children?

22. Do you want to set up trust accounts for our children? If so, how would you like to do it, and what do you think the money should be used for?

23. If you haven't already done so, how do you feel about making a living will? In other words, do you want heroic measures taken if you are placed on life support? (Suggestion: Before making this decision, make it a serious matter of prayer, as there have been people who have gained consciousness after many years of being in a coma.)

24. Do you have any handicaps? If you are handicapped or mentally challenged, what are your needs?

25. If you need to see a doctor, or need medical treatments on a regular basis, or if you take medications, how much do you have to pay for them each month?

26. If you are taking medications what would happen if you got off of your medication(s)? If you need to take medications, are you careful to take them as prescribed?

Conflict Issues:

1. How do you feel about either of us making a decision that affects both of us or our family before discussing it together and agreeing on it first?

2. When something is bothering you, how do you deal with it?

3. How do you deal with conflicts?

4. Do you think we handle conflict well?

5. How do you think I deal with conflicts, differences of opinion and misunderstandings?

6. Do you think we communicate well? If not, why not?

7. Do you consider me a good listener?

8. Do you consider yourself a good listener?

9. If we are having serious problems getting along, are you willing to seek help from our Bishop or a Counselor to resolve our issues? If not, why not?

10. Are you willing to discuss differences of opinion or misunderstandings with me?

11. Are you willing to give the other person the benefit of the doubt or do you have to be right?

12. Do you think we have problems in our relationship that we need to deal with before we get married? If so, what are they? If so, do you think our problems are fixable? If so, how do you suggest we try to work them out?

13. If you think our problems are more than we are willing or able to deal with, are you willing to break off our engagement?

14. If you feel we should not be getting married, would you be willing to discuss it with me? In addition, would you be willing to fast and pray with me about it before we make a decision like that?

15. Do you consider yourself Christ-centered, others-centered, or a self-centered person? Describe the difference between the three.

16. Do you consider me to be a Christ-centered, others-centered, or a self-centered person?

17. Do you keep from arguing because you are a peace maker?

18. Are you afraid to say what you are feeling if it differs from my opinion(s) or other peoples opinions?

19. Are you afraid others will not like you or will reject you if you do not agree with them?

20. How are we different?

21. How are we alike?

22. Can you live with my differences or diversities?

23. Do you consider trials a blessing or a curse? Explain your answer(s).

24. Do you expect me to change? If so, in what way(s)? If so, can you accept me if I don't change?

25. How well do you forgive *and forget*?

26. Are you willing to work on communication skills with me?

27. Are you willing to share emotional, spiritual, psychological, and intimate concerns with me using the Golden Rule?

Potential problems (**answer all of these**):

1. Do you drink? If so, how often?

2. Are you dependent on pain killers? If so, for what condition(s)?

3. Do you take or are you addicted to illegal drugs? If so, which one(s), and what are you doing to get help for your addition?

4. Do you have any former girlfriends or boyfriends you are still friends with? If so, what do you view as a healthy relationship to keep with them and why?

5. Will you be willing to affair proof our marriage? What does that mean for you and for me?

6. Do you have a criminal record? If so, what for and have you paid your debt to society for each crime?

7. Have you been guilty of child molestation? If so, have you paid your debt to society, and through your priesthood leaders, and are you getting counseling to help you to overcome the tendencies? Do you mind if I speak with your Counselor or priesthood leaders about it? Would you be willing for me to be involved in the counseling so I can know how to deal with it?

8. Are you worthy of a temple recommend? If so, do you have one?

9. Have you been guilty of physical or mental abuse against another person? If you have had or still have the problem, are you seeking professional and/or ecclesiastical help to deal with the problem? If you are getting counseling for the problem, do you mind if I speak with your priesthood leaders or Counselor about it? In addition, would you be willing to let me go to counseling with you so we can deal with it together?

10. Is there anything that has not been addressed in the previous questions that you think would pose a problem in our marriage? If so, please write down your concerns so we can discuss them.

If the couple has answered the questions truthfully then they will have an honest assessment to see where they compliment each other and to see if there are any *hotspots* they need to work on before they get married.

If there are too many differences, and/or discussing them causes heated arguments that seem to be irresolvable, then the couple might consider getting counseling to see if they can work them out or consider breaking off their engagement.

If more couples would make the effort to really get to know each other before they get married, there would be fewer divorces. However, even if the couple goes through each question and answers them as honestly and sincerely as possible, neither can know for sure how they will react in every situation once they are married. Nevertheless, going over these questions when those challenges arise, might help dispel the conflicts and put the couple on more solid footing before becoming husband and wife.

Transitioning From "I" To "We"

Making the adjustment from "I" to "we" can be a challenge even for the most *perfect union*. The fact is, all marriages at some time will go through difficult and even frustrating times.

Years ago, I heard a General Authority claim that when he and his wife had a disagreement, he would take a long walk until he calmed down and think rationally. He said he became known as "the Great Outdoorsman".

In other words, no marriage is immune from strife and problems. However, President Spencer W. Kimball believed that while marriage can be difficult and discordant at times, and that frustrated marriages are common, lasting happiness is possible. As I mentioned before, he was a firm believer that marriage can be more an *exultant ecstasy* than any person can conceive; yet, it is within the capability of every couple and every person to experience such euphoric feelings.[1]

President Spencer W. Kimball shared a "never-fail-marriage-formula", in which he guaranteed that the individuals and couples, who follow it, would have a happy and eternal marriage. However, like all formulas, if any of the key or necessary ingredients are left out, reduced or limited, the formula cannot produce the desired outcome.

President Kimball said that the formula is a simple one, and that the ingredients are but a few, though there are many facets and levels to each. Since I do not have permission to include his words here, I will attempt to summarize the important elements. However, I would strongly encourage every reader to go to the resource in the footnote to read and study what he wrote in its entirety.

1. The individuals and couple need to approach marriage with the proper attitudes—which includes a spouse who is as close to perfection as possible in all the areas that matter most. After doing so, both parties need to approach the altar of the temple, ready to *work hard* towards becoming *one* as husband and wife—which President Kimball referred to as, "Successful Joint Living".

2. There cannot be any selfishness in the marriage or the family.

3. Each spouse and family member needs to forget him or herself. All the actions and attitudes of the individual family members should be for the good of the marriage and the family, subjugating or vanquishing their own self-serving attitudes.

4. Complete adherence to living the commandments of the Lord (as found in the gospel of Jesus Christ), cannot be compromised or shortchanged!

5. The husband and wife should continue to court each other as they did when they were dating—show forth expressions of love and kindness, and make concerted efforts to keep their love alive and growing. [It helps to remember that *love* is a verb as well as a noun.]

President Kimball believed that if a husband and wife would faithfully follow the never-fail-marriage-formula, it would not be possible for unhappiness to stay in their marriage—misunderstandings would quickly be dispelled—and breakups would not occur. Thus, divorce attorneys would have to go into other fields of labor; and divorce courts would have to put padlocks on their doors, as they would have no business. I am glad to see that I am not the only person who believes that divorce can become a thing of the past! The challenge is to get every husband and wife to commit to faithfully following those guidelines!

I envision that in a Zion Society, divorce will be non-existent because the people will be so pure in heart. Therefore, I believe what makes President Kimball's "never-fail-marriage-formula" a success, is that it is actually a formula for preparing families to become so pure in heart that Satan will no longer have power over their minds and hearts...thus making their homes a Zion Society.

President Kimball said that a temple marriage is not a "legal coverall", as it requires sacrifice on the part of both the husband and wife who should share and even sacrifice some of the freedoms that they enjoyed as a single person.

A strong marriage requires dedication of the husband and the wife to be economical. They need to realize that children who bless the union will require money, time, service, sacrifice, and will naturally add to their parent's worries.

President Kimball promised couples who keep all the ingredients blended together of the "Never-Fail-Marriage-Formula", that marriage for them will bring about the deepest and sweetest emotions they will ever feel. [1]

The Wisdom of A Well Planned Honeymoon

Laura Brotherson (author of, "And They Were Not Ashamed - Strengthening Marriage through Sexual Fulfillment") wrote, "A positive and mutually pleasing honeymoon begins the foundation upon which the richest and sweetest relationship ever created by God, can be built. Couples need to understand that education...as well as time and experience, will be needed to create a mutually fulfilling intimate relationship." [2]

The purpose of the honeymoon is to provide a comfortable and safe place where the couple can feel free to express their most intimate feelings for each other without the worry of interruptions or distractions. The couple should not be discouraged if their first few weeks, months, and yes, sometimes years of sexual intimacy are not what they expected or hoped they would be.

Passion is a natural outcome as the couple learns to blend their emotional, social, spiritual, and physical intimacies. Moreover, as the couple continues to add elements from *each* of those intimacies into their daily interactions with each other, they will come to enjoy to a greater degree, the feelings of "exultant ecstasy" that the Lord has provided as a gift for every married couple.

In the beginning, it may seem harmless to leave one or more of the intimacies out of the relationship. However, if left out of balance for too long, the imbalance can cause insurmountable challenges, or damage the relationship to the point where the couple may come to believe that their only recourse is to divorce.

Compare each of those intimacies, to the legs of a chair. If one or more legs are missing, or if any are shorter than the others, the chair *can* fall over causing injury to the person who is trying to sit in it (read "The Parable of the Unwise Carpenter" in Chapter Six).

I want to reemphasize that even though marriage can be difficult and frustrating at times, lasting happiness is possible for every couple.

According to President Kimball, one of the leading causes of divorce was that the couple did not get along sexually. He said they did not always say so, but it is still the main cause. [1]

As bold or hard to believe as that statement is, I have to agree with him. In the 4 + years of study and research that I have put into this book, I have learned that there are many couples, including Latter-day Saint couples, who married in the temple, whose marriages are in serious trouble, and sexual difficulties seem to be at the very root of the reasons the people have given as the cause.

Go to: StrengtheningMarriage.com, and read many accounts that people have posted under "Comments". It is interesting to note that no one is immune to this challenge in marriage, not even Bishops, Stake Presidents, or marriage counselors!

If you think these problems come from individuals that lack in dedication and commitment to the Lord and their spouse, think again. Many faithful LDS couples admit to giving their all to building the Lord's Kingdom, and in being very much in love with their spouse, yet, their marriages are falling apart. Many of them tell of being heartbroken that their spouse seems to have lost interest in them sexually. Interestingly, President Kimball made that observation in the late 1970s, and I would venture to say the problem is much worse in 2011 than it was in the late 1970s.

With all the excellent books on marriage written by LDS authors, and with the Celestial Marriage classes being taught in Institutes and Stakes around the Church, we should not be seeing the alarming increase in divorces among young (and not so young) couples who have married in the temple.

Discerning What Is Okay and What Is Not

Everything the Lord has created, including a grain of sand, to the scariest looking creature, to the most beautiful sunset, are all His masterpieces. Yet none can compare to His greatest creations, which are man and woman. In fact, nothing can compare to the beauty and majesty of an exalted husband and wife in the Celestial Kingdom.

Like a loving Father, He finds great joy in showering blessings on all of His children. However, the greatest blessing He has given to His children is the ability to create life.

As joyous as it is for a new parent to be able to look into the face of their new born child for the first time and to realize that they helped to create that precious, beautiful gift from God, it cannot compare to the sweetness and joy that comes to husbands and wives' as they experience the emotions of becoming one flesh, in the way the Lord designed it to be.

The apostle Paul told the Hebrews: "Marriage is honourable in all, and the bed undefiled" (Hebrews 13:4). Dictionary.com defined *undefiled* as: "Pure, spotless, and innocent".

I love that definition, as it dispels the world's distortions about the most sacred part of a husband and wife's relationship; bringing it into the light the Lord intended. Besides the obvious, where the Lord expects the newly married couple to come to the marriage bed *pure, spotless, and innocent*, I believe Paul's admonition is a testament that the Lord has placed great trust in husbands and wives, to allow them to decide together about "what is okay" and "what is not okay" in how they choose to express their love for each other. Of course there are some things that the Lord would not condone. Nevertheless, a good way to judge is if the behavior elevates and inspires, rather than hurts, degrades, or humiliates.

In a covenant marriage that has been sealed in the temple (D&C 132:7, 18-19, 26), it would be inconceivable that either spouse would do anything that would grieve the Spirit. However, far too many people have been taught and/or believe that some intimate expressions between a husband and wife, that are completely acceptable before the Lord, are evil and dirty, or carnal and devilish. So how is the couple supposed to discern between Godly and un-Godly choices?

Laura Brotherson wrote two excellent articles that can help husbands and wives figure out for them selves what would be appropriate, and what is not appropriate in their intimate relations with each other. Her articles are titled, "What's Okay and What Isn't, Part I – Determining What's Okay Within the Intimate Marital Relationship" and "What's Okay and What Isn't, Part II – Dealing with Sexual Differences in Marriage" (found on MeridianMagazine.com & StrengtheningMarriage.com).

In "A Parent's Guide", under "Mature Intimacy: Courtship and Marriage" (found on LDS.org), it suggests that before the wedding night, the engaged couple should study, on their own, to learn about the diversities and functions of the male and female bodies.[4]

A strict word of caution however, is for the couple to set up strict guidelines that they will stick with so they will *be worthy* to go to the temple on their wedding day.

I have included a list below that a few young married couples have shared with me that helped when they were engaged to be able to stay away from situations that would have made it hard for them to use self-control:

1. Never be alone together for very long.
2. NO PASSIONATE KISSING!
3. No discussions about details to do with sexual intimacy.
4. Practice virtuous habits and thoughts. Learn the difference between those and immoral thoughts in regards to the Lord's design for sexual intimacy.
5. Pray for strength to make righteous choices.
6. Follow promptings of the Spirit and have courage to flee from a situation that might be leading up to crossing the line.

Study and Application vs. Being Spoon-Fed Answers

Even when the newlyweds have made the effort to learn about sexual intimacy before getting married, the wedding night can still be very awkward and embarrassing for them. That is why being tender and considerate with each other's feelings when they are intimate for the first time, is an essential part in developing trust that will flow into other areas of their lives, laying a foundation for helping to strengthen their relationship for many years to come.

In ninth and tenth grade, I had very diverse experiences with history teachers. The first one spoon-fed our class the answers just minutes before taking the tests. Getting a good grade in that class, was assured if you showed up on the day of the test and paid close attention as the teacher gave the answers that would be on the test. He was fun and treated the students like friends. As you can imagine, I loved that teacher…and I got a good grade in the class…big surprise!

The second teacher announced on the first day of class, that no student had ever earned an "A" from any of his previous classes. His tests required either a photographic memory, and/or a complete mastery of the subject, as a wrong answer carried a penalty of twice the value of a right answer. Therefore, if the student missed all 100 questions, he could end up with a minus 200 points! To my knowledge, that teacher was never nominated for the Teacher of the Year Award!

Maybe it was the challenge to accomplish what no other student had been able to accomplish before, or maybe it was just my reaction to his arrogance that gave me the incentive to try to earn an "A" in his class. However, despite my best efforts, I just barely missed earning the "A"…thus leaving his record unblemished.

The latter was one of the most grueling classes I had ever taken. Nevertheless, I learned more from that class than I had in any other class up to that point because I tried to make sure I mastered the material. I wish I could say the same about the 9th grade History class. Sadly, the Monday following the tests, I could not recall much of anything I learned, except that I had a great time in class.

We are all gods and goddesses in embryo. If we expect to become as God is, then we cannot expect to get there by being spoon-fed the answers without making any effort on our own to learn, grow, and prove ourselves faithful.

The Savior requires serious study and prayer for husbands and wives to learn about the most sacred part of their relationship. Many faithful Latter-day Saints, can quote chapter and verse about the law of chastity before marriage. Yet once they are married, they often find themselves back in kindergarten, struggling to learn their "A, B, C"s, in regards to what is okay and what is not okay between husbands and wives.

Laura Brotherson pointed out, "The doctrines of God's law allow for couples to move to a higher level of spirituality, growing line upon line, in their own time. To remove the responsibility from husband and wife for understanding God's intent in the sexual relationship would weaken members of the Church spiritually, rather than strengthen them. In the area of sexual fulfillment in marriage, husband and wife can rise to a higher level of spiritual understanding as they draw nearer to each other and seek divine guidance to distinguish between godly behavior and sinful behavior." [6]

The Lord's Design for Sexuality in Marriage Needs More Airtime

Laura Brotherson said, "Satan's preeminence on this topic allows him to spread his perspective like wildfire without much hindrance. There is barely a faint whisper to counterbalance the world's distorted perspective...The Lord's divine design of marital sexuality needs more airtime" [30]

Steven Kapp Perry (Janice Kapp Perry's son) said "...LDS couples hunger for accurate, yet gospel-centered information to help them connect joyfully in this important part of every marriage relationship." [3]

Laura Brotherson said "In our zeal to keep sacred things sacred we hesitate to talk about them at all. Thus, the sacredness slips into a secretness that can shut the door to needed light and understanding. Sex needs to be taken out of the darkness and brought into God's light." [30]

I have a strong testimony that the Lord will answer the humble, sincere prayers of *every* individual and/or couple who wants to know how they can celestialize all of their intimacies (i.e.: spiritual, emotional, psychological, and even sexual). Nothing is too embarrassing to ask the Lord...nothing! The humble petitioner might be surprised at how comfortable he or she will feel when asking the Lord their most intimate questions; and equally surprised when He answers like a loving Father who cares about *everything* in regards to His precious sons and daughters.

I hope that I have gotten the point across that "proper" sex education is vital for engaged as well as married couples! Just because someone has been married for many years and has had children…even grown ones with their own children…does not mean that they have received proper sex education!

"I tell you these things because of your prayers; wherefore, treasure up wisdom in your bosoms, lest the wickedness of men reveal these things unto you by their wickedness, in a manner which shall speak in your ears with a voice louder than that which shall shake the earth; but if ye are prepared ye shall not fear" (D&C 38:30)…[and you will have the power of discernment as you search, ponder, and pray about *what is okay* and *what is not okay* with sexual intimacy in marriage].

Some Excellent Resources for Engaged and More Seasoned Married Couples

The following are some excellent resources designed to help pre-engaged, engaged, and married couples (of all ages) to be better prepared for all areas of married life:

1. BYU's website, http://beforeforever.byu.edu/mprep.htm
2. "300 Questions LDS Couples Should Ask before Marriage", by Shannon Adler
3. Celestial Marriage Class: offered through LDS Institute of Religion
4. "And They Were Not Ashamed — Strengthening Marriage through Sexual Fulfillment", by Laura M. Brotherson (2004).
5. "From Honeymoon to Happily Ever After", by Laura Brotherson, http://www.meridianmagazine.com/LdsMariageNetwork/060802honeymoon.html
6. "The Act of Marriage – The Beauty of Sexual Love", by Tim and Beverly LaHaye (1998)
7. "Intended for Pleasure", by Ed Wheat, M.D. and Gaye Wheat (1997)
8. "Before The Wedding Night: Pre-Marriage Counsel" by Ed Wheat, M.D. (CDs)
9. "What's Okay and What Isn't, Part II - Dealing with Sexual Differences in Marriage" by Laura M. Brotherson, CFLE, Meridian Magazine, October 24, 2005
10. "What's Okay and What Isn't, Part I - Determining What's Okay within the Intimate Marital Relationship" by Laura M. Brotherson, CFLE, Meridian Magazine, September 22, 2005

As I mentioned at the beginning of this book, you can e-mail me at 2HeartsOneDream@gmail.com to find out how to order Dr. Ed Wheat's books if you are unable to find them, as the bookstore that carries all his books and CDs, does not have a website as of the writing of this book.

Laura Brotherson suggests that "The ultimate answer is that individuals must determine for themselves, with the help of the Spirit, when it would be best for them to read and learn more about this subject. Women are generally less affected by sexual information, and can especially benefit from this learning prior to their honeymoon. Men also can benefit from such knowledge, if they are able to maintain control of their thoughts. If not, the man might consider reading this material...shortly before the wedding day. [In addition] Young brides-to-be need to be attentive to the different mental wiring of young men, and not unwittingly put their fiancés in a precarious [unsafe or risky] situation." [2] (Emphasis added)

Meeting Each Others Needs *after* Becoming Husband and Wife

Once the couple is married, they need to make sure to meet each other's needs emotionally and physically. As I mentioned earlier, the number one cause of divorce often has to do with the couple not getting along sexually. [7]

Laura Brotherson wrote, "With 'intimacy issues' as one of the primary causes of divorce and dissatisfaction in marriage, it is important that couples make it a priority to prepare for the honeymoon and the intimate aspects of marriage rather than allow them selves to be consumed solely by the wedding day arrangements. Truly fulfilling physical intimacy is a learned behavior requiring knowledge, time, and preparation." [2]

In regards to the honeymoon, Dr. Ed Wheat told couples (that came to him for pre-marriage counseling) that balancing their funds to be free of responsibility for a few weeks, would allow the couple more time to get to know each other. He suggested that during that time together, they should be able to have clearer communication lines than they may ever have again. He further emphasized that rushing, or shortchanging those lines of communication during those first few days of getting to "know" each other, can cause blocked communication lines that can deteriorate as time progresses. [7]

Did you catch that last line? How many divorced men and women can look back and pin point when the deterioration started to take place in their failed marriage? Moreover, how many of those moments take place on the honeymoon, and had to do with unfulfilled or botched emotional and physical intimacy expectations? In addition, how many of those formerly married men and women dealt with broken lines of communication because they were too embarrassed to talk about sex, and/or the hurt or frustration they felt as they were getting to "know" each other?

The tragic thing is, far too many husbands and wives just shove those feelings aside, then stumble and struggle until they finally decide that it is no longer worth the effort, deciding instead to throw in the towel and give up on their hopes and dreams of a "Happily-Ever-After" with the person they had planned to spend eternity with.

David's Counsel to His Son Solomon on His Wedding Day

"Rejoice in the wife of thy youth…be thou ravished *always* with her love" (Proverbs 5:18-19).

David's wise counsel to his son Solomon, would be very good advice for every groom to hear before his wedding day—and to remember every day thereafter to help his bride to continue to feel like she did on their wedding day…or like she should have felt on their wedding day.

PMS 101

Husbands, if your otherwise sweet and pleasant wife exhibits any of the following symptoms for three to seven days each month, she could be suffering from Premenstrual Syndrome, also known as PMS:

☐ Exaggerated mood swings

☐ Depression

☐ Irritable

☐ Oversensitivity

☐ Anger

☐ Signs of bitterness

☐ Resentment

☐ Seems out of control

☐ Cries for no apparent reason

There are other symptoms that sometimes go along with PMS, but they don't usually cause husbands to want to seek shelter until their wife's symptoms subside.

These symptoms might include any or all of the following:

☐ Being overly tired

☐ Forgetful

☐ Clumsy

☐ Craving sweets, carbohydrates, or salty foods

☐ Bloating due to water retention (making it hard to zip up her pants)

☐ Headaches

☐ Breast tenderness

☐ Sleep disturbances (too much or too little)

☐ Overeating

☐ Weight gain

☐ Backaches

☐ Cold sores

☐ Sinus problems

☐ Asthmatic attacks

☐ Seizures

☐ Acne

PMS Is Not a Character Flaw

PMS can hit any woman at any age, but it seems to target mainly women in their twenties and thirties. However, pregnancy and the discontinuation of taking birth control pills seem to intensify the symptoms.

PMS is NOT a character flaw in the women who suffer from it, nor do the symptoms mean that she is weak or unstable. And most importantly, the struggle a woman goes through when she is suffering from PMS does NOT necessarily mean that her life is out of balance spiritually. Therefore, there is no need for the woman to visit with her Bishop after suffering from these symptoms…unless her behavior is so bad that it is adversely affecting hers and her family's physical and/or emotional well-being. If her behavior gets that extreme, it would be wise for her to seek medical help and/or professional counseling.

Upon reflecting on this dilemma, I could not help but wonder how many women have been thought to be crazy and have been institutionalized for nothing more than undiagnosed PMS symptoms.

Part of the dilemma for the women who struggle with PMS, is in being able to pinpoint what is causing them to be so upset or flying off the handle over things that normally do not bother them.

A woman getting to know her own body with how she reacts with PMS symptoms helps in being able to deal with the troublesome attitudes and behavior when they appear unannounced on the doorstep each month.

Something that would also help for the sufferer's spouse and family is to pay close attention to what the recurrent symptoms are, as well as when and how long they last. The delicate balance is for the sufferer to be able to receive the observations of loved ones, as helps not personal attacks.

Another thing that would greatly help, is for all in the family…including the one suffering from the symptoms…to remember when the symptoms are at their worst…that there is a beautiful daughter of God inside who will reappear once the symptoms subside.

A word to the wise: If the husband decides to point his observations out to their wife, they should consider timing, tact, and most of all LOVE in how they choose to do so. Such an endeavor should NEVER be used to vent frustration, or as an attack, but to enlighten and ease the suffering of a beloved spouse, as well as the rest of the family.

The husband should always reinforce this approach with love unfeigned. The following advice found in D&C 121:41, 43 would be excellent for him to study before taking on such a daunting and RISKY undertaking…no matter how well-meaning his intentions are: "No power or influence can or ought to be maintained by virtue of the priesthood, only by persuasion, by long-suffering, by gentleness and meekness, and by love unfeigned…when moved upon by the Holy Ghost; and then showing forth afterwards an increase of love toward him whom thou hast reproved [admonished], lest he [or she] esteem thee to be his [or her] enemy…" (Emphasis added)

Some women who suffer from PMS symptoms, have found that increasing their spirituality, as well as their relationship and dependence upon the Lord, helps them to be better able to handle the symptoms when they occur.

Some have reported that limiting their intake of salt, sugar, caffeine and increasing their exercise, as well as using vitamins and herbs (that have proven benefits for PMS symptoms), has offer welcomed relief.

Even though not all women suffer from PMS symptoms, about 80% suffer from at least one or two of the symptoms mentioned above. It is estimated, that about 2% to 6% suffer from the more severe symptoms, which are referred to as Premenstrual Dysphoric Disorder or PMDD. A website that describes the symptoms associated with PMDD, as well as the treatments for those symptoms, can be found on the Internet.

A very helpful diagnostic tool is to keep a Menstrual/PMS diary, which documents physical and emotional symptoms, as well as duration over several months. If the same or similar symptoms show up consistently around ovulation (mid-cycle, or days 7-10 into the menstrual cycle) and persist until the menstrual flow begins, then PMS is probably the correct diagnosis. Keeping a Menstrual/PMS diary not only helps the healthcare provider in making a correct diagnosis, but it also helps the woman, as well as her spouse and family members to be better able to deal with the symptoms when they occur…which are usually very treatable.

PMS can be difficult to diagnosis because of the many medical and psychological conditions that mimic or worsen the symptoms. Unfortunately, there are no known laboratory tests to determine if a woman has PMS. However, the healthcare practitioner may want to use laboratory tests to rule out other conditions that can mimic PMS symptoms. [32]

PMS Shelters for Men

Jeff Foxworthy spoke for all men who deal with women who suffer from PMS symptoms when he said, "You may as well check into Ralph's PMS Shelter for Men, because a week is a terrible thing to waste."

All kidding aside, let me ask you husbands a question. "Are you always PRINCE CHARMING in how you treat your wife and family?"

In addition, are there days when your temperament more resembles Shrek? Also, when your wife may be in "one of those moods"…remember…kindness begets kindness. In other words, if you treat your wife like a *princess* when you may be feeling she least deserves it, then she may decide to repay your kindness when PRINCE CHARMING, is NOT what would best describe your behavior or attitude.

When you come home from work or school, instead of seeing a well-kept house and a charming wife, you see disarray, and you could very easily accuse someone of kidnapping and cloning your wife, as the woman who meets you at the door, more closely reminds you of a shrew than the loving wife who usually greets you…do you:

1. Turn and run out of the door saying you forgot to pick something up at the store, and then stay away for a few hours until you think it is safe to return? Then, after entering the house, you quickly bury yourself behind a newspaper or the computer to avoid contact with her?

2. Ask her what she has been doing all day, then plant yourself in front of the T.V. and ask when dinner will be ready?

3. Give her a big hug and kiss, and tell her how beautiful she is and how much you missed her, and then walk right past her and the toys on the floor and plant yourself in front of the T.V. (after pushing the piles of laundry out of the way), and then ask where the remote is…and when dinner will be ready?

4. Offer to help with or fix dinner and then suggest she go relax in a warm bath? Then, while the warm bath water works its magic, you do the dishes, or help the kids with their homework, and then put them to bed. Then, fold the laundry that is piled on the couch, and put it away. And when she gets out of the tub, offer to give her a good back and foot massage…with no strings attached.

Which one of those choices do you think will help your wife feel like a beloved and cherished sweetheart? Better still, which one will help her be more willing to repay your love and kindness when you have had a rough day and are not being your *best-self*?

Let me add an eternal perspective: You are building a relationship that will last the eternities…so why not invest wisely by doing random acts of kindness on a regular basis, while using the Wisdom of Solomon and exercising the patience of Job when your wife is suffering from PMS symptoms, or is just having a bad day?

Moral of the story: How can any woman stay upset with her PRINCE, when he is being so *charming?*

Be Wise with Your Finances

On LDS.org, on the home page, there is a link to "Provident Living" (found under "Related Sites" on the left sidebar); you will find a variety of excellent suggestions by Church leaders in regards to emergency and family preparedness. For many years, Church leaders have counseled Church members to prepare for emergencies and to be wise with their resources. [8]

"...if ye are prepared ye shall not fear" (D&C 38:30). In other words, those who follow this wise counsel will be better able to sleep when the gale force winds start to blow...which they surely do in every life.

Teaching Frugality Should Begin Before and While Planning the Wedding

If the goal is to teach young couples to be frugal, then why is it so many couples begin their life together with elaborate and costly weddings and then they cannot afford to buy groceries or pay their first months rent? Wouldn't it make more sense for the couple and/or their parents to find ways to cut costs with the wedding so the couple can better afford a place to live, or be able to have reliable transportation, or even to have money to put towards schooling?

Pay Tithes and Offerings

"Will a man rob God? Yet ye have robbed me. But ye say, wherein have we robbed thee? In tithes and offerings...Ye are cursed with a curse: for ye have robbed me, even this whole nation...Bring ye all the tithes into the storehouse, that there may be meat in mine house, and prove me now herewith, saith the LORD of hosts, if I will not open you the windows of heaven, and pour you out a blessing, that there shall not be room enough to receive it...And I will rebuke the devourer for your sakes, and he shall not destroy the fruits of your ground; neither shall your vine cast her fruit before the time in the field, saith the LORD of hosts." (Malachi 3:8-10).

I consider tithing as paying my fire insurance.

Avoid Debt like it is the Plague

Spending less money than you make is crucial to your financial security. Avoid debt with the exception of buying an affordable home, for education, or other vital needs. Try to save money when you need to purchase a car or appliances. If you are in debt, pay it off as quickly as possible. To avoid impulse buying, ask yourself, "Is this a need or a want?"

Years ago, when our oldest children were toddlers, my husband bought a car for a dollar from a man he worked with. In New Jersey, you had to pay for the vehicle to be able to transfer the title to yourself, so instead of giving the car for free (which is what the man wanted to do), he asked Eric to pay him a dollar for the car.

Eric towed the car behind a van that we had purchased, to make the trip from New Jersey to Texas. That van was another story! It was a 1966 Ford van that was frog green, with a bad case of rust. But, it got us where we needed to go!

When we got to Texas, my husband's best attempts to get the car to run were unproductive. I told the Lord, if He would help Eric get the car running, I would exercise the faith needed to keep it going until we could afford to replace it. Minutes later, Eric came in the apartment and told me he did not know how, but the car finally started. It literally ran on faith until we were able to replace it.

Eric had to tighten bolts nearly every day to keep the engine from dropping onto the ground, and claimed he poured more oil into it than gasoline. However, it kept running until the moment we coaxed it into the dealership to trade it in on another vehicle. A friend, who worked there, reported that they never were able to get it started after we dropped it off.

I learned from that experience that there is nothing the Lord cannot do when we put our unwavering faith and trust in Him.

Use a Budget

Keep a record of your expenditures. Record your monthly income and expenses. Determine how to reduce what you spend for nonessentials. Use this information to establish a family budget. Plan what you will give as Church donations; how much you will save; and what you will spend for food, housing, utilities, transportation, clothing, insurance, and so on. Discipline yourself to live within your budget.

Budget Worksheet

Budget for: _____ Month/Year: _____

Income	Planned	Actual
Wages/Salaries (after taxes)		
Other Income		
Total Income		

Expenses	Planned	Actual
Church donations		
Savings		
Food		
Mortgage or Rent		
Utilities		
Transportation		
Insurance		
Medical		
Other		
Total expenses		
Income less expenses		

If you find yourself in debt, a debt-elimination calendar can help you reduce or eliminate that debt. It is actually very simple to use. First you make several columns on a piece of paper, like the chart below. In the first column on the left, write the names of the months, beginning with the upcoming month. At the top of the next column, write the name of the creditor you want to pay off first. It may be the debt with the highest interest rate, or the earliest pay-off date. List the monthly payment for that creditor until the loan is repaid, as shown in the illustration below. At the top of the next column, record the name of the second creditor you want to pay off. Now list the payments due each month. After you have repaid the first creditor, add the amount of that monthly payment to the next creditor that you want to pay off. (In the example below, notice that the monthly payments of $110 that were made to the credit card company, was added to the $70 furniture payment, creating a new monthly payment of $180. Continue the process until all the loans are repaid.

	Credit Card	Furniture	Dentist	Physician	Auto Loan
DEBT ELIMINATION CALCULATOR					
Mar	110	70	50	75	235
Apr	110	70	50	75	235
May	110	70	50	75	235
Jun	110	70	50	75	235
Jul	0	180	50	75	235
Aug		180	50	75	235
Sep		180	50	75	235
Oct		0	230	75	235
Nov			230	75	235
Dec			0	305	235
Jan				0	540

Extra Tips on Budgeting

Determine how much money is needed per month to cover expenses. Using a checkbook helps to keep track of income and where the money is going. However, make sure to record each check and deposit as quickly as possible, and balance your checkbook as soon as you get your statement. This way you will catch charges that you may not have entered or may not have been aware of.

Before going shopping for groceries, it helps to make a list of the food you already have, and then see if you can make up a menu for a week or two using just the food in your home. You may also consider using the food storage that has an expiration date so you can use it before it goes bad. Just make sure to replace it. Using your food storage also helps you and your family to get used to eating it in the event that you have to live off of it.

If after making your menu for the week, you need extra items, then make up a shopping list and take it with you to the store. Make sure to stick with it. If you see that you have put things in your shopping cart that are not on your list and/or are not needed, or that you have gone over what you budgeted for, then keep the essentials and put the other items back on the shelf.

It helps to look through sales papers that come in the mail from grocery stores. They often have very good deals. However, burning up gas to run from store to store to save a few pennies per item is not good use of your time or money.

To help with this, find stores that will accept another store's coupons. There are stores that will price match if another store is selling the item for less. Just ask the cashier if you do not see a sign saying so.

Using coupons also helps cut back on what you spend out. One woman I know filled her pantry paying much less, or getting items for free, because she made good use of store and manufacturer coupons.

Turn off the lights in a room when it is not occupied.

If you will raise the thermostat to $78^0 - 80^0$ during summer months, and use ceiling fans to make it more comfortable in the house, and then put on sweaters and lower the thermostat to $68^0 - 69^0$ during winter months, you will notice an improvement in your electric and heating bills.

The Pros and Cons of Dollar Stores

Dollar stores seem to be the answer to the frugal shoppers' prayers. However, there are some things to consider before walking through their doors:

1. A good number of items in dollar stores can be purchased elsewhere for less than a dollar.

2. Since each item is only a dollar, it is easy to lose track of how many items you have put into your cart, until the cashier tells you the amount owed. Then it may be too embarrassing or inconvenient to put things back. So, use caution and pay attention to how many items you have put into your cart.

3. Sometimes the quality is so poor that the item does not last long.

4. On the other hand, I have felt very pleased with many purchases I have made at dollar stores, such as: silk flowers, party supplies, gift bags, picture frames, packs of pens and pencils, birthday and special occasion helium balloons, kitchen utensils, little figurines, and baskets. I have even found quality name brand foods that were less expensive than the regular grocery stores were selling them for.

I want to repeat, with the exception of buying a home, paying for education, or making other essential investments, to avoid debt and the resulting finance charges like they are the plague.

Buyer Beware When Purchasing Vacations and Timeshares

When it comes to taking a vacation, use cash whenever possible. If you are tempted to use a credit card, consider the interest and finance charges that you will pay if you do not pay off the credit card before the month is up.

When considering purchasing a time-share, consider the following:

1. Do not be taken in by smooth talking salesmen who will say anything to sell their product, but will do nothing to stand behind their sales pitch. *Get it in writing, or it does not exist.*

2. Too often, the ruses they use to get the consumer in for the sales pitch, such as: free cruises, airline tickets for two, vacations to different resorts, are often either too hard to find a date that you are able to go on, or you have to sit through a 1 ½ - 4 hour arm twisting sales presentation to get the gifts, or the cost to go on the so-called *free* cruise is more expensive than if you were to purchase it yourself.

3. There are the maintenance fees that usually cost close to $500.00 per year. Then there is the transfer fee of $129.00 or more if you go to a different resort, along with the cleaning fee of close to $50.00 a night to use the resort, and that is if you are lucky to find an available date that you can use your timeshare.

4. If you decide that you are not able to use your timeshare, then good luck trying to rent it or sell it!

5. In defense of timeshares, I know people who have the income and free time where they are able to go from resort to resort all over the world. However, those people are few and far between, especially with today's economic conditions.

Interest From Credit Cards Never Sleeps Nor Takes A Vacation!

Some things to consider about credit cards are the following:

1. Avoid installment credit, and be careful with your use of credit cards. They are principally for convenience and identification and should not be used carelessly or recklessly.

2. Remember, interest never sleeps or takes a vacation.

3. The use of multiple credit cards significantly adds to the risk of excess debt.

4. Buy used items until you have saved sufficiently to purchase quality new items.

5. Purchasing poor-quality merchandise almost always ends up being very expensive.

6. Those who choose to ignore or avoid their creditors are entitled to feel the inner frustrations that such conduct merits, and they are not being honest in all their business dealings.

Bankruptcy should be a Last Resort

Bankruptcy should be avoided, except only under the most unique and irreversible circumstances. In D&C 104: 78 the Lord told Joseph Smith, "And again, verily I say unto you concerning your debts - behold it is my will that you shall pay all your debts".

However, there are times when the couple, whether through loss of a job, business failure, prolonged illness, high medical bills, injury or permanent disability, and divorce or death, that the individual or couple finds that they are unable to pay their bills. In those circumstances, they should be prayerful and make sure to seek counsel with competent legal and financial consultants before making the decision to declare bankruptcy. It will stay on their record 7-10 years. And to be honest, they will have to put down that they have declared bankruptcy when applying for a future loan, even when it is past the 7-10 year time period.

However, having mentioned all of that, due to the economic conditions in the U.S. in 2011, a person or couple can purchase a home or automobile almost as soon as they declare bankruptcy or go through a foreclosure of their home, or a repossession of their vehicle, because so many people are going through financial hardships that the banks are being forced to get more creative.

Self-reliance and Thrift

Our Church leaders have counseled us for decades to become self-reliant and to be wise with the use of our funds. In the past few years with credit being so easy to obtain, there are record numbers of people who have taken on heavy amounts of debt to purchase things that are not necessities. Many of those people are unable to pay their bills, requiring them to default on their homes and other debts they owe on. Some are declaring bankruptcy and others are just walking away from their homes and other financial obligations. I heard on the news a while back, where two different men in our town lost their construction jobs, one due to a heart attack, and the other due to the crash in the building industry over the last few years. Both men lost everything, including their wives (who divorced them); and those men were reported to be living in tents in the desert. The welfare system failed these men because their income last year was too high to get welfare (according to their income tax returns), and now they do not have an address, which is required to be able to get welfare benefits.

Our Church leaders have wisely counseled us to get out of debt and to build a reserve for when emergencies happen. The following are some lessons from the *Provident Living* site on LDS.org that can be given in Family Home Evenings [9]:

1. Family Finance: Family Finance Lesson Materials
2. Financial Responsibility
3. Young Women Manual 2, Lesson 46, 175–78

4. Managing Family Finances

5. Duties and Blessings of the priesthood: Basic Manual for priesthood Holders, Part A, Lesson 21, 153–59

6. Marriage and Family Relations Instructor's Manual, Lesson 8, 35–40

7. Temporal Wealth and the Kingdom of God

8. Teachings of Presidents of the Church: Brigham Young, Chapter 32, 234–41

If we will make the effort to follow the prophets, then we will have a deep sense of peace and security and will be able to sleep when the wind blows.

Build a Reserve

Gradually build a financial reserve to be used for emergencies only. If you save a little money regularly, you will be surprised how much accumulates over time. Save and wisely invest a percentage of your income.

With the economy the way it is, the stock market is not as safe to invest in as it has been in times past. Make a serious study of what is the safest way to invest your money. Keep yourself informed about financial markets and the news to protect your investments.

It would be wise to build a savings account *that can be easily accessed*, that is sufficient to cover at least three months of your financial obligations.

Teach Family about Financial Stability and the Importance of Obtaining a Good Education

Parents should teach their children how to create and work within a budget, and learning to set family financial goals, which should include setting proper examples of the principles of hard work, frugality, and saving money.

Parents should obtain and encourage their children to obtain as much education as possible, in fields where they can make a decent living. There are a number of degrees where the graduate finds it hard to find work, or if they do find a job in their chosen field, it is hard to make a living. It would be wise to study out the different careers and see what degrees provide the most stable and best incomes.

Daily Scripture Study and Prayer

President Marion G. Romney taught that if parents would prayerfully read the Book of Mormon not only on their own, but also with their children every day, that peace and harmony in their home would increase and the spirit of contention would not exist there. In such a home, more kindness and respect would be shown to family members, and children would be more likely to be obedient and submissive to their parents' counsel. Righteousness, faith, hope, and charity would increase, and the pure love of Christ would permeate the atmosphere of their home, as well as in the hearts of family members. Therefore, living in such a home, would bring peace and joy to each family member, even if storms are raging outside of the home. [9]

Many faithful Latter-day Saints find it difficult in their family's busy schedules to find the time for prayer and scripture study. However, I speak from experience when I say, "Parents cannot afford *not* to make time for daily scripture study and prayer with their families."

I saw firsthand as a child and as a parent, the drastic differences in the dynamics in our home and family when we made the time to read and study from the scriptures daily and when we did not.

Temple Marriage

Have the courage and conviction to marry the right person, in the right place, at the right time. Elder Boyd K. Packer said that parents should not feel like failures if their children do not turn out as they wish. It would be different if we lived in a world free of Satan's influences. All too often, parents who have put their heart and soul into raising and training their children in the paths of righteousness, are heartbroken when their children rebel. Such parents often find themselves confused and feeling helpless because they have tried so hard and cannot understand where they failed.

President Packer said that evil influences will one day lose their power over the hearts of men. Such teachings should give great hope to parents with children who have strayed.

There are binding ties that take place in the sealing ordinances of the temple, and it is through those ordinances that children who are sealed to parents, who continue to keep their temple covenants, will be bound to them forever. [10]

Attend Temple Regularly

President Gordon B. Hinckley counseled members of the church to attend the temple regularly so there would be less selfishness in their lives. [11]

At the Manti Temple rededication in 1987, Elder Vaughn J Featherstone promised members of the Church that if they would be more faithful in their temple work that their families would draw closer to the Lord and angels would protect them from harm, as well as Satan's influence. In addition, they would also have an increase in spiritual experiences, and the veil would become very thin. [28]

My husband and I have found this promise to be true. As we increase our efforts in finding our ancestors and providing the saving ordinances for them in the temple, the veil has become very thin at times. The spirit of love has increased in our home, and we have felt the love and joy from those we have performed the ordinances for.

We saw Elder Featherstone's promises fulfilled over and over again as we were raising our children, and we are continuing to see the promises be fulfilled in our sons' families as they are faithful to their temple covenants and make the effort to attend the temple regularly.

Imagine the joy I felt when visiting our son and his wife in Ohio a few months ago, when after scripture study and prayer, our grandkids, ages 2-6, wanted to take their copies of the Book of Mormon to bed with them because they did not want to let the books out of their presence. What our son and his wife are teaching their children will have a lasting impact throughout their lives, especially during their difficult teenage years when so many give into peer pressure.

In his talk, "Our Temples are Havens in a World of Turmoil", Elder Featherstone said that the wickedness in the world will become worse than at any other time in the history of the world. He stressed that in such a world, the only safe places will be found in the temples. He said that law enforcement agencies will not be able to provide the safety we will seek, and that church membership alone will not provide it.

The times will become so wicked that even the most righteous will lose hope if they do not attend the temple on a regular basis. The righteous will not only strive to do the work for their deceased ancestors, but to find safety and peace. Parents will long to have their children go in with them for their safety and peace.

Elder Featherstone said that angels act as sentinels, guarding every door of the temples. It will be like in the days of Elisha where he said, "Those that be with us are more than they that be against us." (2 Kings 6:16)

There will be an increase of hosts of Heaven in the temples as the time draws closer to the Second Coming. Elder Featherstone said that those who attend the temple will feel the spirits of ancient as well as modern day prophets strengthening them and being their companions.

He stressed that our garments will give us the same protection outside of the temple as when we are inside the temple, and that the covenants and ordinances we partake of will fill our hearts with faith that will be as consuming as a fire.

He said when desolating sickness, plagues, disease, and destruction will fill the earth, the latter-day saints will find refuge in the shade of the trees, and will find refreshment in the cool fountains on the temple grounds. The righteous will be lifted up as on eagle's wings, and will find safety from a very evil world. [31]

We cannot expect to understand all the temple ceremonies when we first attend the temple. We need to attend again and again so we can learn the deeper meanings, and how to apply them in our lives. Latter-day Prophets have told us that in the temple we can receive answers to our questions and trials that we are dealing with, and that things that have seemed like a mystery, will become clearer to us.

We should ponder and pray to understand the meanings of the ceremonies. After leaving the temple, we should continue to ponder and pray about what we have learned. As we do so, our understanding will increase and we will gain a stronger testimony and understanding of the Plan of Salvation and God's purposes for mankind. Regular temple attendance will also help us stay in tune so it is easier to recognize when we get off course. [12]

The Prophet Joseph Smith said we become saviors on Mount Zion when we build temples and receive all our baptismal and temple ordinances, as well as when we provide the saving ordinances for our ancestors, so they too can enjoy exaltation and thrones of glory. [13]

Is it any wonder that family research is moving forward at such a rapid pace?

There is no work on earth, that is more spiritually refining, or gives us more power, or that requires a higher standard of righteousness than temple work. However, the blessings only come if we will believe and accept the temple ordinances for ourselves.

If we will take upon ourselves our temple covenants without *hesitation* or *apology*, the Lord will protect us, and we will receive inspiration and strength to meet life's challenges. If you have not already done so, make a commitment here and now to go to the temple and claim those blessings for yourself and your loved ones who have passed on to the other side of the veil. [14]

Husbands Love Your Wife Like Christ Loved the Church and gave himself for it (Ephesians 5:25)

We can expect to get back what we are willing to put into our marriages. So, what will it be...10%...50%...or 100%? The Lord gave all, should we give anything less to the one we have chosen to spend eternity with?

In verse 26 of Ephesians 5, husbands are counseled not to be bitter against their wives. In a covenant marriage, there cannot be *any* room for bitterness, frustration, contention, anger, and dare I say it? ...Self-pity. We are all imperfect beings. Therefore, there will be times, even in the best of marriages, when one, if not all of those emotions will rear their ugly heads. The danger is when we invite them into our hearts and homes with open arms, and treat them as if they are long-lost friends, and then refuse to bid them a speedy farewell.

The Spirit cannot abide in such an environment. Furthermore, if those destructive attitudes are allowed to fester for too long, feelings of love and respect for one another, can quickly feel like strangers in a strange land.

It is a temptation to hold onto the hurt and self-pity that are the natural outcome of being the victim of such behavior. However, it is a temptation we must not give into!

The Savior taught us how to deal with such feelings when He said, "Wherefore, I say unto you, that ye ought to forgive one another; for he that forgiveth not his brother his trespasses standeth condemned before the Lord; for there remaineth in him the greater sin...I, the Lord, will forgive whom I will forgive, but of you it is required to forgive all men." (D&C 64:9)

The Husband Is the Head of the Wife Like Christ Is To the Church: (Ephesians 5:25)

The message in Ephesians 5:25 should not be confused with the husband being overbearing or forcing unrighteous dominion over his wife and children. On the contrary, the husband/father should follow Christ's example in how He loved, taught, guided, counseled, and prayed for His followers.

Our Church leaders have counseled wives' to sustain and support their husbands' as their husbands' sustain and follow the Savior (Ephesians 5:25). It goes without saying, couples that love each other, should want to sustain and support each other in their individual and collective roles as husband and wife.

A true Saint wants more than anything else, to follow the Savior's example and will. However, when it comes to applying those teachings into our every day family relationships, it can be hard to understand how they apply to what we are going through at that very moment in our lives. That is why we are told to search, ponder, and pray as we read the scriptures. For it is in those sacred moments, when a humble, teachable heart and mind, are more likely to be open to the impressions and enlightenment that can come as gentle dew from Heaven. However, keep in mind what happens to dew when the sun comes out. It does not stay long. Therefore, we must quickly record and treasure up in our hearts and/or act on those promptings to those things we are taught from on high, for times when we feel like Lehi in his dream of the Tree of Life, when he was struggling to hold onto the Iron Rod while walking through the midsts of darkness.

How can the Lord deny the humble petitions of a spouse/parent, who gives his/her hands, mouth, mind and heart completely over to Him; being willing to give up all, even their sins and weaknesses to know Him and to become like Him (Alma 22:18).

Such efforts can be especially difficult for a husband or wife when their marriage seems to be thread bare and falling apart. However, when a humble and teachable spouse turns to the Lord...that is when their "Will you fix my spouse?" transforms into, "What is it I lack?"

It was at one of those times, before we had children, when my husband was putting in long hours at school and studying, and I was also putting in long hours at work, that I chose Saturdays to catch up on chores around the house. However, one Saturday, while immersing myself in my chores, Eric was being short and unpleasant with me. Before chewing him out for how he was treating me, I chose instead, the refuge of our bedroom, where I knelt to plead for the Lord's help.

At first, all I could think of was to ask the Lord to "fix" my husband…to make him be nice to me. After all, I reasoned, Couldn't Eric see that I was trying to make the house look nice…*for him?*

Yet, as I knelt, my prayers turned from "Will you please fix him?" to, "Help me see and understand what he is going through. And help me know what to do."

I no sooner uttered that humble, heartfelt plea, when the thought came to my mind, with perfect clarity, that my husband was feeling neglected, and that he needed to know that he was important to me. Therefore, I got up from my knees, and went into the living room, and as tenderly as I knew how, I asked if Eric was feeling neglected and unloved.

The look in his eyes said it all as he tenderly told me that he wished to spend some time with me since we did not get to see much of each other during the week, and he did not want to interrupt what I was doing.

I am always amazed at how quickly the Lord can turn hurt, cold, or lukewarm hearts into feelings of love that can be sweeter than words can express.

I do not believe most couples who divorce, intentionally forget and abandon their wedding vows. I honestly believe in part, that it comes from not having a clear understanding of what it means to support and sustain each other and/or not knowing how to apply those vows and commitments in their own marriages.

It helped me to go to the Thesaurus as well as Dictionary.com, to get a better understanding of what it means to support and sustain. The *Thesaurus* gave the following words in relation to *support*: "Hold up; sustain; maintain; shore up; buoy up; brace; pillar; encourage; back; cheer on; help; assist; aid; be there for; defend; champion; espouse; take care of; look after; and strengthen."

Dictionary.com defined *sustain* as: "…support, hold, or bear up from below"; "…to bear the weight of"; "To bear a burden"; "…endure without giving way or yielding"; "…to keep (a person, the mind, the spirits, etc.) from giving way, as under trial or affliction"; "…to keep up or keep going, as an action or process"; "…to supply with food, drink, and other necessities of life"; "…to support (a cause or the like) by aid or approval"; "…to uphold as valid, just, or correct, as a claim or the person making it"; "…to confirm or corroborate, as a statement".

Those are essential keys for couples to be able to gain entrance into the highest degree of the Celestial Kingdom. The Savior places great trust in husbands in His counsel for them to be like Him, by how He expects them to love and treat their wives. Take a moment and think about how Christ treated his Disciples and followers. Imagine the love and selflessness that it took for Him to go through the Atonement...all alone...while His Disciples slept...even after He pleaded with them to stay awake and pray for Him in His greatest hour of need.

Now, put that kind of love, commitment and selfless sacrifice into a husband's relationship with his wife; and his wife sustaining and supporting him in the same way. Can you get the picture of why the Savior chose those two words to help covenant husbands and wives to know how to build a Celestial marriage?

What causes you to love and to be as devoted as you are to the Lord? I say in part, that it has to do with what it says in 1 John 4:19: "We love Him because he first loved us."

Now, wouldn't it be much easier to love, support, and sustain someone (even an imperfect spouse) who tries to love and treat us as Christ does the Church?

Unfortunately, none can come close to the love the Lord shows us. However, someday, if we will continue to follow His example, we will become like Him...which means, we will love as He loves.

Have you ever wondered what makes His love so deep? I am convinced that it is much easier to understand, than to achieve. Have you noticed when you serve someone, not just give a token effort, or grumble and complain as you serve them, that you cannot help but love them...even if you hardly know them?

The more selfless and difficult the sacrifice, the more we love the person(s) we serve. That explains why the Savior loves us as completely and deeply as He does...even those who will never appreciate it or reciprocate those feelings...even those who caused Him to bleed from every pour and caused His inhumane suffering before He died on the cross.

The Dangers of Role Reversals

A serious problem I have seen in and out of the Church is where the women are becoming independent, and in some cases, they act like they are the heads of their households. Husbands in those homes, are often treated like one of the children, and/or like their opinion, if it differs from their wife's opinion, is stupid or does not have any merit.

Years ago, when we received a letter from a married friend, I was shocked when I saw that the wife had added a few lines, telling how stupid he was because his writing skills were so poor. In addition, she often told others (in front of him) that he was stupid.

I often wondered how he managed to take such verbal and emotional abuse. Then, a few years later, when she wrote and told us that he had left her for another woman, I was heartsick, but not surprised.

There is nothing wrong with women being strong and leaders. However, there is a fine balance with knowing when and how to support their husbands as the leaders of their homes.

The challenge some wives face, is when their husband's will not take the reins, or they will not lead; or if they do lead, they will not lead in righteousness. What then?

There is an old adage that says, "Treat a man the way you want him to be and he will eventually become that person".

This can go two ways. If a wife, who is struggling with a clueless or fledgling husband, will treat him with dignity and respect, and as if he is already a wise and righteous priesthood holder, giving her best efforts to support and sustain him in that role, he will in most cases, rise up to meet her expectations of him.

But, if she brow beats him, and criticizes or demands that he be those things, then she should not be surprised if he mirrors her behavior, or ignores her demands all together...*even if he knows she is right*.

The same advice can go for a husband who treats his wife like she is already a wonderful wife and mother (even if it is hard to see those qualities in her). Then in most cases, the day will come when it will be hard to imagine that she was ever anything less.

Wives Should Reverence Their Husbands

"Nevertheless let every one of you in particular so love his wife even as himself; and the wife *see* that she reverence *her* husband" (Ephesians 5:33).

The following definitions (found in Dictionary.com) add light and greater understanding into how the Lord expects husbands and wives to treat each other: "The outward expression of an inward feeling"; "...a feeling or attitude of deep respect tinged with awe"; "...a gesture indicative of deep respect"; "...to regard or treat with reverence"; "...to honor, esteem; revere, adore."

Can you see why the Lord has commanded husbands and wives to sustain, support, and reverence each other?

In D&C 25:5, the Lord's counsel to Emma, should be a guide for all wives: "And the office of thy calling shall be for a comfort unto my servant, Joseph Smith, Jun., thy husband, in his afflictions, with consoling words, in the spirit of meekness."

In verse 14, the Lord tells Emma, "...let thy soul delight in thy husband"; and in verse 15, He warns what will happen if she does not do those things: "Keep my commandments continually, and a crown of righteousness thou shalt receive. And except thou do this, where I am you cannot come."

Is there anything in the scriptures for wives or for husbands that gives the idea that they should tear down or belittle each other? Then why is it so many spouses take great delight in joking about, belittling, or tearing down each other? Can you imagine God the Father making fun of or belittling Heavenly Mother...or Her doing the same thing to Him? It is inconceivable!

In the temple covenants, we are taught how to reverence each other. If then, our greatest goal and desire is to rule together as kings and queens in the Celestial Kingdom, then, we should start NOW to become more than just gods and goddesses in embryo. We should to move on from the embryo stage to the toddler, then the adolescent, on to the teenage stage, and eventually the adult stage of *becoming, not just thinking about becoming* like our Savior..."Wherefore, my beloved brethren, pray unto the Father with all the energy of heart, that ye may be filled with this love, which he hath bestowed upon all who are true followers of his Son, Jesus Christ; that ye may become the sons of God; that when he shall appear we shall be like him, for we shall see him as he is; that we may have this hope; that we may be purified even as he is pure." (Moroni 7:48)

What a Difference a Month Makes!

The wedding night should be one of the most exciting parts of the wedding plans for a bride and groom..., which is as it should be. That is when they will begin the process of truly *becoming one* as God intended them to be. Unfortunately, in far too many cases, there is only one of the two, who comes away from that first experience with *becoming one;* feeling like it was exciting and enjoyable. Not to be indelicate here, but the man's sexual wiring is quite different from the woman's. Therefore, by design, he is the one who will in most cases; experience the euphoria that comes from sexual fulfillment (that is, if he does not have a medical condition that prevents it from happening).

However, as exhilarating and enjoyable as the experience is for him, it can be short lived, as the flames of passion can be quickly doused by his wife's lack of interest or enjoyment. Such a scenario can be devastating to his male ego; and may even cause him to feel like his wife no longer loves him, or that he is no longer desirable to her.

Far too many divorces have been the result of the wife deciding she is done with sex, and her husband can just suck it up and get used to it. I read a comment about a wife who told her husband that since they were done with having kids, she was done with having sex! His reply spoke volumes when he said, "Retirement is going to be LONG!"

On the other hand, there are those couples who claim it is the Fourth of July every time they are intimate with each other. In those relationships, the man feels like he is Mr. Atlas, and the wife feels like Mrs. America. How can such completely opposite scenarios take place with the same physical act?

I have put a lot of study and thought into this weighty issue, and what I have come to understand are two things, #1) Men are designed to experience the fireworks whether or not romance is involved; #2) The woman on the other hand, has a hard time experiencing fireworks unless there is romance, and possibly, the aid of a good chick flick to help her get in the mood for love!

Sadly, many wives come away from the honeymoon with the attitude of *sex* being something they have to endure to keep their husband happy.

So, why is it the man is wired to be easily fulfilled, and the woman has to work at it? I will borrow Tevia's comment from "Fiddler on the Roof", "I will tell you...I don't know!" I can assure you however, that this is not a design flaw.

Selfless giving of oneself is a key element in becoming Celestial beings. I am convinced, if a husband and wife will learn and apply each other's love language, their love for each other will become ironclad, and they will find great joy in *becoming one.*

First of all, if the couple has no prior experience with sex (and no that is not an endorsement to do so), then the first night, and quite possibly for sometime afterwards, the couple may wonder if they are broken, or if there is something missing in their relationship. They may wonder if it is even worth the effort to keep trying. Some couples go so far as to imagine that they never really did love each other, or that the sparks that were between them before they got married, would still be part of their marriage.

During this transitional stage (that *every* couple goes through), it is very important for both the wife and the husband to understand *before they get married*, that such a thing will happen, and that it is very normal, and usually very easily remedied. That way, a potential train wreck can be avoided...oh, and did I mention that the remedy can be very enjoyable and fun?

It used to be, that the mother or the older women in the family, would take the bride aside and give her pointers for the wedding night, along with how to keep the spark alive in her marriage.

The dad or older men in the family, would usually be the ones to take the groom aside, and give him the "How to please your wife" talk. After all, they have been through it, and have learned, usually from personal experience, that an unsatisfied wife, can be a very unpleasant wife. You know the saying, "When mamma isn't happy, NO ONE is happy!" Well, the same can be said of wives!

The inexperienced couple can go into the honeymoon being well versed in the "How-To's" on making their wedding night an enjoyable and memorable experience for both. Nevertheless, when you combine shyness, awkwardness, unfamiliarity, and the lack of experience with that first-time encounter...oh, and let's not forget the hormones that will surely be in full bloom, especially for the anxious husband...you often have a VERY disappointing experience for both.

For those who find themselves in such a predicament...even if it has been many years since the honeymoon, have no fear, the solution is a very simple one. However, it takes two to tango! One spouse, trying to get the spark back, may find their resolve is diminished rather quickly, if their spouse shows no interest, or gave up their dance card long ago after experiencing too many unfulfilled intimate encounters with their spouse.

That is where both spouses should be willing to go back to the basics, as doing so is quite helpful and highly encouraged. In addition, they should make sure to study together. Even though they should have avoided in depth discussions about sexual intimacy before the wedding day, once married, it is perfectly acceptable to discuss it with each other, and to enjoy the homework assignments. The thing to get over QUICKLY is the embarrassment and shyness about discussing sexual intimacy with each other.

I once overheard a woman who had been married a number of years, say that she and her husband refer to sex as the "s-word". Don't laugh, there are many more couples out there who are just like them…and some of them have grown children!

Remember, practice makes perfect. If a toddler gives up on walking each time they fall down, they will never be able to walk or run. The best part is, it does not take long for a toddler to master the skill of walking…the same goes for creating beautiful music together as husband and wife. You just need to learn some the basics and how to apply them…often. After all, this will be the most important part of your relationship, as it has the potential to either build or break down bridges to other areas of your relationship. Therefore, study, prayer, and application are *all* necessary when things are not going well in this, or any other area of your marriage.

If the flames of desire for each other are dwindling, why not ask the Lord to help them return? You might be surprised and delighted at how quickly your prayers are answered! What a difference a prayer makes!

Learning To Discern Between Unholy and Holy Practices in Marriage

One common problem that seems to plague many faithful Latter-day Saint husbands and wives is poor programming about sex. From an early age, we are told to save ourselves for marriage and not to do anything that would stand in the way of keeping us from going to the temple.

It seems in every General Conference that there is at least one talk or mention about the dangers of pornography. Therefore, if we are striving to be steadfast and immovable, then we should follow our parents and Church leaders counsel…right? Right! However, too often when we hear such counsel, whether from parents or church leaders, our thought process is, *anything to do with "sex" is pornographic, and should be avoided like the plague.*

So, how can we get the proper programming and education without crossing the line into Satan's territory and losing our good standing with the Lord? How are we supposed to go from thinking sex is immoral, to having a firm testimony and conviction that it is ordained of God and

102

should be enjoyed, free of guilt, between a husband and wife who are legally and lawfully married? I have come to realize that it is often our virtues, not our vises that are the contributing factor in this predicament. You may be asking, "How can that be?"

In "Intended for Pleasure", Dr. Ed Wheat told about a man who became deeply disturbed when anyone would mention "God" and "sex" in the same conversation. He refused to see God's views about sex, thinking it was unholy. Sex for him, was a rushed and empty act, followed by terrible guilt. Sound familiar?

Dr. Wheat said there are couples who appear to have good, Christ-centered marriages, but have found very little joy in sexual intimacy, which can lead to lives filled with misery, rather than the joy and pleasure that the Lord intended for His children.

Dr. Wheat said there were other couples that he counseled with, who had suffered such serious blows to their egos, due to their unpleasant and even disastrous experiences in the bedroom, that they have become, for all intents and purposes, complete strangers, rarely talking or interacting with each other. [8] That is not what the Lord intended husbands and wives to go through.

The Good Girl/Boy Syndrome

Laura Brotherson said, "The Good Girl Syndrome may be the great underlying and underestimated cause of sexual dissatisfaction in marriage...The 'Good Girl Syndrome' is a result of the negative conditioning that occurs from parents, church, and society as they teach- or fail to teach-the goodness of sexuality and its divine purposes. This conditioning leads to negative thoughts and feelings about sex and the body, resulting in an inhibited sexual response within marriage." [15]

If the procreative powers are eternal and sacred, then why do we deal with them as if they are some kind of forbidden fruit? No matter how the eternal and godly nature of sexuality is taught, it is difficult to bridge the gap between the *doctrinal and sacred purposes of sex,* and what we inwardly struggle with in regards to it.

Our Church leaders have counseled parents to teach their children about procreative powers and the divine nature of sex. Then why is it, so few parents adequately fulfill that role?

To read and better understand the counsel of our leaders, go to "A Parent's Guide" (found on LDS.org under "Family Resources"). It is a booklet that all parents should read and study, as it is filled with wise counsel and instructions for raising kids in a world filled with the Adversary's influences and counterfeits. [16]

My husband and I had no idea what was okay to teach or sons other than the, "Thou shalt Nots"...and we fulfilled that charge VERY well. Parents today have it much easier, as there are excellent resources that are easy to find, to know what and how to teach such delicate and important issues to their children.

Joseph F. Smith taught that sexual relations between a husband and wife, who are legally and lawfully wedded, are not just for the purpose of populating the earth, but for helping men and women *to develop more noble qualities and Christ-like traits*. It was interesting that he referred to sexual relations between husbands and wives as *sanctifying*. [17]

To be able to gain a better understanding of the meaning of *sanctify*, I went to my trusted resource, "Dictionary.com" where it defined *Sanctifying* as *purification*, which is a *sin forgiving process*!

What ordinances do you think of that have to do with forgiving sins? The ones I come up with are:

- Partaking of the sacrament
- Baptism
- Confirmation of the Holy Ghost
- Temple ordinances

Elder Hugh B. Brown said that marriage should be a *sacrament*. This concept gives new meaning for me, and adds importance, dignity, and glory to what the marriage bed can and should be. [18]

Dictionary.com defines *sacrament* as, "...a sign, token or symbol; something possessing a sacred character".

Let's look at it this way, the *sexual procreative act* is considered an *ordinance* that provides *purification* to its participants, if engaged in with the right intent and authority...like when we partake of the sacrament.

It goes without question, that we reverence the sacredness of the sacrament, baptism, and temple ordinances, which are all symbolic of heavenly and eternal things. To be able to participate in these ordinances, one must receive Godly approval through the proper priesthood authority. Participation in any of these ordinances creates 'new life' in the participant, by helping them to become more familiar with the eternal nature of our Father in Heaven and Jesus Christ.

Do these explanations help shed more enlightenment on how sexual union between a husband and wife, when engaged in with the proper intent and authority, could generate life inside a marriage relationship?

If the sexual union between a husband and his wife is considered a *sacred ordinance*, it would have to be *symbolic*, as all ordinances in the Church are symbolic in nature.

Participating in sacred saving ordinances gives new life, and the procreative act is the way the Lord chooses to generate new life. Therefore, the ceremonial act, or rites of sexual union are heavenly in nature as well as in their origin. After all, the only kingdom after this life where there will be procreation is the Celestial Kingdom, where only perfected and exalted beings will dwell. So, it only makes sense, that after we die, if it is a celestial act that is reserved for Gods only, then why not study, learn while in this life, and perfect what makes it so? [16]

It would be unthinkable to engage in any sacred ordinance outside of its proper priesthood authority. Could you imagine play-acting the sacrament, baptism, or even temple ceremonies? I cannot even make my mind go there! Then why would anyone misuse the sacred ordinance of sexual union which is meant to be engaged in, only in a lawful union, under the proper priesthood authority? In other words, sexual relations in any form, is meant to be sacred, like any other ordinance.

Such activity, such as making out, petting, or just fooling around "a little", is mimicking and mocking the behavior of a husband and wife engaged in that sacred, exalting act of sexual intimacy.

No wonder the past and present prophets have made some strong statements about premarital sexual relations. When a couple or individual takes on him or herself to engage in any form of physical love-making outside of the covenant of marriage, he or she is violating a sacred ordinance that should be reverenced, respected, and unpolluted by worldly influences.

On paper, this all sounds good, but how do you internalize it, so as to remove the guilt and embarrassment? The only way I know of to overcome anything that troubles your spirit, is to follow Moroni's counsel found in the Moroni 10:4-5 where it says: "...ask with a sincere heart, with real intent, having faith in Christ, he will manifest the truth of it unto you, by the power of the Holy Ghost...And by the power of the Holy Ghost ye may know the truth of all things."

"If any of you lack wisdom, let him ask of God, that giveth to all *men* liberally, and upbraideth not; and it shall be given him...But let him ask in faith, nothing wavering. For he that wavereth is like a wave of the sea driven with the wind and tossed" (James 1:5-6).

Where did we Short Circuit?

Laura Brotherson said, "Typically for men, the creation of 'sexual music' might be likened to pressing 'play' on a CD player. But for women, sexual music is more like that of an instrument that must be tuned, warmed up and played masterfully - as in a symphony of sexual interludes." [19]

Therefore, if the husband will exercise patience, making sure his wife is completely satisfied and fulfilled (and her not faking it to keep from hurting his feelings); it will be a huge blessing in their marriage! Remember, patience is a virtue in more ways than one; however, some of the dividends are much more enjoyable than others...hopefully, this one does not need an explanation.

If a new husband is clueless about his wife's need for the *emotional,* as well as the *physical* preparation, the results often turn into one or all of the following scenarios:

1. The wife not being interested in sex and pulling away when her husband touches her, because she thinks he is only interested in "one thing".
2. The wife feels like sex is a duty and a drudgery and only to be enjoyed by the man.
3. Sex is for the purpose of bringing children into the world and after all the children are born, and then she decides she is through with it.
4. The wife cannot understand why any woman would enjoy sex.
5. The wife's lack of interest in sex can leave the husband feeling unloved, undesirable, and frustrated, because his needs are not being met.

Need I go on? Can you see why President Kimball said that sex is the reason for most divorces, whether the couple will admit it or not? [20]

If it weren't so tragic, it would seem comical that a couple who has worked so hard to keep themselves morally worthy to marry in the temple, would end their marriage over one or both not being interested in sex.

Marriage is a Natural Refiner's Fire

In biblical times, the newly married husband was released from all military and business responsibilities for a whole year (see Deuteronomy 24:5) to allow the couple ample opportunity to get to "know" each other (see Moses 5:2), as they discover how to become "one flesh" (see Matthew 19:5).

While most couples cannot afford to take a yearlong honeymoon, just knowing that it will take some time and effort to get to "know" each other intimately, can help to alleviate anxiety and frustration as the husband and wife transition into marriage and adjust to their sexual relationship.

Developing a playful attitude of adventure and discovery, will help the couple look forward positively and more patiently to the journey they have embarked upon, while learning to meet each other's unique needs and expectations for love and intimacy.

In addition, genuine patience and expressions of tender affection and love, helps to maintain the emotional climate needed for couples to learn and grow together. Truly satisfying sex is a learned behavior requiring time, effort, and intimate learning. Full engagement in learning the art of lovemaking must be a shared adventure, because the only true fulfillment in the sexual relationship comes from mutual fulfillment.

The time, experience, and effort required to develop the intimate relationship, makes sex a "natural refiner's fire" in marriage. This delicate, intricate element of sexual expression in marriage was intended to provide many satisfying opportunities for significant development as a couple and as individuals.

The husband and wife who will allow themselves to go through the "sexual refiner's fire" while going through the different stages of sexual development and discovery, will find an ever deepening degree of marital oneness and bliss.

As hard as it may be for some to imagine, God does care about the intimate relationship between a husband and wife. As I mentioned before, it was God who created sex, not Satan. Our Father gave it as one of His most precious gifts to husbands and wives.

When couples invite God into their sexual relationship, by seeing sex as a sacred and spiritually bonding experience, they will come to understand the importance and power of sex in marriage.

Sex was not meant to be a solo self-gratifying act. It is a mutually bonding experience, which not only provides bodies for our Father's spirit children, but it helps a husband and wife to become beings that are more Celestial in nature. After all, it bears repeating, that the ONLY kingdom where sex will be allowed and enjoyed after this life, is the highest degree of the Celestial Kingdom, for that is the only place procreation will take place.

Seeking ways to improve sexual relationships in your marriage should be a high priority when petitioning our Father in Heaven in personal and couple prayers. You will not offend Him if you will ask for help to develop and/or restore sex to its proper place in your marriage and in society. After all, it is ordained of God; and it is paramount to your progression as husband and wife towards godliness, and maintaining a marriage that feels like it was "made in Heaven"…while still on the earth.

What Happened To The Person I Thought I Married?

As the engaged couple becomes more familiar with each other, they should recognize hot spots or red flags in their relationship. In other words, if the one they are considering marrying has a tendency to be unkind, hurtful, or thoughtless and immature, they should ask themselves if they can live with those traits in a spouse, as those traits that seemed a little bothersome before marriage, will be magnified a thousand-fold after marriage.

If the husband or wife was not wise enough to keep the blinders off before marriage, then they had better become very skilled in holding them over their eyes when the honeymoon is over.

Sadly, too many spouses let their better selves go by the wayside after they get married. The reason for such a phenomenon is not always clear, but nonetheless, it happens more times than many couples would like to admit to. I have heard more than one wife say, "Now that I found my man, I don't need to worry about how I look!"

Yikes! That is not fair to him, or the other way around for that matter.

The tale-tell signs come when the bride wakes up one day and wonders if someone has kidnapped her knight in shining-priesthood-armor, leaving instead, someone who forgets her birthdays, anniversaries, no longer tells her how beautiful she looks, and seems to have forgotten where the florist shop is.

It is not uncommon for the new husband to replace his once well-groomed appearance with a favorite sloppy t-shirt that is usually stained and full of holes. His socks...when he wears them...may be full of holes and are often mismatched. His pants may be wearing thin in the knees, and look like they have never been introduced to the inside of a washing machine. In addition, when his wife offers to wash them, or better yet, replaces them with new ones, he protests, asking what is wrong with what he is wearing.

One husband went as far to say, when he wore his paint covered, holey coveralls to the hardware store that he was dressing for success. His wife did not find his comment amusing, and he has since improved his attire when going in public with her.

On the other hand, it may be the groom who comes home from school or work one day, and instead of seeing his bride, who he believes could have previously won a Miss America contest, sees instead, a woman who more closely resembles someone who misplaced her brush and makeup. In addition, he may find himself wondering if his wife's grandmother has been giving his once very stylish wife, her hand-me-down clothes.

To make matters worse, like I previously mentioned, no one prepares these young (and sometimes not so young) husbands for the times that usually occur once a month, where his wife (who most days possess the demeanor of an angel), without warning, turns into someone more closely resembling a mother bear who is protecting her cubs from harm.

I am convinced when marriages start to become stale, that those traits that first attracted the couple to each other are still there, but for some reason, once the husband and/or wife no longer feels they have to win their true love's affection, they often let their best self, and romantic ways go by the wayside. To those who can relate to this scenario, I will borrow words of wisdom and warning from the robot in "Lost in Space" (a T.V. show from when I was a kid), "Danger! Danger! Warning! Warning!"

Need I say more?

Cooking - No Guts - No Glory!

My euphoric feelings of becoming a new bride were quickly replaced with frustration and discouragement, when I realized that getting married did not come with an automatic guarantee that I would magically be transformed into a domestic goddess. The reality was that I had no idea how to cook anything other than Ramen® and few other simple dishes. Oh yeah...I could also heat up a bagel in a microwave, and it only took one time to figure out, you do not put a bagel into a microwave for 3 minutes...unless of course, you want a broken tooth!

Then there was the time before my husband and I were engaged, that I decided to be nice and make him a birthday cake. One of his roommate's and I went to the store to purchase the cake mix. However, after returning back to their house and following the instructions on the box, neither I nor his roommate could find what temperature to put neither the oven at, nor the time needed to bake the cake. I chalked it up to the cake mix being a discount brand, and decided to call Eric's Aunt Mary for the elusive instructions.

After about 20 minutes of baking, I looked into the oven to check and see how the cake was doing, and noticed the batter was clear and bubbling. Since I had never made a cake before, I had no idea what batter was supposed to look like as it cooked. However, the longer it cooked it became more obvious that something was not right. So once again, I called Eric's aunt for help! She agreed with my suspicions that cake batter was not supposed to be clear or bubbling.

I put the blame once again on the manufacturer and removed the cake pan from the oven.

With the concern that Eric would be home soon, his roommate and I quickly returned to the store to pick up an angel food cake, along with a can of ready-made frosting.

Trying to frost a cake in a dark, dingy bathroom that was a little larger than a shower stall, is *not* something that I would care to repeat! However, it provided the privacy I desired in case Eric arrived home before I had finished.

As I heard Eric come through the front door, I quickly added the matches to the top of the cake...okay, so his roommate and I forgot to buy candles, and matches were the closest thing I could find to act as substitutes.

Eric seemed genuinely surprised and pleased at our pitiful efforts to make him feel special on his birthday. However, when I told him about what happened with the cake mix, he walked over to the trash can and removed the box. Lifting the box for me to see, he asked: "You mean this frosting mix?"

Hey, at least I was not alone in making the mistake, as his roommate was a part of the buying *and* baking process!

Eric and his aunt got a good laugh out of it...and I am not sure if I'll ever live that one down. However, one redeeming thing came out of it though, as a few days later, Eric told me that he and his roommates enjoyed the candy that was the result of letting the baked frosting cool. Hey, at least something besides a good laugh came of my blunder.

That was not the end of my cooking disasters, as a couple of days after we got married, I decided to put a crock-pot to use that we had received as a wedding gift. Stew seemed like a good choice, so I cut up potatoes and carrots and put them in the crock pot. I then put the stew meat in the pot and covered the contents with water.

I had no idea that you are supposed to dredge the meat before putting it in the water (which is where you sprinkle a few tablespoons of flour over the meat and then brown it in a pan with a few tablespoons of hot oil). However, it did not matter that I did not do it right, because when I was looking for something to season the stew with, I decided to sprinkle the stew with a generous amount of red pepper flakes (which came from a box of groceries we also received as a wedding gift).

When we got home that evening, instead of enjoying a tasty bowl of stew, we both ran for the sink to douse the flames that were coming from our mouths!!!! Needless to say, the stew was inedible!

It gets better! Since our first anniversary fell on a Sunday, I decided to make a nice dinner at home instead of going out to eat. So I decided to splurge on two steaks.

Did you know that a little bit of smoke flavoring is all that is needed to add a hint of a smoky flavor to your meat? I do now!

I thought baked potatoes would be a good addition to the meal, so I scrubbed them and placed them next to the steaks that were already in the oven. At least I knew enough to scrub the potatoes.

Did you know you are supposed to pierce the skin of the potato a few times with a fork or a sharp knife before baking it? I do now! My first clue came after my husband and I heard the explosion from inside of the oven.

While I was trying to salvage the potatoes that were all over the inside of the oven, I decided to check on the steaks...or should I say "...the two pieces of shoe leather".

Did you know that you are NOT supposed to cook steaks as long as you cook baked potatoes? I do now!

Since it was the Sabbath, we decided not to go to the store, so we put up with the measly remains of the potatoes and the smoke flavored pieces of shoe leather. I assumed that sucking the smoke flavoring off the inedible pieces of meat, would keep the meal from being a total disaster...but I made a discovery...let me explain it this way...have you ever tasted smoke flavoring straight from the bottle? The memory of the overpowering noxious taste that assaulted my taste buds, still makes me feel sick to my stomach every time I think if it! I have not been brave enough to cook with bottled smoke flavoring since.

Consequently, not wanting my husband and children to die from malnourishment was enough motivation for me to try to improve my culinary skills. And it only took me a few years to figure out that when I used the recipes in the cookbook (that was also a wedding present), that my family seemed a lot happier at meal time.

I have heard it said numerous times, "If at first you don't succeed…then try reading and following the instructions".

Hey, it actually works for cooking!

However, just because you have followed the recipe, is not a guarantee that the dish will be edible…like when the finished product makes you want to find the nearest napkin. Take for instance the fruitcake I made a few Christmases ago. I thought if I used fresh ground wheat along with real fruit and nuts, that it would be delicious.

As I carefully added each ingredient, while making sure to include the love, I envisioned my family showering me with praise for creating the first fruitcake that was not only delicious, but healthy!

However, instead of shouts of praise…let me just say that using it for a doorstop would have been an improvement…and less embarrassing for me!

So women (and men), for the sake of your spouse and children, it would be a good idea to learn how to cook BEFORE getting married. However, if you have already tied the knot, and your attempts at cooking have become a sore spot in your marriage, then do not despair. That is why recipes were invented.

Women, if your mother, mother-in-law, or grandmother(s) are good cooks, you could ask if they would be willing to teach you to cook and/or share some of their cooking tips and recipes with you…your husband will thank you for it…especially if you ask his mother for his favorite recipes. That way, you do not have to hear those words that most wives dread hearing: "That is not the way my mother used to make it!"

A little hint: Before attempting to tackle a recipe, it would help to get enlightened on cooking terminology…such as, learning what the word *dredge* means; and learning the difference between a tsp and a TBSP; and why sifting the dry ingredients can make all the difference in how light or heavy a cake turns out.

I have worn out the cookbook my mother gave me for a wedding gift. Nevertheless, it is still the first place I go to try to find a recipe. However, if I am unable to find what I am looking for there, then I move on to the bookshelf full of cookbooks and recipes. If I still cannot find what I am looking for, then I simply get on the Internet and type in a name of the recipe or the main ingredients into a search engine and then hit the enter key. The hard part with that one is, deciding which recipe best suits my husband's and my tastes.

Cleanliness is Next to Godliness

Years ago, my husband and I brought home a kitten that had been taken from his mother before he learned to clean himself. He would often come in the house with hardened feces stuck to his fur from laying in the area outside that he used for a litter box.

My husband decided to teach the kitten to bathe himself by putting him under a stream of water under the faucet in the bath tub, and then pulling the kitten's tongue out of his mouth as he rubbed it on his wet fur. To our surprise, instead of freaking out, the kitten began to purr, and it was not long before the kitten was cleaning himself on his own.

Part of the parents job is to teach their children proper hygiene, such as bathing or showering every day; washing their hands with soap and water after using the toilet or if their hands to get dirty; brushing their teeth daily; making sure their hair is clean and well groomed; wearing clean and wrinkle-free clothing; making sure their clothes are in good repair and are not missing buttons; and making sure their shoes are clean and/or polished. However, any mother or father knows that this is easier said than done.

With couples, one of the biggest turn offs, is when one or the other spouse has not bathed, brushed their teeth, or shaved before engaging in intimacy. The wife's unshaved legs are as much an intimacy killer as her husband's unshaved face. An adage to adopt here is, "Do unto others as you would have others do unto you".

Home Can and Should Be a Heaven on Earth

A seedbed for Saints starts in a home where "Heaven" is built into the foundation. The challenge however, is for parents to make their earthly home mirror the Heavenly one that they lived in before coming to the Earth, and where they hope to return to someday. It is in such a home, that it takes courage, vision, dignity, and grace, for a mother to stay committed to her divine role when all around her voices refer to it as demeaning and unfulfilling. Accepting and being faithful to her divine calling (when given the opportunity), is part of a solemn promise that daughters of God made before coming to the Earth. It is through being faithful and magnifying those roles, that some of the choicest and sweetest blessings are experienced.

George Q. Cannon said that God saved for this dispensation, the most valiant spirits, who possess the courage and determination to withstand all the fiery darts that Satan can throw at them; and who will have the vision to build the Kingdom of God on earth, without fear of what the Adversary or man can do to them. [20]

Righteous wives and mothers are needed now more than at any other time in the history of the world. Never underestimate the power of a righteous woman in the winding up scenes of the world. Her righteous influence in the home cannot be minimized or trivialized.

A home that is clean and orderly, and reflects the love family members feel for one another as well as the hard work and industry of all the family members; and it builds confidence and pride in the people who live there. Such a home also creates an atmosphere where the family's faith and testimony can grow; and is a refuge from the storms that are bombarding the earth at an ever increasing rate.

112

In Doctrine & Covenants 88:119, the Lord said, "Organize yourselves, prepare every needful thing; and establish a house, even a house of prayer, a house of fasting, a house of faith, a house of learning, a house of glory, a house of order, a house of God".

With mothers often needing to supplement, or in some cases, provide all of the family income, very few are able to juggle their roles, which includes being a wife, mother, homemaker, and earning a living.

When the mother is required to work outside of the home, the role of homemaker is often spread out among family members, because too often, the mom comes home exhausted from putting in a long day at work. If she then has to cook dinner, clean house, help the children with their homework, bathe, and help the children get ready for bed, as well as meet her husband's needs (so she can keep the home fires burning)…all before going to bed…then she will probably not be a very happy camper…remember, "If mama's not happy, no one's happy!".

If either the single man or woman has not learned to cook or maintain a clean and orderly home, they should become committed to learning at least the basic skills before getting married. After all, an ounce of prevention is worth a pound of cure. In other words, the couple will forestall many arguments and a lot of frustration if *both* will pull their weight with cooking and cleaning…and not wait for the other to do it; or worse yet, to have to say something about needing the other's help with a chore. A little hint: such comments are often borne out of deep frustration.

Skills to Learn Before Getting Married:

1. Cook nutritious and well balanced meals, plan menus, and buy groceries
2. Sort, wash, dry and iron, sew and repair clothing
3. Do house and yard work
4. Work within a budget, learn to write checks and balance a check book at the end of the month
5. Decorating and painting a home inside and out
6. Grooming tips, style and *cut* hair, and apply makeup (for girls)
7. Cake decorating, arts, crafts and card making
8. Buy clothes that are modest, fashionable and compliment their body shape(s)
9. Child care (including newborns)
10. Replace and repair dripping faucets and unclog a stopped up toilet or sink
11. Know how to turn off electricity, water to the house and toilet, as well as the gas, in the event of an emergency
12. Know how to put out a fire, especially an oil fire, and when to call 911
13. Discuss the family plan for emergencies, or if the house is on fire

14. Know what to do in the event of a natural or national disaster

15. Change a tire, oil in a car, fill the tank with gas, and how to do minor auto repairs

16. Administer first aid and CPR

If family members are lacking in any of those skills, and there is no one in the family with the knowledge, then maybe friends or Ward members would be willing to teach them. Classes at church or in the community (through parks and recreation or extension programs) offer some of these classes for free, or for a minimal fee. However, there is help closer to home. YouTube.com is a great resource for just about any skill someone wants to learn. The best part is, you can go back and review it as many times as you wish. I looked up each of the skills (in the list above) and each one of them can be found on YouTube.com...you're welcome!

Hopefully, you can see, there is no reason to remain homemaking-challenged, as there is a wealth of information on just about anything you want to learn yourself, or teach to your children. Go ahead, get on YouTube.com and type in any skill you can think of, and see if there is a video about it. If you cannot find one, then reword your search.

How many of you husbands or soon-to-be husbands assume(d) that your bride or bride-to-be, not only possessed the beauty of a goddess, but the domestic skills to match, only to find out later that her beauty far out weighed her domestic-goddess skills...and any desire to acquire them?

To those men, I am here to tell you, this is not the same world your mother's and grandmothers started married life in! When I was in high school, I had to talk my school counselor into letting me take college prep classes in the event that I might go to college someday. The prevailing attitude when I was in high school was that a woman's place was in the home. In fact, that attitude was so prevalent when I decided to go to college, I purposely choose not to take any classes that had to do with homemaking skills, as I wanted to avoid the condescending attitudes that implied that any woman who went to college, went for one reason...and that was to find a husband.

So instead, I chose secretarial classes. I could kick myself for being so shortsighted and naïve back then, because when I got married, my homemaking skills resembled those of a clueless teenager, who gives no thought to how the house stays clean, how their clean and ironed clothes manage to find their way into their closet and drawers, or how much work and planning go into the meals their mother makes for the family.

I am grateful that where I grew up, they required every student to take cooking and sewing classes in Junior High. However, about all I remember from my cooking class, is where the knife, fork, and spoon go when you set the table. As for learning to sew, let's just say my sewing skills leave a lot to be desired. Of course, it could have something to do with my teacher being more interested in the male teacher that visited her every class period, the whole semester, which made it very difficult for us to get her attention when I had a question or needed help with my project.

I finally decided to cut out the skirt (which was the class project) from the pattern my mother had purchased for me. It only required my mother needing to sew a few pieces of the material back together, so that there was enough fabric to cut out all of the pattern pieces properly…and she wondered why I never wore that skirt.

Fortunately, in today's world, young women (even in the Church) are encouraged to go to college. However, to my knowledge, it is getting harder and harder to find any homemaking classes in Middle or High Schools.

With the trends in modern Western society, fewer and fewer women (even in the Church) have very little desire to stay at home and raise a family. Moreover, when they do decide to have a family, oft times, the children are farmed out to babysitters or daycare so the mother can work or go to school. Therefore, very few marriages (even in the Church) resemble the ones from my parents and grandparents' generation.

With the growing acceptance of such attitudes, along with ones that are trying to either redefine or destroy the family unit, it is easy to understand why so few men and women in the Church understand what their God-given roles are. Quite honestly, such attitudes are contributing greatly to the disintegration of the family unit, as the Lord intended it to be.

However, I am encouraged by my daughters-in-law, as well as other young mothers that I know, who have chosen to be stay-at-home mothers and wives. I love watching them as they strive to develop their domestic and mothering skills. It is reassuring that these valiant and courageous women are choosing to go against the mainstream attitudes about the roles of women. It is also interesting that many of the wives and mothers that I associate with, are highly educated and have earned, or are in the process of earning their college degrees, but who choose instead, to stay at home to raise their children.

One such woman came to the realization that her place was at home with her children. She gave up a lucrative career as an attorney, to do so. However, I have no doubt that the blessings she and her family will gain will far outweigh any money or prestige she would've gained pursuing her career outside of the home.

My not realizing the need to develop my domestic skills before getting married, led to some unnecessarily humiliating and painful experiences for me, as well as for my poor husband, whose taste buds deserved better treatment than what I inflicted on them. However, in spite of my culinary disasters, they were not all in vain, as they provided quality entertainment for my husband, and taught me what NOT to do when preparing a meal.

If a clean and orderly home is important to you, then you better think twice before marrying someone who does not seem bothered if there is not a clean dish to be found in the kitchen; or who cannot find a clean shirt, or a clean pair of pants because every article of clothing they own, is making it hard to tell if they have hardwood floors or carpeting.

Another tale-tell sign of a clean and/or order-challenged potential mate, is if you can see the layers of your courtship on the dashboard or seat of their car. However, if I had let such a pile hinder me from marrying my husband, I would have missed out on all of the other wonderful qualities he possesses. Besides, it was amusing as I helped him pack up his things just before we got married, because each piece of paper that I picked up brought back fond memories of our courtship.

If a person does not like to keep a clean and orderly home before marriage, then expecting them to change after marriage, is pretty slim. I knew a woman who asked her mother-in-law if she had taught her son any homemaking skills when he was growing up. The mother-in-law reassured her that in most of the things she had taught her son, he had been very receptive and obedient, except when it came to domestic skills...hmmmm, I wonder if there will be maids in Heaven.

There are no hard and fast rules for this, as I have known kids whose rooms looked like a Tasmanian devil resided there. Yet now that they are adults, their homes are very neat and tidy.

One summer when my friend and I were hired as live-in nannies for a family, we learned that no matter how clean-challenged a person is, when given the choice between a messy room and a clean room, they will choose the clean one to congregate in.

The day we first walked through the front door of that family's home, my friend and I were sure that a tornado had passed through. Yet, no one in the family seemed to notice. After a week or so of wondering how high piles of clothes and debris could get before the furniture disappeared underneath them, my friend and I decided to de-clutter and deep clean each room from top to bottom.

However, by the time we moved on to the next room, the previously cleaned room starting to rapidly return to its former disheveled condition because the family would congregate there. Because no one in the family lifted a finger to clean or pick up anything, my friend and I had assumed that they did not mind the messy condition of their home, but we could not have been more wrong. It is easy to see why the Spirit will not dwell in unclean and disorderly conditions (D&C 88:119, 124).

For those couples who prefer a clean and orderly home, but do not like doing the housework, there is hope! I am sure if you ask friends, family, coworkers, or check out CraigsList.com, or even want ads in the newspaper, you will be able to find a maid who could use the extra income. However, after paying a maid to clean your mess, you may decide it is more affordable and less embarrassing to do it yourself.

When my brothers and I were too young to be left alone at home while she was at work, my mother hired a babysitter who cleaned house and fixed meals. It was great! Consequently, I did not know anything different; because that was all I had known until my mother decided my brothers and I no longer had need of a babysitter. That is when I discovered that houses do not clean themselves, and that a messy house, and no dinner on the table, made my mother cry when she came home from a long day at work.

Therefore, in an effort to make her feel better, I tried to find ways to make the house look cleaner. However, in my 9-year-old reasoning, I figured if I could not see the clutter when I walked into a room, then that was all the cleaning that needed doing. I therefore became very skilled at shoving things under beds, behind couches, and under the top shelf of our end tables in the living room.

That lasted until my mother discovered that most of the clothes that needed ironing, were crammed under my bed. Since I was the "designated-ironer" for the family (NOT by choice), she called me in and asked how the clothes and sheets got there (yes, my step-dad made me iron sheets and pillowcases!). Not wanting her to think I had done something wrong, I acted clueless. However, she persisted until she was in tears.

In my young and immature thinking, all I could see was how hurt she would be if she knew I had put the clothes there. I did not realize that my lying to her about it was hurting her much worse. I do not think I ever fessed up to the crime until years later when I had matured enough to realize how badly my lying had hurt her.

The next defining moment took place on my 12th birthday when my mother invited some of our female family and friends to a slumber party at our house and one of my cousin's saw the clutter that I had crammed under the top shelf of the end table in our living room, and she made a comment about it.

I am not sure why I had thought that no one would discover my secret hiding places for clutter, but I am grateful that she helped me pull my head out of the sand and see what others were seeing when they entered our living room. It is amazing that that single comment that she made over 40 years ago, comes to my mind nearly every time I enter or clean a room in my home.

Since no one taught me how to clean a house, my domestic skills were mostly self-learned and were very minimal when I got married. Therefore, in an attempt to help my sons avoid the embarrassment I went through as a teenager, I tried to implement charts to track keeping their rooms clean, as well as other chores they were assigned to do around the house. I made sure to offer rewards that would give them incentive to complete their tasks. However, if I remember right, not one of them ever earned a reward for doing the chores on *any* of the charts I made for them.

Even though I became a master chart maker, they serve no purpose unless you are willing to LOOK at and Do what is on them! Needless to say, I have made more unused cleaning and organizational charts for my kids and myself than I care to think about. I have even resorted to putting up visual reminders or quotes around the house that had to do with the importance of keeping clean and orderly homes. Alas, the visual reminders and quotes only work if you look at them on a regular basis!

Something I learned years ago to avoid embarrassment when unexpected guests would stop by is to keep the rooms that visitors would see, clean and orderly on a daily basis. However, I made sure to keep the door closed to the catch-all room.

Was I alone with that approach? I do not think so, as I recall Fibber McGee (from the old radio show "Fibber McGee and Molly", from my parent's generation), had a closet where all his junk was stashed. Every-so-often, someone would open the closet door, and all the junk would come falling out. I never understood why they had a closet like that because Molly took such pride in keeping a clean and orderly home.

I have since put more effort into disciplining myself to keep all my rooms clean, even the ones that are not frequented by guests. The garage however, is a work in progress.

Helpful Cleaning Tips:
1. If you hang up an article of clothing when you take it off, then you will not have to deal with a huge pile of clothes to put away, and your bedroom looks much neater.
2. A good rule to follow to keep a clean and clutter-free home is: It takes a few seconds more to put things where they belong the first time.
3. If you make your bed as soon as you get out of it, then your bedroom looks more pleasing to the eye.
4. Deal with the mail as soon as you get it. Have you noticed, if you let mail stack up, it is easy to lose important papers and to forget about bills that are due? Then, before you know it, the pile has turned into Mount Everest, and the slightest bump or jostle will cause it all to come tumbling down like an avalanche.
5. If you do the dishes and clean the kitchen as you cook the meal, or as soon as you finish eating a meal, then you will not have to deal with large piles of unwashed dishes, and you will not have to hunt down and wash dishes when you need them...nor will you be embarrassed when guests drop by unexpectedly.

6. If keeping your house clean is not high on your priority list, then you can find creative or cleaver excuses for the condition of the house when the unexpected guest appears at your door.

7. If you need more of a reason to keep a clean and orderly home, then remember, "…the Spirit cannot dwell in unholy temples" [this includes our homes]. (Helaman 4:24)

8. Here are some websites with instructions on how to make your own natural homemade cleaners that are environmentally friendly:

- www.creativehomemaking.com/articles/051005i.shtml
- http://save.lovetoknow.com/How_to_Make_Natural_Cleaning_Products
- http://eartheasy.com/live_nontoxic_solutions.htm
- http://earthnotes.tripod.com/clnrecipes.htm
- http://hubpages.com/hub/Making-or-Buying-Organic-Cleaning-Products
- www.aboutmyplanet.com/daily-green-tips/cleaning-products/
- www.demesne.info/Sustainable-Living/Greener-Cleaning.htm

Being Prepared for any Emergency

Check with your city, county, or state government offices to see if they have a book or pamphlet on what to do in the event of a disaster of any kind. The Internet is a great place to search for ways to prepare for emergencies. Being prepared may save yours or your family's lives someday.

The Kid Factor

It is always a good idea before becoming husband and wife, to find opportunities to observe each other taking care of other peoples' children. That way you can get an idea about how your potential mate deals with kids. In addition, the more rambunctious and challenging the kids are, all the better! The risky part here is that your potential mate, if they are smart, will be doing the same thing with you.

However, this scenario is not always a good monitor in how someone will deal with his or her own children, as I was never one to make over other peoples kids before becoming a mother. Yet, with my own kids, I tried to be the best mother I knew how to be, and I loved having them around. I hated it when summer breaks were over, because it meant my kids had to go back to school, and were not at home with me.

Then there is the magic of becoming a grandmother and looking into the face of your child's child, and hearing that child call you "G'ma" for the first time, and tell you they love you! Nothing can compare to that feeling! And it just keeps getting sweeter with each grandchild that is added to your family tree!

It is amazing to see the change that comes over a new mom or dad when they hold their own flesh and blood baby (or adopted baby) in their arms for the first time. Something magical takes place. We have all seen an otherwise self-absorbed man or woman who transforms over night into super dad/mom when they become parents.

Therefore, just because a potential spouse does not seem to be the best with other people's kids, it is not always a reason to throw red flags onto the playing field of the courtship. Therefore, this would be another good reason to seek the Lord in fervent prayer, to find out His will about whom to marry.

Leave Father and Mother

"Therefore shall a man leave his father and his mother, and shall cleave unto his wife: and they shall be one flesh." (Genesis 2:24, Matthew 19:5; Mark 10:7; John 16:32; Ephesians 5:31; 1 Nephi 2:11; Moses 3:24; Abraham 5:18)

To gain a greater understanding of that counsel from the Lord, I once again turned to my trusted friend...*Dictionary.com*, to discover a better understanding of what it means to *cleave;* and once again, I received the enlightenment I was hoping for: "To adhere, cling or stick fast; ...to be faithful; ...come or be in close contact with; ...stick or hold together; ...*resist separation*". [21]

I especially like the imagery of *resisting separation*. If husbands and wives would make that counsel their breastplate and shield, then I could conceive divorce becoming a thing-of-the-past!

There is no husband and wife, who either has not, or will not have conflicts at some time in their marriage. If they think they have a good relationship because they have not had a disagreement or an argument, they can rest assured that the time will come when they will join the ranks of other married couples who have had their bubbles burst when they had their first heated disagreement.

However, couples should not despair if they have an argument from time to time, because it is part of life. It does not mean that their marriage is doomed to fail.

Therefore, instead of using their points of contention as battering rams, or as a reason to break their wedding vows, they should prayerfully seek to adhere to the Lord's counsel for them to *cleave* to one another, and to find ways to cement their bonds.

It is the unwise husband or wife, who calls their mother or father to complain about their spouse; and will not forgive, nor forget; and continues to dredge up "should-be forgotten past misdeeds" in their relationship, each time they disagree or get into an argument.

To illustrate the dangers of allowing such behavior to go unchecked or unresolved, a number of years ago, a woman I knew, told me that when she was a newlywed, she often called her mother to complain about her husband each time he and she got into an argument, or when he did something that hurt her feelings. However, what she neglected to do was to call her mother to let her know she and her husband had made up.

Since her mother lived a long ways away from her, she could only go on what her *only* daughter told her about her son-in-law's behavior. Therefore, the mother, acting like a mother hen protecting her chicks, used every opportunity to convince her daughter that her husband was a horrible person. Hence, after a number of years, the daughter finally gave in to her mother's insistence that she divorce her husband.

What made it so tragic, is she and her husband still deeply loved each other, but neither figured out how to show it to each other.

Another challenge most, if not all couples face, is how to maintain close and loving relationships with their parents, extended family and friends, without neglecting their own marriage and children.

In addition, as difficult as it may be, learning not to depend on parents for financial aid is advisable, because it teaches the couple to be self-sufficient.

It would also help the couple to remember when starting their own family, that both come from different upbringings, and often have very diverse family values and traditions. The couple can choose to let these diversities broaden and enhance their relationship and family dynamics, or they can allow the diversities to become stumbling blocks, and even worse, huge impassable chasms.

Once they get married, they should decide if they are going to incorporate family traditions from when they were kids, or start their own. However, they need to make sure they are sensitive to each other's feelings in these matters.

Make Time for Each Other – Remove Distractions

"Ye husbands, dwell with them according to knowledge, giving honor unto the wife…Be ye all of one mind" (1 Peter 3:7, 8).

Too much time spent watching television and playing computer games, can steal away those moments that the husband and wife should be devoting to each other and their family. They can take away the most wonderful hours of a couple's day – which could be spent in personal communication and sharing moments when they can best learn to relate to each other. There is no giving and no receiving when time is spent in front of the television or playing computer games. Television doesn't produce prime time; it steals prime time from couples and their families.

The talk given by Elder David E. Bednar titled, "Things as They Really Are", bears reading and studying, as it offers great insight into the dangers of cyberspace. I am not just referring to pornography, but mind controlling effects through seemingly harmless things where you stay in constant contact with others through phones and computers. I would strongly suggest that you read the talk in its entirety and share it with your loved ones and friends. In addition, remember, one of the Lord's mouthpieces (that we have said we would sustain and support), gave this inspired and timely message. [25]

Never Go To Bed Angry or With Unresolved Issues

"Let not the sun go down upon thy wrath" (Ephesians 4:26).

"...forgiving one another, if any man have a quarrel against any: even as Christ forgave you, so also do ye." (Colossians 3:13)

It is not easy to get along at all times with your spouse, especially when you are first married and still adjusting to each other's diversities. I am convinced, one of the reasons the Lord has said that every worthy young man should serve a mission, has to do in part, with learning to get along with others who live with them. A mission teaches how to resolve conflicts and to live in harmony with a companion, even when the two may have very different likes and dislikes.

Two weeks before my husband and I got engaged to be married, my husband's roommate asked if I had ever considered marrying Eric. I told him, "We do not have much in common". Yet, within a couple of weeks, I found myself engaged to someone that I did not share many interests with. And over three decades later, I learned firsthand that couples can learn to accept and/or blend each other's diversities, as well as use them to strengthen their relationship, instead of allowing them to tear it apart.

It is never good to go to bed or leave the house when you are angry at your spouse. A friend of my mother's said as a newlywed, she and her husband used to get into a lot of heated arguments. One day as her husband was leaving for work, she ran after him screaming, "I hate you!"

He died in an accident that day, and the woman said she would give anything to be able to take back the last words she yelled at him.

We should all live like it is our last day or hour on Earth with our spouse and family...for it may well be. Norma Cornett Marek wrote the following insightful poem she titled, "Tomorrow Never Comes":

If I knew it would be the last time that I'd see you fall asleep,

I would tuck you in more tightly, and pray the Lord your soul to keep.

If I knew it would be the last time that I'd see you walk out the door,

I would give you a hug and kiss, and call you back for just one more.

If I knew it would be the last time I'd hear your voice lifted up in praise,

I would tape each word and action, and play them back throughout my days

If I knew it would be the last time, I would spare an extra minute or two,

To stop and say "I love you," instead of assuming you know I do.

So, just in case tomorrow never comes, and today is all I get,

I'd like to say how much I love you, and I hope we never will forget.

Tomorrow is not promised to anyone, young or old alike,

And today may be the last chance you get to hold your loved one tight.

So, if you're waiting for tomorrow, why not do it today?

For if tomorrow never comes, you'll surely regret the day

That you didn't take that extra time for a smile, a hug, or a kiss,

And you were too busy to grant someone, what turned out to be their one last wish.

So hold your loved ones close today, and whisper in their ear,

That you love them very much, and you'll always hold them dear.

Take time to say "I'm sorry," "Please forgive me," "thank you" or "its okay".

And if tomorrow never comes, you'll have no regrets about today.

Because if tomorrow never comes, you certainly will regret for the rest of your life

Not having spent some extra time for a smile, a conversation, a hug, a kiss,

Because you were too busy to give that person what ended up being their last wish.

Then hug tight today the one you love, your friends, your family, and whisper in their

ears how much you love them and want them close to you.

Use your time to say, "I'm sorry", "Please", "Forgive me", "Thank you", or even,

"That was nothing", "It's all right",

Because if tomorrow never comes, you will not have to regret today.

The past doesn't come back, and the future might not come!" [22]

With Major Unresolved Conflicts, Seek Outside Help

"Brethren, if a man be overtaken in a fault, ye which are spiritual, restore such an one in the spirit of meekness" (Galatians 6:1).

Notice the words *major* and *unresolved* in the subtitle. That does not mean spats or arguments that get resolved within a few days or weeks. It also does not mean if you do not see eye to eye on something, and ever so often have an argument over it. It means that the two of you are not talking and possibly choosing to sleep separately, or one of you has moved out of the house for a period of time. It can also mean you two cannot go a day or two without arguing or being angry with each other. It can also include physical, emotional, or sexual abuse...hint, a husband who wants sex every day, does not qualify for sexual or emotional abuse unless he is forcing or degrading his wife in any way. And a wife who refuses her husband sex to punish him, or because she has issues about it, can be considered abusive behavior.

When it seems a couple has done all they can (as a couple) to resolve the issues, and cannot seem to get past them, then they should swallow their pride and go see their Bishop or a competent marriage counselor who shares their values and morals. Their Bishop may not be an expert on marital problems, but he is their spiritual counselor and is entitled to receive inspiration for them as their Bishop.

It is important not to let seeds of bitterness take root and grow up to smother or destroy their marriage.

The following scriptures encourage forgiveness, reconciliation, and restoration:

"Brethren, if a man be overtaken in a fault, ye which are spiritual, restore such an one in the spirit of meekness" (Galatians 6:1); "Follow peace with all men, and holiness, without which no man shall see the Lord: Looking diligently lest any man fail of the grace of God; lest any root of bitterness springing up trouble you, and thereby many be defiled" (Hebrews 12:14-15). "...forgetting those things which are behind..." (Philippians 3:13).

For Unresolved Sexual Difficulties, Seek Outside Help

"Let the husband render unto the wife due benevolence: and likewise also the wife unto the husband. The wife hath not power over her own body but the husband: and likewise also the husband hath not power of his own body, but the wife. Defraud ye not one the other" (1 Corinthians 7:3-5)

When couples came to him and let on that they were having serious sexual difficulties, Dr. Wheat would suggest that they seek help from a marriage counselor that shared their values and standards, not waiting until their problems were so serious that they considered divorce as their only option.

Divine Roles of a Husband and Wife

We made covenants before coming to earth, that if Heavenly Father would see to it we were given bodies and an earthly experience; we would keep the commandments and marry in the temple, and rear a righteous family. President Spencer W. Kimball referred to it as a *solemn oath and promise.* [31]

President David O. McKay said that motherhood is near to divinity and is the highest, holiest service a woman can assume. [23]

C. S. Lewis made the following bold statement that bears repeating over, and over again: "Homemaker is the ultimate career. All other careers exist for one purpose only—to support the ultimate career!"

President Spencer W. Kimball said righteous women are needed in all dispensations of time, but to be a righteous woman before the Savior returns to the earth is even more noble a calling. He said a righteous woman's strength of character and righteous influence in the winding up scenes of the world, can be of a much greater worth than in peaceful times. He said a woman's role is to enrich, protect, and to be a guardian of their home, and that she should not be deceived into thinking her time would be better served in places that would take her out of, or cause her to neglect her duties and roles in the home. [24]

Elder Richard L. Evans said the world will be no better than its homes. [25]

Hopefully, you can get the idea of the importance the Lord places on the role of a righteous mother in the home.

Get a copy of "The Family: A Proclamation to the World". Don't just read through it. Prayerfully study it with your spouse (and children), and make it a mission statement for your home. If you do not have a copy, you can get one on LDS.org, or at one of our Church bookstores and distributions centers.

We have one on the wall in the waiting room of our office, which includes pictures of our family making a frame around it, and another on the living room wall of our home as constant reminder of the Lord's standard for the family.

As I mentioned before, the Lord's counsel to Emma Smith could be given to all wives: "…the office of thy calling shall be for a comfort unto… thy husband, in his afflictions, with consoling words, in the spirit of meekness…Continue in the spirit of meekness, and beware of pride. Let thy soul delight in thy husband, and the glory which shall come upon him…Keep my commandments continually, and a crown of righteousness thou shalt receive" (D&C 25:5, 14, 15)

President Kimball said that his call to be an Apostle was so overwhelming that he literally sat on the floor and sobbed like a baby until his wife came and knelt next to him on the floor, and stroked his hair while offering words of encouragement. Because of that act of love, he said his wife was his salvation, because she comforted and encouraged him and continued to reassure him that there was only one road for him to follow.

President Kimball went on to become a great apostle and prophet. Sister Kimball's role as a wife and helpmate played an important part in her husband's life. She was to her husband, like Emma was to the Prophet Joseph Smith, a comfort in his times of trial. [29]

Attitude determines destiny. Learning the basics and *sticking with them* can help couples accomplish any goal that they desire...even in building a Celestial marriage that will last the eternities.

Notes:

1. President Spencer W. Kimball, First Presidency Message, "Oneness in Marriage", *Ensign*, March 1977

2. From "Honeymoon to Happily Ever After—Preparing for an Intimately Fulfilling Relationship", StrengtheningMarriage.com

3. Steven Kapp Perry, "Brotherson*: And They Were Not Ashamed*", Mormon Times, 19 June 2008

4. "A Parent's Guide under Mature Intimacy: Courtship and Marriage"

5. Laura Brotherson, "And They Were Not Ashamed", p 139

6. "The Teachings of Spencer W. Kimball"*,* ed. Edward L. Kimball [Salt Lake City: Bookcraft, 1982], p. 311

7. Wheat, Ed, MD and Wheat, Gaye "Intended for Pleasure" (1997)

8. LDS.org, under *Family Living*, there is a link to *Provident Living*

9. Marion G. Romney, "The Book of Mormon", *Ensign*, May 1980, 65

10. Boyd K. Packer, "Our Moral Environment", *Ensign*, May 1992, 68

11. An address given to the regional representatives of the Church on 6 April 1984, President Gordon B. Hinckley

12. Lesson 7: *Continuing to Enjoy the Blessings of Temple Attendance, Endowed from on High: Temple Preparation Seminar Teacher's Manual,* 31

13. Joseph Smith*, History of the Church,* 6:184

14. Boyd K. Packer, *The Holy Temple*

15. Laura Brotherson, "And They Were Not Ashamed", Chapter One

16. "A Parent's Guide", LDS.org

17. Joseph F. Smith, *Improvement Era*, vol. 20, p. 739

18. Hugh B. Brown, Sacred Power of Procreation, Lesson 33, Young Women Manual 2

19. Laura Brotherson, "And They Were Not Ashamed", Chapter Three

20. Spencer W. Kimball, "The Teachings of Spencer W. Kimball"*,* p. 312

21. Dictionary.com

22. Written by Norma Cornett Marek in 1989 as, in her words, "a tribute to a beloved child I lost, in hopes it would cause people to never be careless or too busy to let our loved ones know we love them...I give anyone permission who wishes to use the poem to go ahead as long as I get credit and the date is correct." Norma Marek

passed away July 18, 2004, after a prolonged battle with cancer. BreaktheChain.org

23. David O. McKay, *Conference Report*, Oct. 1942, pp. 12–13

24. Spencer W. Kimball, *Ensign,* Nov. 1978, p. 103

25. Richard L. Evans, *Area Conference Report* (England) 8/71:71

26. "The Family: A Proclamation to the World"

27. Edward L. Kimball and Andrew E. Kimball Jr., *Spencer W. Kimball* [Salt Lake City: Bookcraft, 1977], pp. 191–92

28. Vaughn J. Featherstone t*aken from an address given during the Manti Temple Rededication events of April 1987*

29. President Spencer W. Kimball, "Be Ye Therefore Perfect"*,* devotional address, Salt Lake Institute of Religion, 10 Jan. 1975

Chapter Seven

Paradigm Shifts

About a year and a half after graduation, two kids, and four years into our marriage, Eric was working as a mechanic, due to the fact that he was unable to find work in the field he had graduated in. Even though his job paid the bills most weeks, and was work that he had enjoyed before his mission, we were impressed that it was not the field that he should spend his life working in. Therefore, after much study, fasting, and prayer, we felt impressed that he should return to school to become a Chiropractor.

This decision took a leap of faith for us, as it required our moving from New Jersey to Texas, leaving the security of a job and home, to go to an area where we had neither.

When we arrived in Texas, Eric left me and the children with some friends in San Antonio, while he went to Houston (where the Chiropractic school was located), to look for a job and a place to live. However, while he was there, he had the distinct impression to check out a newly opened Chiropractic school near Dallas. I knew from the peace that filled my mind and heart, that it was the Lord guiding him in that decision.

We quickly found an apartment, and Eric was able to find a job as a mechanic, which provided for our basic needs.

Although I had anticipated that Eric would immediately be able to enter Chiropractic school, the reality was that he needed an additional two years of prerequisites. And to be able to qualify for in-state tuition, he needed a year's worth of residency. It helped to have the sure knowledge beforehand, of what the Lord wanted Eric to do, so the setback did not cause us to lose sight of our goal.

During the two years he was earning his prerequisites, I was a stay-at-home mom, while Eric worked multiple part-time jobs. This schedule allowed him the opportunity to spend a good amount of time with me and the kids, as well as allowing us to get together with friends.

However, that way of life came to a screeching halt when Eric started Chiropractic school. Then, to add to our growing stress, three weeks into his first term in school, we moved and I had an emergency cesarean section (to deliver our third child), all within less than a 24 hour period of time!

The stress of being (for all intents and purposes) a single mother, who was recovering from major surgery, while trying to keep up with two very active preschool aged children and a new born baby, while dealing with the stresses of running a household alone, was a lot more of a challenge than I could possibly have anticipated beforehand. Those things, combined with the realization of just how much time my husband was going to be away from home, let me know that life as we had known it, was going to be quite different and difficult, and would require a lot more strength and faith to be able to handle all that the next three years would require of us.

Eric and I feel strongly that the husband/father should be the bread winner, making it so the wife (whenever possible) can be a homemaker and a stay-at-home mom. Our commitment to that principle was strengthened by President Ezra Taft Benson, in his General Conference talk in October 1987 ("To Fathers in Israel", *Ensign*, November 1987, page 49). So, even though it took a lot of time away from his studies and our family, Eric continued to work a number of part-time jobs while he went to school. I will be forever in his debt for allowing me that priceless blessing of being able to be in the home while our children were growing up.

While in Chiropractic school, his schedule was pretty hectic. He continued to get up at 2 am to deliver newspapers, and after a long day of mind bending classes, he worked another part-time job assembling motorcycles at a bike shop. In his third year, he had to add three hours a day for treating patients at the campus clinic to be able to meet the requirements for his internship.

He often arrived home so tired that he could hardly keep his eyes open. But he always made sure to have family prayer and scripture study with me and the kids before we put the kids to bed. Then, he would retire to the bedroom to put in a few hours of study before we went to bed, which was usually between 10:30 and 11:00 pm.

However, even with very difficult classes, and not near enough time to study for them, he chose not to study on Saturdays or Sundays. His decision about not studying on the Sabbath came from when I was a student at Rick's College. President Henry B. Eyring, who was the President of the college at the time, promised the student body, that if we would study hard for our classes on the other days of the week, and not on the Sabbath, we would be blessed to do well in our studies.

Eric felt Saturdays should be for family. Therefore, except for when he needed to put in extra time studying for midterms and finals, he was able to stick with his Saturday commitment. I have no doubt that the Lord blessed him to be able to maintain a high GPA because of his being completely committed to those ideals.

My husband compared the following adage with our trying to stay focused on our goals, when the stresses and hardships seemed overwhelming: "When you are up to your necks in alligators, it's hard to remember that the original objective was to drain the swamp!" (Unattributed)

As admirable as his accomplishments were, I was naïve and clueless about most of what he was going through physically, emotionally, and mentally, because he never talked about any of it with me. And it wasn't because I didn't ask. As a matter of fact, I often asked how he was doing, as he usually looked like he had the weight of the world on his shoulders. I wanted to ease his burdens and suffering, because I loved him. But his short, abrupt retort saying he was fine, felt like a door had been slammed in my face.

I honestly believe if he had filled me in on some of what he was going through, I would have been much more understanding, and would not have taken his behavior so personally. It wasn't until I started writing this account, that he helped me understand what he was going through that made it very difficult for him to be pleasant and conversant about much of anything.

He had no idea how much I craved his attention and love. Yet, even if he had comprehended it, there was not much of him to give to me or the kids when he got home in the evenings. However, he did the best he could with that, as between school breaks, we would find someone to watch the children for a day or two, and we would go somewhere fun. A couple of times, we went to a Renaissance Faire. On one of those trips, I smiled so much my cheeks hurt by the end of the second day. Those respites, and having him to ourselves on Sundays and most Saturdays, helped us each week, to get through the rough 5 days in between. However, he was usually so tired or had things with the cars and around the house that needed his attention, that we rarely got any real family or couple time on Saturdays. And Sundays were usually spent in church meetings and taking literally the meaning of, the Sabbath being a day of rest.

His schedule made him so sleep deprived, that when we were able to get together with friends, he would hardly say a word. He half jokingly said recently, that he was so tired on those occasions, that he had one eye at half mast, and the other eye catching a catnap.

It was about that period of time, that a friend of mine asked how I stood being married to someone who was so cold. Even though it made me uncomfortable that she would think such a thing of the man I loved and I knew loved me, that I tried to brush it off as her not really knowing him like I did. Yet, the seed was planted, and as Eric became more distant and moody, my friend's words started to take root in my weary mind and heart.

It was not long before all I could see in him was her observations. So, in an attempt to "fix" him, I expressed my desire that he would be more loving, and that he would spend more time with me and the kids. For some reason, I had delusions that he would magically be transformed into the knight in shining priesthood armor that I longed for him to be.

As you can imagine, he *not* only did not react how I had anticipated, but he became even more distant and moody. Alas, after numerous failed attempts at trying to help him see himself as I was lead to believe others saw him, it became painfully obvious, that my efforts were only making things worse.

Then, to complicate things, about that same period of time, I learned that a number of young couples we knew were going through divorces. When that startling news came to my attention, I first had to rule out whether we should declare a "divorce epidemic", so married couples could run for shelter to avoid catching it. Secondly, I tried to consider if there was a common denominator in each of these failed marriages. Let me explain it this way: Have you noticed that when you complain about something, it is easy to find fault with other things, until it escalates into all sorts of things that annoy you? In addition, have you noticed that the other people involved in the conversation, will often start griping about things that annoy them as well? Need I go on?

I have since wondered if the same type of thing happened with those couples…who all happened to know each other. You know how it goes: Mary says, "My husband forgot my birthday."

Susie, adds, "That's not so bad, Jim, forgot our anniversary last week!"

Then Jill tells what her husband did that was equally insensitive. Thus, they fuel each others frustrations and hurt to the point that they all feel like victims, instead of wives, going through the normal situations that occur in *every* marriage.

Side note: Now, in the defense of the supposed insensitive and thoughtless husbands, little did any of us wives realize at that time, that our husbands were probably doing the best they knew how; as most, if not all, had not taken "New Husband's 101" or "New Dad's 101". They were pioneers on a maiden voyage in their roles as husbands and fathers. However, the same was true of my friends and I, who were all young, first time wives and mothers.

Finding fault with one's spouse is NEVER healthy in any marriage. Doing so makes it difficult to see any redeeming qualities in them…even if their good qualities far out weigh their weaknesses and failings.

It is interesting to note, that the moment I started to allow those negative views to *take root* in my mind and heart, a strong impression came to me that I should not allow myself to be critical of Eric. However, thinking I was justified in my feelings, I shoved the impressions aside.

Fortunately for both of us, it was not long after that when Eric shared a startling statistic that he had heard in class that day, where his professor said that couples, where one or both have earned a professional degree (i.e.: doctor or lawyer), that 50% of those marriages ended in divorce, either during school or within a year of graduation.

Needless to say, my jaw dropped! Not only was I shocked at the alarming statistic, but it made me sick inside to think that our marriage could end up on the same garbage heap of those other failed marriages.

That solitary wakeup call was all it took for me to humble myself and to intensify my prayers and efforts in trying to get the Lord's help to heal the gulf that was rapidly widening between me and my husband. I knew the Lord would not have had me go through all I did to make sure I married the right person, in the right place, at the right time, just for our marriage to fail.

I poured over every marriage book that I thought would offer help. However, for a short period of time, all my increased efforts seemed to drive my husband further away. He became more distant and moody...which caused me deep pain and heartache. Yet, looking back with a different perspective, I can see that he was also suffering from deep heartache and pain because of my comments to him. However, because I was so focused on my own feelings, I could not see it.

Something I will be forever grateful for, is no matter how dark things seemed during that period of time, neither of us gave up on our marriage. In fact, neither of us ever hinted at giving up. I just kept hanging in there doing the things I knew to be right and hoping and praying that somehow the Lord would help us build the Celestial marriage I longed for.

A short while later I found renewed hope when I heard about a marriage seminar that focused on values which were similar to ours. However, once again I was crushed, as my attempts to tell my husband about it met with his acting like I was still trying to find ways to "fix" him.

I was desperate for help, so with all the heartfelt sincerity and conviction I could muster, I looked into his eyes and expressed my deep love and commitment to him and our marriage. I shared that all I wanted for us, was to have the sparkle that the more seasoned couples have, who, in spite of the loss of their youthful beauty, still hold hands as if they are newlyweds, and glow whenever they see each other enter a room.

I grew even more frustrated when my husband said, "That's not normal", to which I quickly replied, "I do not want us to be normal. I want for us to have something special."

After saying that, I was delighted to see his countenance soften, and a sparkle come into his eyes as he expressed a sincere interest in our checking out the seminar. This seemed to be the answer I had been praying for. However, once again, my excitement was short lived when my husband said he would not be able to attend the seminar because he could not afford to miss any of his classes.

I *very* reluctantly went alone, and evidently my disappointment must have shown in my body language and facial expressions. I had rationalized my attitude by the fact that I had been hanging on to the hope that this was the answer to my *many* prayers. I had gotten past the delusion of thinking I wanted the romantic love you read about in fairytales. But I really wanted the sparkle and magic that I saw in other couples, which I felt we lacked.

During a break on the second day of the seminar, I approached the instructor to tell him about something I had read in a self-help marriage book. Yet, before I could say anything, he blurted out, "You're upset your husband is not here, and it is *you* who needs this seminar, not him!!!"

I was shocked and embarrassed that he would say such a thing to me, especially in front of all those people. It was all I could do to keep from running from the room. I felt he had falsely accused me, as I had not said a word about my husband during that seminar.

However, in spite of the humiliation I was dealing with, and the frustration I felt towards the instructor, I somehow managed to get back to my seat...all the while praying hard not to let my hurt feelings and embarrassment get in the way of what I had paid a lot of money to learn. It proved a good thing that I made that choice, because the instructor took time to clarify what he said to me.

A miracle took place as I applied the enlightenment I received from that seminar. My relationship with my husband started to improve, and he started treating me with more tenderness and love.

Then, not long after that experience, I was driving down the road, not thinking about much of anything, when the following words came to my mind, "If you could see your husband in the eternities, you would drop to your knees in humility."

It was not a harsh voice, but, nonetheless, I knew I was being chastised.

When the Lord enlightened my mind with that gentle but powerful chastisement, I had a paradigm shift, where I realized that my negative attitude and self-pity, had caused me to be so blind and self-absorbed, that the Spirit was *unable* to teach me what I desperately wanted and *needed* to learn.

In Dr. Stephen Covey's, "7 Habits for Highly Effective People", he told how one Sunday morning when he was in New York riding on the subway, the silence was broken when a man and his unruly children entered the car he was in. The children ran around the car annoying everyone in their path. Finally, someone spoke up and asked the man if he could control his kids, as they were bothering people.

The man looked up from his downward gaze and said, "Oh...I am sorry...I suppose they do not know how to act. You see...we just left the hospital where their mother died a short while ago."

Immediately, the other commuters had a paradigm shift and rushed to assist the man and his children, to try and ease their burdens.

The Indians have a wise saying; "Do not judge a man, until you have walked a mile in his moccasins".

Sometimes, when someone in the family is being cross or difficult, they may be dealing with some heavy burden, or they may be feeling as if they are a failure, or like they have no worth to anyone. However, it would be wise to remember during those times when tempers are short, and arguments seem to be the only communication that takes place in the home, that that spirit can be very unproductive and destructive to the fabric that holds the marriage and family together. The Spirit cannot and will not dwell in such an environment (Helaman 4:24; Isaiah 57:15).

When there are misunderstandings between spouses or family members, it is wise to try and see the other person's point of view before trying to express your own. If you will make that effort, you will be surprised at how wrong you were about the reasons for the other person's behavior.

To the Lord, we are all gods and goddesses in embryo. Can you see the value of making the effort to see each person, including your spouse, in that light? If we would, our relationships would take on new meaning, depth, and beauty.

I am grateful the Lord opened my eyes and understanding, to be able to see and appreciate the choice son of God that holds my hand and heart!

Chapter Eight

Getting Back to the Basics

In the movie, *The Sound of Music*, Maria, the new governess to the von Trapp children, discovered early on, that the children did not know how to sing. Therefore, she decided to start at the very beginning by teaching the children to sing the notes on the musical scale.

Once the children mastered the notes, she then taught them to sing parts so they could blend their voices in beautiful harmony. With their newfound talent, they decided to enter the prestigious Salzburg Folk Festival, in which they won first place. It was not long before they were performing all over the world.

Years ago, my husband and our son Jeremy heard the world-renowned concert pianist Wladimir Jan Kochanski, play in a concert. Jeremy, who was about 7 or 8 years old, became an instant fan. After the concert, he went up to Wladimir and asked how he got so good.

Wladimir's words to him spoke volumes when he said, "Practice, practice, practice!"

Wladimir knew becoming an accomplished pianist did not just happen, that it takes hard work, dedication and commitment. He studied six years at the prestigious Julliard School of Music, where he was mentored by some very talented musicians, one of which was, Rosina Lhevinne, who described him as "a dazzling pianist reminiscent of the masters." [1]

Countless people have devoted similar dedication and commitment like the Von Trapp Family Singers and Wladimir Kochanski to become accomplished musicians. Many have put the same dedication into earning a degree, mastering a sport, or to be able to excel in their chosen professions and careers. Yet, with their most precious commodities, which should be their spouse and children, too many neglect, or put very little effort into building and strengthening those relationships.

Dig in Your Fingernails and Hold On

Years ago, in south Florida, a little boy decided to go for a swim in the old swimming hole that was behind his house. In a hurry to dive into the cool water, he jumped in, not realizing that as he swam toward the middle of the lake that an alligator had entered the water.

In the house, his mother was looking out through the window. To her horror, she saw the alligator headed towards her son. She ran out of the house toward the water, yelling to her son as loudly as she could.

Upon hearing her screams, he turned to swim towards his mother. However, as his mother grabbed her son in her arms, the alligator grabbed hold of the little boy's legs with its jaws of steel. Even though the alligator was much stronger than the mother, the mother would not let go.

A farmer happened to drive by and upon hearing the screams, he grabbed his shotgun from his truck and raced towards the horrible scene, he aimed his gun and shot the alligator.

It was a miracle, but after spending a number of weeks in the hospital, the little boy was able to return home. His legs were covered in deep scars from where the alligator had held onto his legs, and his arms had deep scratches from where his mother dug in her fingernails to be able to keep the alligator from taking her son from her.

The newspaper reporter, who interviewed the little boy, asked if he would show him his scars. The boy lifted his pant legs, and with pride in his voice, he said, 'But, look at my arms, I have great scars on my arms, too. I have them because my Mom wouldn't let go." [2]

Would you have done the same as the mother in that story did for her son? I should think most, if not all of us would fight that hard to save our spouse, our children, or any member of our family in a similar situation. Then why not hold on and fight that hard if our marriages or families are falling apart?

It is Time to Succeed with Those Goals

A few years ago, I decided to start a scripture journal. I wanted to start by writing down all the quotes and impressions that were on the scraps of paper that I had placed in my scriptures over the years. I had no sooner started writing them in my journal, when I noticed an unsettling trend, where one scrap of paper after another had the same goal written on it.

Seeing the same thing written on so many pieces of paper, was a stark wake up call for me, because I could not figure out why each time I started making the effort to follow through with that goal, it was not long before I lost my resolve and commitment to stick with it. Then, each time I got off track with that goal, it was harder to get back on track.

A short while later, a Relief Society teacher had the class write down things that make us happy. Then she had us write the things that make us unhappy. After comparing our lists, we were asked to see if there was anything on our "unhappy list" that we could change, so we could move it to our "happy list". Upon looking over my "unhappy list", that same goal loomed out at me! I resolved at that moment, that it was time to get to the bottom of what kept sabotaging my resolve to stick with my goal. After giving it some serious thought and prayer, I realized that I needed to decide on a *clear* and *workable* plan of action that I not only *could*, but *would* stick with.

It was not long before I started seeing real progress in accomplishing that goal, and the best part was how good I felt about myself. However, it did not take long before I started to back slide again. Then one morning after praying for further insight into what was causing me to lose sight of my goal again, I started pouring through my scriptures to find anything and everything to get me past the massive roadblock that stood in my way, I opened my scriptures and saw the following words: "And as all have not faith, seek ye diligently...out of the best books words of wisdom; seek learning, even by study and also by faith...Organize yourselves; prepare every needful thing; and establish a house, even a house of prayer, a house of fasting, a house of faith, a house of learning..." (D&C 88:118-119)

I realized that faith without works is dead! If I expected to get and KEEP the results, I needed to DAILY apply what I was learning and not let go of my goals when I get discouraged or side-tracked. However, as with any goal, we need to remember the following words of wisdom: "...see that all these things are done in wisdom and order; for it is not requisite that a man should run faster than he has strength. And again, it is expedient that he should be diligent, that thereby he might win the prize; therefore, all things must be done in order." (Mosiah 4:27) And in D&C 10:4 it says, "Do not run faster or labor more than you have strength and means...but be diligent unto the end."

So there you have it, the formula to be able to accomplish any worthy or righteous goal is:

1. Seek diligently out of the best books, which should always include the scriptures, the words of the prophets, and Church leaders.
2. Seek learning by study and by faith.
3. Organize yourselves; all things should be done in wisdom and order.
4. Prepare every needful thing.
5. Pray
6. Fast
7. Have faith.
8. Do not run faster than you have the strength and means.
9. Be diligent until you win the prize (or reach your goal).

A big goal inhibitor is *discouragement*. Within a few months of applying the above words of wisdom, I was able to get back to my commitment to follow through with my goal...which was getting to a healthier weight. I was pleased when I lost weight quickly, but then I got discouraged when the weight loss slowed down. For a while I thought I was not progressing, until I looked back over my track record for the previous few months and noticed that I had lost 3-4 lbs and 5-6 inches in that time. It was not a lot, but it was still progress that could be measured.

That helped me get over *the discouragement* and I got back on track. From that experience, I learned an eternal principal about how the Lord teaches us line upon line, precept upon precept, here a little, there a little (Isaiah 28:10, 13; 2 Nephi 28:30).

Now, I would like to say that I have stuck with those goals, but, like everything else in life, if we do not stay committed and focused we will not be able to accomplish the goal, whether it is physical, educational, or spiritual.

I like to write things down so I will not forget them. Therefore, as I studied and prayed for what I needed to do to accomplish the goals on my list for ways to be happy, I wrote them down. That made it easy for me to review them on a regular basis. Also, when I started getting off track, or would get discouraged, I could pull out the paper and review the area I was struggling in.

If you are interested, here is the list I came up with that helped to inspire me with not just weight loss, but other goals as well:

1. Write down on a paper the things that make you happy. It can be anything that comes to your mind.

2. Next, write down the things that make you feel unhappy, sad, or frustrated. Again, it can be anything that comes to your mind. This is not for posterity; it is for you, unless you choose to share it with others.

3. Next, look at the list of things that make you unhappy, and write down things you can do to change those things.

4. Now, read Ether 12:27: "And if men come unto me I will show unto them their weakness. I give unto men weakness that they may be humble; and my grace is sufficient for all men that humble themselves before me; for if they humble themselves before me, and have faith in me, then will I make weak things become strong unto them."

5. Really put some thought, prayer, and effort into studying that verse and how it applies to this growth process; and then write down your impressions in a scripture journal, so you can refer back to it.

6. Now, turn to Alma 32:26-43 in the Book of Mormon. Really, pay close attention to verse 27: "...*if ye will awake and arouse your faculties.*" You must first, *awake and arouse* your faculties with any undertaking or goal you wish to accomplish, or you may lose your desire to accomplish it.

7. Now, read and ponder D&C 93:12-13: "I, John, saw that he [meaning Christ] received not of the fulness at the first, but received grace for grace...until he received a fulness..."

8. Next, turn to 2 Nephi 28:30: "...thus saith the Lord God: I will give unto the children of men line upon line, precept upon precept, here a little and there a little..."

9. We all need to learn line upon line and precept and precept. Why was the Lord required to learn that way and not us? So, be patient with your growth process, and do not expect to be perfect overnight...or even in your lifetime.

10. Now, write down how you can apply what you are learning as well as the impressions that may be coming to your mind about the things you want to overcome or change. This way you will be able to move items from your unhappy list to the list of things that make you happy.

It is not the big things that count in our families, so much as the little efforts that we do not think amount to too much that makes a difference. "...by small and simple things are great things brought to pass..." (Alma 37:6).

This is true in marriage, as well as for other goals we strive to accomplish.

Notes:
1. http://en.wikipedia.org/wiki/Wladimir_Jan_Kochanski - cite_note-2#cite_note-2
2. Author unknown

Chapter Nine

Decisions Determine Destiny

Dr. Douglas Brinley, co-author of "Between Husband and Wife" and "Living a Covenant Marriage", shared a story about a couple who called him after attending one of his marital relationship seminars. They told how they were on the brink of divorce, and that he was their last hope. They told him they had been to three other marriage counselors who were unable to help them, and if he did not give them the advice and help they needed, then, they would have no other choice but to divorce.

He told how he felt overwhelmed with the task that lay ahead of him, feeling if he failed to help this couple find solutions to their marital problems, then another temple marriage would fail, and he did not like that option.

He pleaded with the Lord to help him be able to know what to use from his education and training as a family therapist, to help this couple.

"Teach the Saints to live the Gospel", was not what he expected the Lord to tell him. Could it be that easy? He realized that the answer was as simple as a Sunday school answer that any couple or individual could figure out on their own, without the help of a trained marriage counselor. [1]

Many times, the Lord answers our prayers through another person, and in some cases, they include family or marriage counselors, and/or priesthood leaders. However, we cannot leave the Lord out of the process. After all, He is the One who knows better than anyone else, what our deepest heartaches and needs are. He is able to heal all wounds and heartaches...even seriously damaged relationships.

Every Family Has the Tools to make it To the Celestial Kingdom

The Lord has provided the way for every family to be able to make it to the Celestial Kingdom. There may be some of you who feel your marriage is unsalvageable, and that you have nowhere else to turn.

To you I say, *dig in your fingernails and hold on like your life depends upon it*. The answers will come. They will however, be in the Lord's time and way. So, be patient, and have trust and faith in His guidance.

Joseph Smith was one who understood all too well, the deep pain and suffering which comes from the betrayal of trusted friends. He endured failed business ventures, homelessness, and false imprisonment on a number of occasions, as well as severe pain and suffering brought on by angry mobs. There were times when even the elements turned against him. There were numerous times when hunger and sickness became constant companions for him and his family. However, probably the deepest pain and suffering he endured came when Martin Harris lost the 116 pages that Joseph had translated from the Gold Plates. The loss of that manuscript caused him to spend six long, miserable months in the pit of despair, believing he had lost his soul (D&C 3 & 10).

The following formula (given by Joseph Smith), gives excellent insight into how your mind and heart can be restored to peace and light, even if you are at the darkest time of your life: "If you have any darkness [or heartache or worry], you have only to ask, and the darkness [heartache or worry] is removed. It is not necessary that miracle[s] should be wrought to remove darkness [heartache or worry]. *Miracles are the fruits of faith...*" [2] (Emphasis added)

I know these words of wisdom to be true, because I have applied them many times in my life, and peace and comfort filled my mind and heart.

Alma gave the following formula, to be able to get answers and help from the Lord, "...awake and arouse your faculties, even to an experiment upon my words, and exercise a particle of faith, yea, even if ye can no more than desire to believe, let this desire work in you, even until ye believe in a manner that ye can give place for a portion of my words...Now, we will compare the word unto a seed. Now, if ye give place, that a seed may be planted in your heart, behold, if it be a true seed, or a good seed, if ye do not cast it out by your unbelief, that ye will resist the Spirit of the Lord, behold, it will begin to swell within your breasts; and when you feel these swelling motions, ye will begin to say within yourselves—It must needs be that this is a good seed, or that the word is good, for it beginneth to enlarge my soul; yea, it beginneth to enlighten my understanding, yea, it beginneth to be delicious to me." (Alma 32:27-28)

James, who was Christ's Disciple, said, "If any of you lack wisdom, let him ask of God, that giveth to all men liberally, and upbraideth not and it shall be given to him...But, let him ask in faith, nothing wavering..." (James 1:5-6)

So, let me recap what Alma said about getting answers and help from the Lord:

1. We need to *awake and arouse* our faculties (verse 27). There are those words again.
2. We need to *ask with faith* (verse 27).
3. We need to *desire to know* (verse 27).
4. We need to *give place for a portion of the words* [or ideas] *that come to our minds and hearts* (verse 27).
5. *Do what is required* to gain answers and a testimony (verses 27-37, 41-43).
6. *Do not cast them out with your unbelief* (verses 38-40). This part of the formula is often overlooked as being an integral part of getting answers and help we desire from the Lord.

Listen and pay close attention to the feelings and impressions that come to your mind and heart as you study and pray. *If it enlarges your soul, enlightens your mind, and is delicious to you,* you have your answer. However, more times than not, the answers are not so easy to discern. They may come as a still small voice with no powerful feelings.

You should not ignore those impressions, as it may be the very answer(s) you are looking for, and if ignored, you may pass up blessings that the Lord is more than willing to pour down upon you. The key is in being able to discern when it is or is not the Spirit speaking to you. So, pray for discernment to recognize when it is from the Lord.

After you receive your answer(s), you must go forward with faith and hope, with *nothing* wavering (Alma 32:38-43).

That process seems like it would be easy doesn't it? Then why is it so few people know where and how to find the answers they seek?

And, why is it, we see so many couples who have been sealed in the temple, who chose to divorce, when, if they would put forth more effort and trust in the Lord's guidance, they could qualify for ALL the blessings He has for husbands and wives who have been sealed in the temple?

Sunday School Answers Are the Answers

A number of years ago, a man who had served as a Bishop, shared (without divulging their names) how numerous couples had come to him for advice on how to strengthen their troubled marriages and families. He told how he asked them if they were having family and individual prayer and scripture study every day, as well as Family Home Evening every week. He was not surprised, when the answer that he received was often a resounding "No".

He then challenged them to commit to adding these practices to their daily and weekly family activities. Those that followed his counsel found their marriages and home life improving drastically. Those that did not, continued to have serious problems. Granted, their problems may have been so deeply rooted, that they may have needed a marriage counselor to help work through them, but the Lord knows our hearts and needs better than anyone else, and therefore, He is the best marriage and family counselor there is.

Every Family has what it takes to get to the Celestial Kingdom

Because of the Atonement, the Lord has the power to heal *all* wounds, even damaged relationships. Therefore, *every* family has what it takes to get to the Celestial Kingdom!

Sometimes, we may be doing the things we have been counseled to do by our Church leaders, as well as what the scriptures teach, but it seems like our prayers are falling on deaf ears, and that there is no hope or relief in sight. It is during those times, one could ask for the

142

Lord to bring peace of mind or to have the quiet assurance that He is there, and has not forgotten them or their family.

As I mentioned before, when I have asked for peace when my heart and mind have been weighed down with worry or grief, it never ceases to amaze me how quickly the Lord answers those requests. The quiet assurance He sends, is like a healing balm that gives me strength to continue to bare my burdens and trials no matter how difficult they may seem. The peace that He sends also helps me to have a happier disposition, and *hope* for brighter days ahead.

Sometimes, there is no obvious manifestation of the Spirit, but I notice hours later, that my burdens seem lighter, and I have the heart to keep holding on to the Iron Rod, and to keep exercising faith and trust in the Lord.

I would rather have peace in the midst of raging storms, than the absence of trails. After all, this life was meant to be a proving ground, not a bed of roses. Besides, how can we hope to dwell in the same kingdom with Jesus Christ…Joseph Smith…Nephi and Lehi…King Benjamin…Alma and Ammon…the Two Thousand Stripling Warriors…Moroni…Abraham, and others like them, if we are not forged from the same metal that they are?

Nothing is too difficult for the Lord

Not long ago when Eric and I were walking from the parking lot to his office, he saw a $20.00 bill in a pile of debris that was from the previous day's storm. As he stooped down to pick it up, he noticed another $20.00 bill buried deeper in the pile. We both got a chuckle as we asked why there couldn't have been larger bills.

However, almost immediately, I remembered my prayer that morning, where I made a simple petition asking the Lord to send us money that day without my needing to go through all the humiliation and stress of trying to collect from companies that owed us money.

The amount of money found that morning wasn't anything close to what I was hoping for. But it was one of those tender mercies that let me know that the Lord had indeed heard my prayer.

It is interesting that my husband hung on to those $20.00 bills for a long time. I assume, as a reminder that with the Lord, nothing is impossible (Luke 1:37). Because of that experience, my mind was drawn to the account in Matthew 17:27, where Jesus told Peter to go to the sea to catch a fish, and in its mouth, he would find a coin for them to be able to pay their taxes. I wish it were that simple to come up with money to pay our taxes…hmmm, maybe we should take a fishing trip the next time taxes are due.

All kidding aside, it is hard to keep exercising faith when it seems like our prayers go unanswered for long periods of time. One morning when asking the Lord why He had withheld some blessings that we were desperately in need of, I had the impression that what I was praying for would not be in our best interest if they were granted at that time. That helped me realize that He had not forgotten us, and that our prayers were being heard. During such times, we should not give-up, even if we think it is impossible or unimportant to the Lord.

Years ago, our middle son came into the house and told me there was a mother cat with her kittens in a shed in our back yard. A kitten's neck and right front leg where entangled in a string. The string had been there long enough to wear away the hair, and had cut off circulation to the kitten's leg, which caused it to lose the use of that leg.

I untangled the kitten and took it into the house where I used a medicine dropper to feed it some warm milk. Our rental agreement did not allow us to have cats, so until I could figure out what to do with the mother cat and her kittens, I decided to put them in a large, empty bird cage that previous renters had left in the backyard.

I provided food and water for the mother cat every day, and checked on her and her kittens to make sure they were okay. However, I became alarmed after a few days, when I realized the kitten was still not walking on its right front leg. It was getting around by pushing with its shoulder and its other three legs.

I tried splinting the kitten's leg to see if it would help the kitten to be able to use it, but nothing I tried seemed to work. I asked my husband, who had medical training, to check out the kitten's leg. He pricked its paw with a pin, but to my dismay, the kitten did not respond. That told us that there was nerve damage.

I was sick because I knew we could not keep the cats, and if we could not find a home for them, we would have to take them to the animal shelter; and I worried they might put the kitten to sleep, if it could not walk on its leg.

The next Sunday, one of the Sacrament meeting speakers told the story about when Mary Fielding Smith (widow to Hyrum Smith) crossed the plains with the Saints, when they left Winter Quarters for the Salt Lake Valley, in the spring of 1848.

In spite of the wagon train captain's protests that Mary and her company would be a burden, Mary very calmly told him that she would not ask for his help, and that she would beat him to the Valley. One very hot day, one of Mary's oxen fell to the ground and appeared to be dead. Mary asked her brother, Joseph Fielding, and a friend, James Lawson, to administer to the ox. After doing so, the stiffened ox stirred, and rose to its feet, and started pulling the wagon as if nothing had happened.

Then, before arriving in the Valley, some of Mary's cows wandered off, and John, Mary's step-son, went to find them. The wagon train captain, not wanting to wait, ordered the rest of the company to move on. While praying and patiently waiting for John and the cows' safe return, an unexpected rainstorm sent the company, which had moved ahead of Mary's group, into a mass of confusion, which caused their cattle to scatter. In the meantime, John had returned with their lost cows, which allowed Mary and her group to move past the other group.

Her faith and courage allowed her and her group to arrive in the valley 20 hours ahead of the Captain and his group that had deserted her. [3]

As I listened to the Sacrament Meeting speaker, I had the thought to suggest to my husband that our family do the same thing for the kitten. So, when we got home from church, my we sat our children down, and discussed the story about Mary Fielding Smith and her ox; suggesting that we as a family, should pray with faith for the kitten's leg to be healed.

I do not know what my husband and kids went through with that experience, but, it was not easy for me because I had a hard time making myself believe that a stray cat was important enough for the Lord to heal. After all, He has allowed horses and cows (who provide income for families), to become lame without healing them; and this was a stray kitten that offered no means of support for our family, and we could not even keep it for a pet.

However, as hard as it was, I shoved all of those doubts from my mind and suggested that my family do the same. My commitment to continue to pray with faith waned late Monday evening when I saw that the kitten's leg was still lame. Then on Tuesday morning as I was getting dressed, I was surprised when the following words came to my mind: "Do you believe I *can* heal the kitten's leg?"

I was elated because I knew the Lord had heard my prayers. Therefore, I forced myself to push away all doubt as I answered with a firm, "Yes!"

Then, the following words came to my mind, "Do you believe I *will* heal the kitten's leg?"

Wow! I knew the Lord *could* heal the kitten's leg. But *would* He? However, as difficult as it was for me, I knew to be able to get the results I had been praying for, I could not doubt or *waver* (James 1:5-6). So before I allowed myself to go down that path, I forced myself to answer with a firm and unwavering "Yes!"

Then the real test came. I knew I had to immediately go out to see the kitten, as it would show a lack of faith if I put it off. Even though it took me a minute or two to get there, it felt like a very long journey, because I had to stay focused with shoving out all doubts and having *unwavering* faith.

As I walked closer to the cage, I could hardly believe my eyes, as I saw the kitten was walking on all of its legs…rather wobbly…but it was *walking* on all four legs!

I shed tears of joy! I had not only witnessed a miracle, but I realized something that I thought would be viewed as of little worth to the Lord, actually had great worth to Him! I also learned a priceless lesson…that faith can literally move mountains and heal what seemed impossible to heal (Matthew 17:20).

The kitten's leg was healed because of prayer, unwavering faith, and belief that the Lord not only *could* but *would* heal it. The same applies to what is needed in healing and building a strong, loving marriage that *will* last through the eternities.

The Lord will answer the sincere, humble prayers of one who will submit his or her heart to Him. I saw a billboard recently that read, "A mother's prayers are stronger than her child's addiction(s)". I do not think the Lord plays favorites with mothers. I believe it has to do with the sincerity and faith of the petitioner to Him.

I am convinced that the same is true of a spouse who is dealing with the heart break and hopelessness of the other spouse's addictions, whether they are pornography, alcoholism, or drugs.

No matter how hopeless things may seem at times, *never forget*, *every* family has the potential to make it to the Celestial Kingdom…even yours!

Reaching Celestial Shores

When Noah began building the ark (which took 40 years), the sky was clear. Yet, his unwavering obedience to the Lord's commandment to do so, made it so the Lord could fulfill His promises and purposes. Likewise, if we will follow the Lord's commandments and counsel for families, *we will be better prepared to handle the storms that too often capsize marriages that started out for Celestial shores while the seas were calm.*

Some couples may think, "All's well in Zion" because they do not seem to have any serious problems in their marriages or families. I say to those who feel that way, "Good for you"; but would caution, "Wait, you're young yet."

It has been my experience, that shortly after thinking, "All is well in Zion", I soon see the storm clouds appearing on the horizon, and it is not long before the storm begins to rage, and the mists of darkness start to surround me, and I find myself wondering where my refuge from the storm is.

It is during those times, when "being prepared" like the Boy Scout motto says, pays off, and I realize to an even greater degree, that being spiritually, emotionally, and physically prepared, is the only way to build a safe refuge from the storms that *every* marriage and family *will* encounter.

In "The Family: A Proclamation to the World", it states that the family is at the center of the Creator's plan. For families to be successful, they should make the following a part of their family life:

1. Faith
2. Prayer
3. Repenting of sins

4. Forgiving others of sins
5. Showing love, respect, and compassion for others
6. Learning the value of work
7. Having wholesome recreational activities as a family
8. Fathers are commanded (not suggested) to lead their families in love and righteousness, as well as being responsible for providing for their family's needs and protection.
9. It is the mother's role to nurture their children.
10. Parents should offer assistance to each other as equal partners in their respective roles.
11. Our church leaders warn that anyone who violates the laws of chastity, who are abusive to their spouse or children, or fail to be faithful in their discharge of their role to their family, will have to answer to God.

A strict warning was given by our Church leaders that which the disintegration of the family will bring upon nations, communities, and mankind, calamities that have been prophesied by prophets of ancient date as well as in modern times. [4]

If becoming a righteous, responsible spouse and parent is at the center of the Creator's plan, then individuals would be wise to prepare for those roles *long before* filling them. Therefore, wise parents will start early with teaching and preparing their children for when they will take on those roles with their own families someday.

Joseph Smith said parents should teach their children correct principles, so they can govern themselves. In Proverbs 22:6 it says, "Train up a child in the way he should go and when he is old, he will not depart from it."

All throughout history, there are examples of how parents made the difference for good or bad, where future generations were concerned.

Therefore, to ensure a safer and a more sure passage to *Celestial Shores* for themselves as well as for their family, parents need to teach by *word* and *example*.

Being able to sleep when the Wind Blows

We have been told if we are prepared, we shall not fear (Doctrine & Covenants 38:30). Some years ago, a farmer who owned land along the Atlantic seacoast, constantly advertised for hired hands. Most people were reluctant to work on farms along the Atlantic coastline, because the storms that raged across the Atlantic Ocean, wreaked havoc on buildings and crops.

As the farmer interviewed applicants for the job, he received a steady stream of refusals. Finally, a short, thin man, well past middle age, approached the farmer.

"Are you a good farmhand?" the farmer asked him.

"Well, I can sleep when the wind blows." answered the little man.

Although puzzled by his answer, the farmer (who was desperate for help), made the decision to hire him.

The farmhand worked hard around the farm, staying busy from dawn to dusk, which pleased his employer. Then one night, the wind howled loudly. Jumping out of bed, the farmer grabbed a lantern and rushed next door to the hired hand's sleeping quarters. He shook the little man and yelled, "Get up! A storm is coming! Tie things down before they blow away!"

The little man rolled over in bed and said firmly, "No sir. I told you, I can sleep when the wind blows."

Enraged by the response, the farmer was tempted to fire him on the spot. Instead, he hurried outside to prepare for the storm.

To his amazement, he discovered that all of the haystacks had been covered with tarpaulins. The cows were in the barn, the chickens were in the coops, the doors were barred, the shutters were tightly secured, and everything was tied down. Nothing could blow away.

The farmer then understood what his hired hand meant. So he returned to his bed with the assurance that he also would be able to sleep while the wind blew. (Author unknown)

Our decisions will determine ours and our family's destiny...one decision at a time.

Notes:

1. Dr. Douglas Brinley – Marriage Seminar in Tucson, AZ Spring 2007

2. Joseph Fielding Smith, comp., "Life of Joseph F. Smith", 1969, p. 131

3. Mary Fielding Smith's story can be found in the following sources: Don Cecil Corbett, *Mary Fielding Smith: Daughter of Britain* [1966], 228; Corbett, *Mary Fielding Smith*, 237; Intellectual Reserve, Inc , www.LDS.org, 2002; History of the Church, 5:355

4. "The Family: A Proclamation to the World", LDS.org

Section Two

His Image in our Countenances

We should live so it makes it easier for others to know the Savior.

The following chapters will help the reader better understand how to become "beings of light".

Chapter Ten

Becoming One without Losing Your Identity

Oneness, in regards to couples, doesn't mean they lose something, but that the twain become so much more. So, how do couples become *one* without losing their individual identity?

I was watching the *Dr. Phil Show* one day, where a young husband (who was a guest on the show) said he did not understand why his wife could not be more like him. Dr. Phil first made sure to understand what the real issues were by asking some qualifying questions. After doing so, Dr. Phil ascertained that in the beginning of their relationship, one of the things that attracted the husband to his wife was her spontaneity. The husband pointed out that in the beginning; it was refreshing because it contrasted his being so careful and calculating. However, not long after getting married, he viewed her spontaneity as recklessness and immaturity.

Dr. Phil then pointed out that the wife had not changed, but that the husband had done what so many spouses do, and that is to expect their spouse to be just like them; and when they are not, they view it as a roadblock, or an insurmountable problem between them.

Dr. Phil then pointed out that couples should celebrate their diversities, turning them into strengths in their relationship; and not allow them to become brick walls or battering rams that have the potential to destroy their marriages.

So why and how does a couple become one and still retain their individuality? Does it mean that they give up hobbies, interests, foods, movies, music, TV shows, and dare I say it?...the temperature that each prefers the house to be set at; or even where the furniture and pictures on the walls should be if it differs from what the other spouse would like?

In "Seven Habits for Highly Successful People", the author, Dr. Stephen Covey, teaches about being synergistic; which means, all parties come out winners. What a concept!

One of the things I struggled with as I was growing up was what my mother gave up to be able to be supportive of my step-dad, who was very different from her. In the early years, it *seemed* all he thought about was him self; seeming to care nothing about what was important to the rest of the family, or anyone else for that matter.

However, after years of selflessness and being totally committed to supporting him as the priesthood leader of our home, my step-dad got to where he did more and more to insure my mother's needs and wants were met before his own. He became completely devoted to her, and often said she was one of his greatest blessings. He lovingly referred to her as "My Joy"...did I mention her name was Joy?

Now, there were those that wondered why she relinquished the reigns to my step-dad when they got married. It was hard for me to understand why she was so supportive of him in that role, when for so many years, he treated her and others with very little respect or consideration.

However, looking back on her behavior, I believe that she understood the divine roles of men and women and wanted that for her and my step-dad. Therefore, she was willing to sacrifice her independence and need to have her own way, to patiently and lovingly show him by example, what a covenant marriage should and could be. Her decision and commitment to never vary from that stand brought eternal blessings that are continuing to influence her posterity, and all who knew her.

It was not until years later that I realized she never did give up her personal identity. She continued to do things she loved, and even retained the things that made her who she was. She understood the importance of what it takes to "become one", without losing your identity and individual worth. Her efforts and example worked, because she and my step-dad truly were "one" in their commitment to the Lord, as well as with their eternal goals. It was because of their dedication to those things, they were able to learn to blend their diversities.

Keeping the Delicate Balance While Growing Into Your Own Family Unit

Picture a triangle with Heavenly Father at the top, and the husband on one of the bottom corners, and the wife on the other. Where on that triangle do their parents, children, or friends fit in? If you answered "Nowhere!", then you answered right.

When a man and woman marry, their commitment should be to each other and the Lord, not to other family members and friends. As hard as it is at times, and yes, sometimes it is gut-wrenching to be able to cut the apron strings and/or umbilical cords that attach a child to their parents; yet, it is a NECESSARY process for the newlyweds to be able to grow and define their own family unit.

The couple should rely on Heavenly Father, not their parents, extended family members, nor their friends, to help them make decisions that have to do with each other and their children. This does not mean that they cannot ask for advice, nor listen to advice when it is offered by others. However, in the end, they (as a husband and wife) will need to discuss their options with each other, and come to a decision that they BOTH agree on, and then take it to Heavenly Father to get His approval.

The hardest part of this is when after painstakingly going through this process the Lord has other ideas for them. In that case, they need to have the courage to do His *will no matter how hard it may be*, and no matter how many people may disagree with their final decision(s).

Family and friends may love the couple with all their hearts, but they are not entitled to the inspiration or revelation for them or their children. Moreover, as much as extended family and friends wish they did, they certainly cannot know all that is best for the couple and their children...only the Lord knows that.

There is no doubt that the couple will make mistakes when they are left on their own. We all do. That is part of the Lord's plan (Matthew 19:5). But, they still need to be given their own space to make those decisions without interference from parents, other family members, or friends.

And when they make mistakes, family and friends should show the maturity and consideration about how they want to be treated in similar situations. And as difficult as it may be, the well meaning family and friends should exercise restraint and bite their tongues, instead of uttering those dreaded words that we all hate to hear... "I told you so!"

Every Couple Needs to be Allowed to Define Their Own Family Unit

Parents do not think that your child no longer loves you if they choose to miss a family get together, or make the decision to spend a holiday or birthday with their spouse and children and no one else. Likewise, you young couples, be considerate of family and friends feelings if you decide to bow out of a family get-together, or want to spend a holiday or birthday without them. When you convey the message, make sure to practice the Golden Rule. After all, *you will be in their shoes some day* when your kids get married and choose to do the same thing.

Parents, do you want your kids to be considerate of you on those occasions? Then set the proper example for them. When those situations arise, you might consider asking if you could get together on another day other than the holiday or birthday. It may take some getting used to, but if family members want to stay close, they make adjustments and sacrifices, making sure to include a heavy dose of the Golden Rule. This is especially true when couples marry and want to do things with both families. If you will treat others the way you want to be treated, your family tree, no matter how many branches get added, will be beautiful and a joy to be around.

Chapter Eleven

Becoming Beings of Light…One Countenance at a Time

True and lasting change comes from within, not through legislation or force. And remember, *lasting change can only take place through the miraculous power of the Atonement.*

In 1973, I was a participant in a Church Regional Dance Festival, which took place in the Seattle Coliseum. Hundreds of dancers had come from all over the region to participate in the festival, and thousands had come to watch the performance. We were honored with the presence of the prophet, President Harold B. Lee and his wife.

At the end of the performance, they had President and Sister Lee, walk to the middle of the stadium floor, where they were surrounded by all the dancers.

As I looked at President and Sister Lee, I noticed that the whiteness of President Lee's face was much whiter than the spotlight that was shining on him and his wife. As I gazed in awe on his countenance, the Spirit bore a powerful witness to me that he was a Prophet of God. It was not until years later, that I came to understand that what I had witnessed was the purity of his spirit.

In 3 Nephi 19:25, it tells about this type of whiteness in the countenances of Christ's newly called Apostles (on this continent): "…and behold they were as white as the countenance and also the garments of Jesus; and behold the whiteness thereof did exceed all the whiteness, yea, even there could be nothing upon earth so white as the whiteness thereof."

If you will read the whole chapter, you will see the process the Apostles went through to become beings of light.

Years ago, I attended the memorial service for a dear friend named Rudy Thompson. It was almost as well attended as a Stake Conference. There were many in attendance who had been students of this exemplary man who had been their high school choir director.

Many of his students had been so inspired by him that they went on to become accomplished musicians. I listened as one after another family member, former student, and fellow church member paid tribute, to how his gentle and loving ways had inspired them to want to excel.

This gentle man always had a twinkle in his eye and a huge grin on his face. Everyone who met him, felt like a cherished friend. No one was a stranger to him. He was definitely a being of light that helped others to become beings of light.

The last time I shook hands with Jim (who had just been released as a member of our Stake Presidency, and was moving far away), the following words came to my mind: "We love him, because he first loved us." (John 4:19).

What made us love Jim? Well, let me tell you. No matter how busy he was, he always took the time to look you in the eyes as he took your hand and sincerely asked, "How are you?"

Then he waited for an answer. He never let on that he had any cares or worries of his own, and he never made you feel like you were a bother, or like he was too busy to talk to you. I always felt like I was a beloved daughter of God when I spoke with him. I have no doubt that many felt the same way about him. He makes it easy to know what it means to be a being of light.

The first time I saw President David O. McKay, was at General Conference in April 1965. For years, my mother told my brothers and me, that someday she would take us to see him. However, I could not see how, as she was a single parent, and often told us she did not have money. Nevertheless, I trusted that somehow, my mom would find the way to keep her word. I was elated, when five months after she and my step-father got married, she and he found the way to keep her promise to us.

After waiting in line for hours outside the Salt Lake Temple gates, and then sitting in the balcony for what seemed like an eternity, I began wondering if the prophet was ever going to arrive. However, within a short amount of time, I noticed everyone around me rising to their feet. As they did so, the tabernacle filled with a brilliant light. Then, almost immediately, tears filled my eyes, as a warm feeling poured through my whole being. Then, what sounded like a choir of angels, strains of, "We Thank Thee O God for a Prophet" started to get louder and louder.

In an attempt to gain understanding, I turned to my mother and asked what was going on. She very reverently, told me that the Prophet had entered the room. That was the first time I remember having the Spirit bear testimony to me about anything; and gratefully, it was about our beloved prophet.

President McKay always had a radiant countenance, twinkling eyes, and an infectious smile. It was easy to know he was a Prophet of God, because of that glow. There has never been a doubt in my mind, that he was a being of light.

In Alma 5:14 & 19, Alma asked: "…have ye spiritually been born of God? Have ye received his image in your countenances? Have ye experienced this mighty change in your hearts? …I say unto you, can ye look up to God at that day with a pure heart and clean hands? I say unto you, can you look up, having the image of God engraven upon your countenances?"

You may wonder how you can have His image in yours when you try so hard to do what is right, and anger or other human failings seem to be too hard to overcome. You may even find yourself lamenting with Nephi, when he said, "Nevertheless, notwithstanding the great goodness of the Lord, in showing me his great and marvelous works, my heart exclaimeth: O wretched man that I am! Yea, my heart sorroweth because of my flesh; my soul grieveth because of mine iniquities." (2 Nephi 4:17)

The Lord has promised, "And if men come unto me I will show unto them their weakness. I give unto men weakness that they may be humble; and my grace is sufficient for all men that humble themselves before me; for if they humble themselves before me, and have faith in me, then will I make weak things become strong unto them." (Ether 12:27)…and they will become a being of light!

Almost is NOT Enough

Elder Bruce C. Hafen said that *almost* giving everything is not enough; that when we *almost* keep the commandments, we can *almost* expect to receive blessings. He said that we must be willing to give *everything* to the Lord, including our fears, our sins, and even our little cottage in Babylon, and "…becometh as a child, submissive, meek, humble, patient, full of love, willing to submit to all things which the Lord seeth fit to inflict upon him, even as a child doth submit to his father." (Mosiah 3:19). [1]

Why is it we pray for the Lord to help us to become more like Him, yet when correction comes, especially from those we love, we tend to reject it, thinking we are being unjustly criticized? Do we mean it when we ask for help to overcome our sins and failings, or are we just giving lip service?

We need to *mean* it when we pray for correction, and then have the humility and wisdom to accept the answers…as well as the courage and determination to apply what we learned. In Alma 7:23 we read, "And now I would that ye should be humble, and be submissive and gentle; easy to be entreated; full of patience and long-suffering; being temperate in all things; being diligent in keeping the commandments of God at all times; asking for whatsoever things ye stand in need, both spiritual and temporal; always returning thanks unto God for whatsoever things ye do receive."

When was the last time you thanked the Lord for correcting and humbling you? If you are like me, after receiving correction, you are so busy nursing your wounded feelings, it is hard to see the correction as coming from the Lord. And, it is even harder to be humble and submissive enough so He can give you the help you asked for.

You might find it is easier to receive correction when it comes from the Lord, rather than from a friend or loved one. I suppose it has to do with knowing the Lord loves and accepts us, no matter how many sins or failings we have. Yet, when it comes from those closest to us, it can feel like they are rejecting us…even if it is done in a spirit of love.

It may not be easy to keep feeling like we have worth to anyone if we receive correction on a regular basis. But, once we truly understand the Plan of Salvation and the Atonement, we will look forward to correction when it comes, as it is a sign that the Lord loves us, because it is His way to help us to become like Him.

Finding Joy in the Midst of Trials

Years ago, a speaker at church suggested we thank the Lord for our trials. I was ill at ease about following her suggestion, because quite honestly, I did not like trials. As a matter of fact, I had the mistaken notion that if I thanked the Lord for them, He would think that I could handle more, and I did not want to take a chance of making things more difficult for me than they already were. In fact, I usually prayed to be spared hardships and trials. Yet, as hard as I tried to ignore what she said, her words gnawed at me until I decided to follow her suggestion.

Now, it was not said by her, but I assumed that just saying "Thank-you", was not good enough. Therefore, as sincerely as I knew how, I forced myself to come up with detailed reasons for what I was grateful for. And as I did so, immense joy and peace filled my mind and heart. I could no longer remember the anguish and heartache I had previously been weighed down with. The world seemed more beautiful, and my relationships (even those that had previously caused me a great deal of grief and heartache) improved drastically. And the best part is, it felt more natural to be Christ-like in my thoughts and actions.

Now, it did not make it on the evening news, but it was newsworthy to me, and I share that experience every chance I get because of my desire to help others discover how to find the joy that comes from true gratitude.

King David, from the Old Testament, understood this principle when he said: "To the end that my glory may sing praise to thee, and not be silent. O Lord my God, I will give thanks unto thee for ever." (Psalms 30:12)

Job understood praising God in the midst of severe and unrelenting trials. He refused to curse God, even when every one he knew told him to do so. Because of his faithfulness, and continually praising and thanking God for all he had, the Lord restored to him much more than He took from him (Job 1-42).

So, are you up to the challenge? Why not try it for a week? What have you got to lose? It won't cost anything but your time and energy...and most everyone can do something for a week. However, be warned, your family, friends, and co-workers may ask what you did with their friend and loved one.

At first you may find the natural man/woman rearing its ugly head if the trials seem too hard to bear. You may feel beat up, picked on, unfairly judged, and mistreated. However, if you will shove those feelings aside, and ponder about what you are grateful for with each trial, and then share those feelings with the Lord, I promise that you will have joy and peace beyond anything you can imagine. You will also have greater insight and understanding of what true gratitude is, and what it takes to feel the pure love of Christ, not only for everyone you meet, but for yourself as well.

Line upon Line

Becoming a being of light does not happen over night. In 2 Nephi 28:30, we are given insight into how the Lord teaches us to become like Him: "For behold, thus saith the Lord God: I will give unto the children of men line upon line, precept upon precept, here a little and there a little; and blessed are those who hearken unto my precepts, and lend an ear unto my counsel, for they shall learn wisdom; for unto him that receiveth I will give more; and from them that shall say, We have enough, from them shall be taken away even that which they have."

I used to get frustrated with my kids (when they were little), wondering if anything their father and I said to them, got through. One day, after reaching my limit, I decided to pray more fervently for help. While doing so, I had the impression come to my mind, that they were children; to enjoy them and not expect them to act like adults.

I am very grateful that the Lord taught me those things while my sons were young, so I did not miss out on how unique and wonderful they were with each stage of their lives. I even enjoyed their teenage years, when many parents wonder what possessed them to want children.

Because of that insight, I learned to pick my battles, and was able to show tough love without building an impassable wall between us. I used every opportunity I could think of to teach them correct principles, while trying to build happy and lasting memories. I am grateful that the Lord sent me children who were easily taught, and a husband who shared the same dedication and commitment to these things as I did.

Our combined efforts paid off, because now that our children are grown and have families of their own, they have turned out to be exemplary adults, husbands and fathers, and are some of our best friends.

When I look back on those years, I cannot help but feel overwhelming gratitude for a Father in Heaven who sets a perfect example for parenting...which is, loving unconditionally, while patiently helping us to grow line upon line and precept upon precept.

Jesus and Joseph Smith had to learn the same way we do. They both put in countless hours in diligent study to be able to gain enlightenment and inspiration from Heavenly Father. Joseph had many visitations and conversations with angels, and I can only assume Jesus did as well. Christ became very familiar with our Heavenly Father, because He tutored Him in who He was to become, and what His life's mission was to be. Joseph became very familiar with the ancient prophets and patriarchs, who had passed on before him, because they tutored him in the things he needed to know to be able to carry out the great work the Lord had for him to do. [2]

I am very grateful for a loving Father in Heaven who lets us grow line upon line and precept upon precept. I have no doubt that His Father did the same for Him.

You Can Only Love the Lord to the Same Degree as He Whom Ye Esteem as Least

Years ago, I heard an interview on "Focus on the Family", between the host, Dr. James Dobson, and a recipient (name unknown) of the "Teacher of the Year" award. When Dr. Dobson asked him what the defining moment was that helped him in his journey towards becoming a beloved teacher, the man shared a story from his college days that while eating at a diner, a badly disfigured man and woman, along a beautiful little girl, came through the door. He said the couple's faces were so badly disfigured that it made it hard to look at them without feeling repulsed. Then he told how the woman called the beautiful little girl over and asked her for a kiss. As the little girl did so, the woman asked, "Do you know Jesus loves you?"

The man said he was so sickened that that mother could ask such a beautiful child to kiss such a grotesque face, that he left the diner without finishing his food. As he entered his dorm room, still sickened and fuming from the ordeal, he noticed a poster on his roommate's wall which showed a drunk passed out in the street with an empty bottle of whiskey in his hand. The caption read, "You can only love Jesus to the same degree as he whom you esteem as least" (Matthew 25:40; John 13:34).

He immediately had a paradigm shift and vowed from that moment on, he would treat others as he would the Savior, whom he loved with all His heart.

I love the quote, "Be patient with me, God is not finished with me yet", as when I feel the tendency to be critical of someone, I try to remind myself that like me, he or she is a beloved child of God that is still in the learning process.

Years ago, I was observing a Seminary class, where the teacher asked a student to come and stomp all over a piece of large, white paper that was face down on the floor. When the student finished, the teacher picked up the picture and turned it over for all to see, we were horrified as we looked at a very dirty and scuffed picture of Jesus.

I cannot express the deep pain I felt in my heart that the teacher would have someone do that to our beloved Savior, even if it was only a picture. Yet, before saying anything else, she read: "For the things which some men esteem to be of great worth, both to the body and soul, others set at naught and trample under their feet. Yea, even the very God of Israel do men trample under their feet; I say, trample under their feet but I would speak in other words—they set him at naught, and hearken not to the voice of his counsels" (Nephi 19:7).

None of us would intentionally stomp all over a picture of our beloved older brother, yet, how do we treat others? What about the person who just cut you off in traffic? What about the bully who beat you up when you were in grade school, or who made your son or daughter cry when they made fun of them? What about the person who took no thought about your feelings, and caused you serious embarrassment, or betrayed a confidence? What about a spouse or parent who deserted your family and thought nothing of the lives they damaged? "…Inasmuch

as ye have done it unto one of the least of these my brethren ye have done it unto me"
(Matthew 25:40).

It Is Hard To Live With an Angel and Not Change

Years ago, I saw the movie "The Prodigal Son" [3] (Luke 15:11-32). In the movie, the wayward son returns home after squandering his inheritance and living a life of sin, which included drug addiction. After being released from a rehab clinic, his brother, who was "the good son", becomes resentful and bitter about the attention his father showers on his brother. One day, when complaining about the injustice, his wife gently and lovingly puts things into perspective for him. It was a gentle reminder for me that God loves all of His children alike, and that we should not judge others, as we cannot possibly know their hearts and potential as He does.

That taught me a great lesson about how easy it is to become self-righteous when you feel like you are the only one trying to do things right. It was also a gentle reminder that God loves all His children alike. We cannot possibly know their hearts and potential as He does.

Has anyone forgiven you for something you did that was thoughtless or unkind? Has anyone been thoughtful or considerate of you when you least deserved it? Have you done the same for others? And, have you noticed it is easier to be forgiving and considerate of strangers, than it is your own family?

When our oldest sons were in elementary school, they joined soccer teams. It was painfully obvious who the coaches sons were, as they were the ones the coaches were more demanding and impatient with. I always felt bad for their kids; yet, as I thought about it, I realized I did the same thing with my kids…more times than I care to think about.

Why is it we are more inclined to treat friends and strangers better than our own family members? One moment we can feel overwhelming love for our spouse, and within minutes, they will say or do something that comes across as thoughtless or hurtful, and it is hard to remember that we ever felt love for them. What changed?

The old saying, "Sticks and stones may break my bones, but words will never hurt me.", is not usually how it works. Broken bones can heal, but too often, we let hurt feelings fester until the wound is so large, it may as well be a cancer that has the potential to kill love between spouses and family members.

Consider how our own family would feel if we treated them like honored guests that we are trying to impress? My mother shared a story about a woman whose husband and father-in-law (who lived with them) were often harsh and thoughtless towards her. In an effort to make her home life more tolerable, she decided that no matter what they said or did, she would respond as if they were treating her the way she wanted to be treated. It was not easy, but with persistence and commitment to her goal, eventually they started treating her with the same love and respect that she showed them.

In "7 Habits of Highly Effective People", Stephen Covey shared the importance of *being a light, not a judge,* when he told a story about a woman who attended a seminar where he taught that principle. She was so impressed by the idea that she decided to give it a try.

So the next morning, as she and her children were leaving for church, she asked her husband, who was watching sports on television, if he was going to go with them. He gave his usual sharp reply (which was intended to put her off). Yet, instead of reacting, she remained silent and walked out the door. It was not easy, but she continued to stick with her commitment, until being a light, was no longer a struggle for her.

About a year later, while talking with Brother Covey, she pointed to her husband (who was across the room), telling how he was now a Counselor in the Bishopric. So, after asking her for permission to speak to him, Brother Covey went over and introduced himself and asked if he would mind sharing with him what had caused his miraculous change of heart.

The husband told how the first morning after his wife went to Brother Covey's seminar; he could tell something was different about her. He went on to tell the same account about his and his wife's responses to his choice not to go to church. However, on that particular morning, instead of giving her usual self-righteous retort, she bit her lip, and walked out the door. He said at first, he could tell it was an effort for her to be nice and not critical with him. But after a while, it became more of her nature. His next comment showed the level of change that took place in his wife's heart when he said, "It is hard to live with an angel and not change!"

The Lord Chastens Those He Loves

We should be very careful not to become prideful when the Lord allows us to endure chastening, which is meant to purge from us those things that keep us from becoming like Him.

C.S. Lewis understood the natural man when he wrote, "Oh Adam's sons, how cleverly you defend yourselves against all that might do you good!" [4]

Solomon said: "...despise not the chastening of the LORD; neither be weary of his correction...for whom the Lord loveth he correcteth...Happy is the man that findeth wisdom and the man that getteth understanding" (Proverbs 3:11-13).

When Alma was speaking to the people of Gideon, he said: "And now I would that ye should be humble, and be submissive and gentle; easy to be entreated; full of patience and long-suffering; being temperate in all things; being diligent in keeping the commandments of God at all times; asking for whatsoever things ye stand in need, both spiritual and temporal; always returning thanks unto God for whatsoever things ye do receive." (Alma 7:23)

As difficult as it may be, if we will bear correction well, and prayerfully and diligently apply the Divine characteristics the Lord is helping us to incorporate, we shall know Him when He appears, for we shall be like Him (1 John 3:2).

Developing an Attitude of Gratitude

When the children of Israel complained about their sufferings in the wilderness, the Lord told them, "Neither murmur ye, as some of them also murmured, and were destroyed of the destroyer" (1 Corinthians 10:10).

The Lord had rescued them from their captors by parting the Red Sea so they could pass through on dry ground; and then drowning Pharaoh's army when they followed after them.

When there was no food, he provided manna from Heaven; and when there was no water to drink, He provided water in a miraculous way. Yet, instead of showing gratitude, all they could do was murmur.

"And in nothing doth man offend God, or against none is his wrath kindled, save those who confess not his hand in all things..." (D&C 59:21)

For years I thought Laman and Lemuel cornered the market on murmuring. However, one day as I was telling one of our patient's about the ongoing saga I went through with trying to get insurance companies to pay what they owed us, it dawned on me that I was...*gasp*... dare I say it?..."MURMURING!!!"

You would think that revelation would have been enough to stop me in my tracks, especially when you consider what happened with Laman and Lemuel and their posterity, because of their murmuring.

But alas, it did not stop there. As the insurance companies seemed to find more creative ways to keep from paying my husband the money they owed him, my attitude continued to deteriorate to the point where being Christ-like (in how I dealt with them) became increasingly difficult for me.

Then one night as Autumn (a young adult friend who was living with us) said family prayer, she thanked the Lord for our trials, saying how they were helping us to become more like Him. As I pondered on what she said, my thoughts went to the speaker in church who challenged us to thank the Lord for our trials. I will be forever grateful for that dear sister for opening my eyes to what true gratitude is; and for Autumn, for bringing that back to my memory when I desperately needed to be reminded of it.

I knew I was doing better when one day, the only check we got in the mail, was for $2.04, and I remembered to express sincere gratitude to the Lord for sending it...remembering, that even small blessings, are still signs of our Father's love and care for us. Having an attitude of gratitude makes it easier to see that trials are His way of saying "I love you enough to give you opportunities to become like Me."

Can you see why it is also important to have an attitude of gratitude for our spouses and family members? When was the last time you thanked your spouse, mother and/or father for the tiny and seemingly unimportant things they have done for you…and it was not their birthday, or Mother's or Father's Day? However, I want to warn you…make sure they are sitting down before trying this experiment, for if they are not used to it, they may pass out from shock.

All kidding aside, one of the highest forms of gratitude is to serve those we love. When we serve selflessly, we grow in our love and appreciation for those we give our hearts and hands to.

Gratitude has a way of healing wounds, rebuilding bridges, mending broken down fences, and rekindling and increasing feelings of love. In addition, the best part is, it works for the giver, as well as the receiver.

Sometimes, all that is needed to end a raging argument, is to hear those simple but magical words, "Thank-you!", "You're welcome", "I'm sorry" and most importantly, "I love you!"

There is a story about a young man who did something to get in trouble. The father, in a rage, sent the boy to his room, ordering him to stay there until he came for him. However, as the father stormed out of the boy's room, the tearful son yelled, "Dad!!"

Fuming, the dad returned to see what he wanted. Upon entering the boy's room, the boy, very tearfully said, "Dad, I love you."

As you can imagine, the father's heart melted, and the thing that had caused him to be so angry with his son, quickly went to the farthest recesses of his mind and heart. Fences were mended, and hearts were healed by those four three simple words.

Imagine what homes would be like if more family members would be willing to use those redemptive words when tempers are flaring…and mean them…especially when the recipient seems to be undeserving, I honestly believe that divorce courts would be rarely used, and more families would come to know what Heaven on Earth is like.

Notes:
1. Bruce C. Hafen, "The Atonement: All for All", *Ensign,* May 2004, 97
2. Joseph B. Wirthlin, "The Restoration and Faith", *Ensign*, Jan. 2006, 35)
3. *Video item #53061000, Distribution Center for The Church of Jesus Christ of Latter-day Saints*
4. C.S. Lewis, "The Chronicles of Narnia"

Chapter Twelve

Keeping Things in Perspective

Jenny was loading baskets of tomatoes to take to town when the children came running to tell her there was a nicely dressed woman at the kitchen door. The woman was lovely with a look of youthfulness. Jenny became aware of how haggard she looked in her worn and dirty clothes.

The stranger spoke, "I hope you don't mind but we parked in your shade to have our lunch and to rest for awhile. I was wondering if I could buy some of your apples."

As they walked to the orchard, Jenny had never been so aware of how unkempt it was. She reached the orchard and began to drag a long ladder from the fence to the apple tree.

The stranger cried, "That's too heavy. Please let me pick a few apples from off of the ground." To which Jenny abruptly replied, "Heavy! This ladder? I lift bushel baskets of tomatoes onto a wagon all day and this feels light to me."

The stranger then asked, "Can we sit down here in the shade and would you mind telling me why you have to work so hard?"

Jenny began her story. "John and I bought this farm when we were first married. We had great plans, but the long hours and hard labor began to take its toll on both of us, and we have nothing to show for it. The work is so demanding I do not have time for the children or the house. The mortgage is due, the owner is talking about foreclosing on our farm, and we do not have the money to pay him."

The stranger asked if Jenny thought what she was doing was really helping John. Jenny was shocked and blurted out, "I work hard to help him!"

The stranger exclaimed, "Men are so peculiar, especially husbands. For instance, they want us to be economical, and yet they love to see us in pretty clothes, looking young and beautiful. They aren't really sure which they want more, so sometimes we have to choose for them.

"Just after we were married, my husband started his own business and at first I helped him in the store but we would both be tired and discouraged after a hard day at the office. The house got run down and dinner was always a hasty affair, and soon we both started complaining and bickering with each other.

"Finally, we decided that maybe I should stay at home and let him take care of his work at the office. I worked to make my house a clean, happy place. My husband would come home dead-tired and discouraged, ready to give up. However, after he had eaten and sat in our bright little living room, and I found uplifting, or funny things to talk about, I could see him change. By bedtime, he had his courage back, and by morning, he was all ready to go out and fight again. At last, he made a success of his business.

"There was a queen once, who reigned in troubled days, and every time the country was on the brink of war, and the people ready to fly into a panic, she would put on her showiest dress and take her court with her and go hunting. When the people saw her riding by, they were sure all was well with the Kingdom. Therefore, she tided over many a danger.

"I've tried to be like her. Whenever a big crisis comes into my husband's business, or when I'm discouraged, I put on my prettiest dress, and make the best dinner I know how, or I give a party. Somehow, it always seems to work out.

"That's the woman's part you know...to play the queen."

A faint honk came from the lane, and the beautiful stranger said, "I must go. Please don't bother about the apples."

She then handed Jenny some coins, saying, "I'll just take a few from under the tree."

Jenny thought, *I don't got no choice, John needs my help!*

The stranger left, and Jenny returned to her kitchen. Upon looking at the dishes left from the previous two meals, Jenny repeated, "I don't got no choice, John needs my help!"

As she looked around the room, she noticed something small and white on the floor. As she leaned over to pick it up, she noticed that it was a dainty, fragrant handkerchief. The fragrance made her think of gardens in the spring; of rooms with the moonlight shining in, of elegant women in flowing dresses dancing in a grove.

Jenny had nothing that was beautiful in her life. Everything about their lives was coarse and soiled. Jenny thought, *suppose I spent my time on the house and let the outside work go...*

Jenny ran in the house and brushed her hair, changed her shoes, and put on the one good dress she owned. Then she cleaned her kitchen and started supper.

She decided on ham, potatoes, homemade biscuits, fresh cold lemonade, and a homemade pie for dessert. She then spread her only white tablecloth on the table.

The pan of flaky brown biscuits were being removed from the oven as she heard Mr. Davis' car come up the lane. Cold fear struck Jenny's heart. He could be coming for only one reason. As she stood wondering how to deal with him, she remembered the beautiful stranger's words, "There was a queen once..."

Upon meeting Mr. Davis at the door, Jenny found herself saying, "Well, howd' you do, Mr. Davis? Come right in. I'm real glad to see you."

Though he entered a bit reluctantly, Henry Davis replied, "I just stopped to see John on a little matter of business."

Jenny quickly blurted out, "Come right in. John will be in from milkin' in a few minutes, an' you can talk while both of you eat. Supper is ready, and you never tasted my hot biscuits with butter honey, or you wouldn't take so much coaxin'!"

Henry Davis then relaxed a little, and sat at the table.

Jenny then asked, "And how are things goin' with you, Mr. Davis?" to which Henry replied, "Oh, so, how are they with you?"

Jenny mustered up a cheerful, "Why, just fine, Mr. Davis. It's been hard goin', but I sort of think the worst is over. We'll be 'round to pay that mortgage so fast that you'll be surprised."

By now, Henry's demeanor was more genial, as he replied, "That's fine. I always wanted to see John make a success of the old place. I'm glad things are pickin' up a little."

John stopped at the kitchen door, staring blankly at Jenny moving about the bright kitchen, while chatting happily with Mr. Davis, whose sharp features had softened. John made no comment, merely shook hands with Henry Davis, and then washed his hands and face at the sink.

Jenny put the food on the table, and they started to eat. Henry and John seemed to grow more and more relaxed and talkative as they ate. By the time the pie was set before them, they were laughing over a joke Henry told. As they rose from the table, Henry brought the conversation awkwardly around to why he had come.

Jenny quickly jumped in, "I told him John, that the worst is over now. I told him we'd be getting him regular payments pretty soon. Ain't that right, John?"

John, mustering up an air of confidence, responded, "Why, that's right, Mr. Davis. I believe we can come up with those payments pretty soon, if you could just see your way to renew the terms."

It was done, the papers were back in Mr. Davis' pocket, and they had bid him a cordial good-bye from the door. Jenny cleared off the table and began to wash the dishes while John sat down at the table with pencil and paper. "I believe I'll do a little figurin' since I've got time tonight. It just struck me, if I used my head a little more; we could be outa debt faster."

Jenny was pleased. She polished a big apple and placed it on a saucer beside him.

John looked pleased and replied, "Now, that's what I like. Say, you look... sort of pretty tonight."

Blushing a little, Jenny gave a shy little girl reply, "Go along with ya."

John looked more grateful over her setting that apple beside him, than he had the day last fall, when she had lifted all the potatoes herself, into the truck!

Jenny walked to the doorway and stood looking off through the darkness. A sweet fragrance rose from where she had tucked the handkerchief in her dress. She wished that she could somehow tell the beautiful stranger that her words had helped, that she was going to fulfill her woman's part. Yes, wives had to choose for their husbands sometimes.

At that very moment, driving along the highway, the stranger leaned suddenly close to her husband and replied, "I can't get that poor woman back at the farm, out of my mind. I know it's silly, but I wanted to help her, and I know now that she didn't understand what I was talking about. She just looked up with that blank, tired face. I don't want to cry, but, could you please lend me your handkerchief dear? I seem to have lost mine..." [1]

The Mother is the Heart of the Home...Whether She Likes it or Not!

When Karen Hughes (a former counselor to President George W. Bush) quit her job to be able to devote more of her time to her family, I cheered for her. However, the media and women's rights groups criticized her for giving a black eye to women who want to "have it all". More women are waking up and realizing that the author of that philosophy does not have the Lord's design for families in mind. Fortunately, it is getting more common for women who have tried to "have it all", to give up their prestigious and time-consuming careers, to be stay-at-home moms.

Because of the failing economy, more and more moms are being forced to be in the workplace; thus, making it where their children are raising themselves. Sadly, with no one at home to mentor or guide them, children are becoming more independent, without having the maturity or training to help them make correct or wise choices. Tragically, many of those children grow up to be irresponsible and problematic adults.

When moms and dads return home after a long day at work, they often want time alone to be able to unwind from the demands of their jobs; and in some cases, to escape the deteriorating and sometimes volatile relationships in their homes. In dealing with such struggles, many couples are choosing to end their marriages, thinking that there are no solutions to their overwhelming problems. In addition, children in such homes, tend to look elsewhere for love, acceptance, and mentoring. It is tragic and heartrending, to see the outcome of those choices.

Fortunately, there are answers that are easily found, that can bring harmony and stability to the home. The safest and most sure ones can be found from the counsel of our Church leaders. "Follow the Prophet", is a Sunday School answer that is taught to our children in Primary. However, too often, it is forgotten or abandoned by the time our youth become teenagers or young adults.

President Gordon B. Hinckley said that men and women are incomplete without each other. There is no other design for them that meet with the divine purposes of the Lord's plan. [3] During her speech at the 1990 Wellesley College graduation commencement, former First Lady, Barbara Bush, offered the following words of wisdom: "...As important as your obligations as a doctor, lawyer, or business leader will be, you are a human being first, and those human connections with spouses, with children, with friends are the most important investments you will ever make. At the end of your life, you will never regret not having passed one more test, not writing one more verdict or not closing one more deal. You will regret time not spent with a husband, a friend, a child, or a parent."

Elder Dallin H. Oaks said that the existence of our Church, as a people, and as nations, relies upon men and women that are willing to give up their own pleasures for the good of others. He went on to suggest that this includes parents who are willing to give up their own pleasures and comforts in life to bring children into the world, and being willing to teach them correct doctrines, to be faithful members of the Church, as well as responsible citizens. [4]

Abigail Guzman, who spoke at the 2008 BYU Hawaii graduation commencement, told the group that she had already started her full-time post-graduate employment as a stay-at-home wife and mother. She went on to say that even though her chosen field of labor is not a typical job for a recent graduate in today's world, she could not think of a better use for her fine education, than to use it in loving and serving her family. [4]

If parents, will see to it their family is armed and protected everyday with the whole armor of God (Ephesians 6:11 & 13), it will be much harder for the Adversary's arrows to pierce their shields and breast plates.

A War We Must Win

Job exclaimed: "I know that my Redeemer shall stand at the latter day upon the earth" (Job 19:25).

"And because of the righteousness of his people, Satan has no power; wherefore, he cannot be loosed for the space of many years; for he hath no power over the hearts of the people, for they dwell in righteousness, and the Holy One of Israel reigneth." (1 Ne 22:26)

The hearts of the people will be so pure during the Millennium that Satan will have no power over them. The polarizing has already begun. The righteous are becoming more refined and valiant and the evil and devilish are becoming increasingly more wicked…past feeling, and void of conscience as we draw closer to the Second Coming. All one has to do is read or listen to the daily news; or go into our schools and work places to see how far the world has moved away from the Lord's standards.

It is vital, that we as parents and members of the Church do all we can to teach and train our children to be prepared to meet the Savior when He returns. However, to do so, requires our complete dedication and commitment to righteous principles.

If parents are too busy to be at home where they can teach their children correct doctrines, how will their children learn to govern themselves in righteousness? And, if parents fail to teach their children, who else will? What excuse will you give the Lord if you fall short in your role? The time is here and now for parents to have the courage to stand up and make the difference. We need to be willing to make a bond and covenant with the Lord that cannot be broken, where we will hold fast to these things.

Satan is getting more cunning. His time is running out and he knows it. Our family's eternal lives are at stake; and it is a war we MUST win. Even if at times, it appears that Satan will be the victor, we must never give up the fight...until we cross the finish line!

Notes:

1. *When Queens Ride By* (Published in 1888; 1930 award winning story by Agnes Slight Turnbull; *revised by Terry Olsen*)
2. President Gordon B. Hinckley, "The Women in Our Lives", Ensign, Nov. 2004, 84
3. "Strengthening the Home", pamphlet, 1973, p. 7
4. "Marriage Is Honorable", in *Speeches of the Year*, 1973, Provo: Brigham Young University Press, 1974, p. 263).

Chapter Thirteen

The In-Law Factor

At some point in our lives, most of us will be an in-law to someone. Have you ever wondered why so many jokes and derogatory comments are made in regards to mothers-in-law? Could it be that mothers-in-law are inherently evil? Or, could it be that a mother-in-law's main goal in life is to ruin the otherwise seemingly tranquil lives of her children and their spouses?

All kidding aside, I do not believe any person, even a mother-in-law, would intentionally sabotage the relationship between themselves and their son/daughter-in-law. I do believe however, that the inability to get along at times, has to do with what I will refer to as, "The In-law Factor", which is often fueled by a lack of experience and education on how to adjust to the diversities that come when merging families through marriage.

There are times when life within extended families is beautiful and all seems right with the world. Then before you know it, the clouds appear on the horizon, and it is not long before gale force winds threaten to destroy the peace and harmony, tossing as it were, puzzle pieces in the wind.

During those times, it is hard to imagine anything ever being right again between the upset family members. Yet, given enough time, effort, determination, and *patience*, the winds die down; the puzzle pieces are gathered together again and put back into their place of the picture of their previously happy family.

It is amusing, that in the aftermath of such storms, family members often find it hard to remember what started the rift in the first place. Even though the Hatfields and the McCoys (famous feuding families you can read about on Wiki.com) were determined to keep their family feud going, even though no one is completely sure what started the feud. However, it went on from 1878-1892; and in that time, there were some brutal murders that were fueled by the hatred between the two families.

Too often, that is the case with family arguments. An unwillingness to forgive and forget can cause many lost opportunities and memories that would have otherwise been enjoyed by the individual and collective family members.

Years ago, a friend of ours became very agitated when he learned that my family and I were moving to a town where my parents and other family members lived. I was elated to be moving near them, as the miles between us, made it where we rarely got to see each other. However, no amount of talk could convince our friend that our decision was a good one. I am grateful that we did not let him talk us out of the move, as our children and my parents were able to get to know each other before my parents died; and our children also built stronger bonds with their cousins, aunts, and uncles before most of them moved away.

However, even as wonderful as it has been, ever-so-often, diversities create potentially contentious situations, even with the closest family members. So, when those times arise, applying the *Golden Rule* is usually all it takes to smooth down ruffled feathers, and to heal hurt feelings. Then, it is not long before the storm clouds dissipate, and the birds return, and all seems right with the world again. When such upsets occur, it is good to remember that prayer is a great healer when our efforts alone are not enough to bring to our memory, that *we are a happy family*.

Tune-up Your Communication Skills

We have all been there - not knowing why our spouse and/or other family members cannot see our point of view. Sometimes, all it requires is an "easy fix". Nevertheless, there are other times when it seems that each person is determined that an all-out-war is going to be declared if the other person does not change their behavior or opinion(s). To help in those situations, I have shared the following techniques, as they have proven to be effective in soothing tempers, hurt feelings, or a general unwillingness to see another person's point of view:

Learning to Communicate Effectively:

1. Talk less and listen more. Seek first to understand the other person's point of view. Remember, the other person wants their point of view to be heard as well. Allow them to talk freely about their viewpoint without interrupting them. This will help you to see their side of things and may open up the lines of communication. It may not happen over night, but your efforts will help to soften their heart towards you, and opens the door to their being willing to pay you the same courtesy as you try to explain your point of view. When we allow our emotions to be what rules our thought process, it becomes extremely difficult to think and behave rationally.

2. Do not interrupt while they are talking. Interruptions tend to make people angry and may shut down the lines of communication. If that happens, the outcome can be very bad. Think of those serving time in prisons for crimes of passion. It is sobering when you realize, most of them wouldn't intentionally hurt a fly, much less, intentionally kill another human being…yet, there they are, serving sentences for doing that very thing. That is why what they have done is referred to as crimes of passion, because they often occur when a person loses their temper, or tries to deal with a situation in the heat of the moment before

170

calming down. When we allow our emotions to be what rules our thought process, it becomes extremely difficult to think and behave rationally.

3. Do not get defensive. While it might be difficult to remain calm, avoid being harsh in your responses. Choose instead, a soft-spoken approach, as it will help the other party to do the same. Remember, you catch more flies with honey rather than vinegar. An argumentative attitude is rarely successful in getting the other person to change their opinion.

4. Make sure to repeat back what you think the other person is saying. People like their opinions and views to be validated. You do not have to agree with them, but just repeating back what you thought they said, to make sure you understand, builds bridges towards more amiable grounds of communication. This costs nothing but your time, and it helps you to be a better listener, and to be more empathetic of the other person's reasons for feeling as they do.

5. Identify the key elements that you need to cover. However, stick to one point at a time. Support your point of view with facts that are true, including time, place, and yours or someone else's knowledge of what happened. Avoid overwhelming with facts, and do not allow the spirit of contention to take over if what you are saying is not being taken well.

6. Do not go off on a tangent. Try to keep the other person from digressing as well. It helps to agree on nonessential points, until the facts are known.

7. If you reach an impasse, or the discussion is becoming too heated, then agree to postpone the discussion until you both can calm down and are better able to focus on areas where you are more likely to agree.

8. Have the attitude of reaching a win/win outcome, rather than trying to force your point with no consideration of the other person's point of view.

9. Make sure the other person is satisfied with the outcome and not just giving in to stop the friction or bad feelings. The other person needs to leave the discussion feeling like they were allowed to state clearly their views, and that you understood their side of things. You do not have to agree on all points, or any points for that matter. But, just knowing you made the effort to understand all their points, is enough to improve your relationship of trust. It will also set the stage for future discussions if you find you have another disagreement that requires a discussion.

Cutting the Apron Strings

I have no doubt that those mothers and mothers-in-law, who give themselves a bad name, have no intention of causing ill feelings with their loved ones. Yet, the best laid plans of the mother/mother-in-law, to shower her child and their new spouse, with love and affection, is often viewed as meddling. However, in defense of the devoted mother who finds it very difficult to cut the umbilical cord that connects her to her son or daughter, her struggles could be viewed as a mother bird pushing her fledgling out of the nest so they can learn to fly on their own. Not running to their aid when she perceives they need her, can cause serious growing pains for the new empty-nest mother.

How does a mother keep from giving unsolicited advice, when from the time her child was born, until he or she leaves home, it was part of her job requirement as a mother? In addition, how does she keep from offering money, or running to their assistance, when she thinks it is needed? Putting it a different way, how can she be expected to slam on the brakes, park the car, get out, and hand over the keys to her married child and their spouse, and then walk away from being a major part of her child's life?

The "Empty Nest Syndrome" takes on new depth when one realizes what it means for a mother to lose the identity that has been engrained in her since the first time she heard the words, "Congratulations, you are going to be a mother!", until she sees her last child move out of the house to live on their own.

It is the wise mother, who prepares her children to become independent, so they will be able to make it on their own some day. On the other hand, if she is unwise, she will make her children so dependent on her and their father that they will never want to leave home. Then, if her children do get married, they may call every day, asking for advice, with questions ranging from what to wear for the day, or what they should eat for breakfast or dinner. Do not laugh! My husband and I knew a young bride who called her mother every night to ask what she should wear the next day!

Another problem, as I mentioned in an earlier chapter, is when married kids call home to complain about their spouse or their lot in life; or when they expect mom and dad to bail them out of every financial difficulty. Parents who give into these things, only cripple their grown child and their spouse from being able to work these challenges out together as husband and wife, as well as being able to mature into their own family unit.

The good news is, millions of mothers have endured transitioning from being a mother with kids at home, to a mother of married children, which brings with it her title and role as a mother-in-law. Some women have done this with such grace, finesse, and charm, that their children and their spouses feel blessed, not cursed that she is in their lives. However, for those mothers who have not figured out how to let go of their married children, imagining that their heartache will never heal, there is One who completely understands, who can heal all the pain, heartache, and loneliness she feels. And He is only a pray away.

I know from personal experience, that it helps to have a strong testimony of the Lord's design for families, as I experienced great joy when our sons got married. It helped that our sons had found young ladies who loved them and shared their commitment to the Lord and their religious beliefs. Seeing the loyalty and love these precious daughters-in-law still feel towards our sons, even after having children and going through the ups and downs of married life, continues to add to the joy I feel.

The Golden Rule for In-laws

"In as much as you have done it unto one of the least of these, you have done it unto me" (Matthew 25:40). By no means are in-laws to be thought of as "least". It is actually quite the opposite. My reason for including that scripture is to illustrate that we should be treating our in-laws with the same love and respect as we do the Savior.

Besides, when we treat others like they are royalty, they often respond in kind. Even if there are those (as every family has) who make it hard to remember that they are children of Divine parentage, we should never be tempted to treat them as if they are anything less than the most beloved child of God.

Walking a Mile in their Moccasins

When I was a young wife and mother, I was sure I possessed the Wisdom of Solomon. Yet now that I am much older and hopefully wiser, I am sure I possess the knowledge that Solomon had wisdom! Bill Cosby put it best when he said the older he gets, the more he realizes how much he does not know as a parent.

For those who need more clarification about the difference between *knowledge* and *wisdom…knowledge,* is an understanding or familiarity of facts and truths obtained over a period of time or through study; *wisdom,* is a knowledge of what is true, coupled with just judgment as to action, discernment, or insight (Dictionary.com).

No one prepared me to be a daughter-in-law, and later, to be a mother-in-law. When I was a young girl, I heard a story about a young woman who came home from school to find her younger brother had gotten into her bedroom and played with her jewelry and makeup. In a fit of anger, she railed her brother until he was in tears.

The next morning at the breakfast table, with quivering chin and tears in his eyes, her brother asked if she would forgive him. Even though she was no longer upset with him, she thought she would teach him a lesson by letting him go through the day thinking about his actions before she would let him know she forgave him.

However, she would never have that opportunity, as later that day as she was walking home from school she noticed an ambulance and her brother's mangled bike in the street. Upon finding out that he had been hit by a car and died from his injuries, she cried inconsolably as she wished she could go back and let him know how much she loved him, and that she forgave him.

Never wanting to live with that type of regret, I have made the effort throughout my life to treat everyone like it was his or her last day on earth. However, no one prepared me for how hard it would be to remember that vow when I became a daughter-in-law. If only I had possessed the Wisdom of Solomon during those years when my mother-in-law was alive, then I would not have to live with the regret and heartache that came from lack of experience and maturity. If I could go back in time with the experience and hind site that I have gained with age and since her death, I would be a much different daughter-in-law.

Mark Twain said, "When I was a boy of 14, my father was so ignorant I could hardly stand to have the old man around. But when I got to be 21, I was astonished at how much the old man had learned in seven years."

Life is too short to live with regrets, so why not fill it with lots of Kodak® moments with your family?

Chapter Fourteen

Is it Worth the Effort?

I once knew a woman I will refer to as Annette, who gave the impression that the only topic she wanted to discuss, was how evil her first husband was. I will refer to him as Jacob. Annette would spend hour after hour confessing what she thought were Jacob's sins, to anyone who would listen to her.

From what she said about him, you would think he was the poster child for all that was insensitive, thoughtless, and down right mean and loathsome. Okay, so she did not accuse him of tying her to the railroad tracks with a train coming, but she claimed she could not remember anything that he ever did that was loving or kind. In fact, from what she said, and with the passion she said it; one would logically assume that she hated him. Yet, shortly before she died, when asked if she still loved him, she responded with a heart felt, "YES!!!"

This was not a revelation to me or anyone else who knew her very well, as it was easy to figure out how she felt about Jacob, from observing what she said, the passion she said it with, and because she could not seem to get over it.

She once told how after nearly 20 years of hearing her mother's constant complaints about how rotten Jacob was, that she finally decided her mother was right, and therefore, like an obedient child, chose to divorce him. However, no amount of finding fault and criticism could kill off Annette's love for him, as well as her deep heartache over losing him.

Joseph Smith said apostates may try to leave the Church, but they can never leave it alone, whether through murmurings, criticizing its leaders and its members, its doctrines, or engaging in persecution, whether verbal or physical.[1]

The same proved to be the case with Annette, in regards to her feelings for Jacob. I have heard that time heals all wounds, yet in her case, it hadn't. In fact, when she died, it had been close to 3 decades since she had divorced him, and two decades since his death, and in that time, she had remarried, and become a widow to her second husband (whom I will refer to as Bradley). It is interesting that she rarely spoke of Bradley after his death, and according to her, he was the "good husband"!

After she died, the evidence of how she felt about Jacob was discovered in the bottom drawer of an end table she and Bradley (not Jacob) had purchased together. The evidence was enclosed in two long, thin boxes, full of 100s of cards that accompany flowers from a florist. The cards were from…you guessed it…Jacob — telling how much he loved her, and that he wanted to be with her for eternity.

In Annette's pictures and keepsakes, there were evidences that she and Jacob had had many happy times throughout their marriage. However, being deeply and hopelessly in love was not enough for this couple to make their marriage last a lifetime, much less an eternity.

Refusing to Give Up

In contrast to Annette's story, is the story about my mother, who showed how Christ-like love and a firm commitment to her baptismal and temple covenants can heal and save even seriously damaged marriages and families.

My mother joined the church a short while after marrying my father. Within a few years, they were sealed in the temple. My mother wrote in her journal, that she took her temple marriage very seriously. Yet, within a few months of their sealing, my father quit going to church.

When my mother was pregnant with me, my father tried to convince her to have an abortion, because he did not want any more children. Then, when she refused, he tried to put my two older brothers up for adoption, which she also refused to do.

Things went from bad to worse, and when my youngest brother was 11 months old, my father took off with another woman…leaving my mother alone with four children, and no way to provide for us.

My mother left my brothers and me with our paternal grandfather and step-grandmother (that we had never met), while she went to a town that was a few hours away to look for work and a place to live. After three long months, we were finally reunited. However, my mother struggled as a single parent not knowing how she was going to provide for herself, much less for four children.

Years later, when reading in her journal, I found out that she considered putting my brothers and me up for adoption, because most weeks she could not pay rent and buy groceries, and there were no family members or welfare systems available to help. I am so grateful that the Lord provided the way for us to stay together!

My mother did her best to shield my brothers and me from the uncertainties and fears that she dealt with on a daily basis. She also never showed any signs of bitterness towards our father, nor the woman he ran off with.

However, when I was 9 years old, the strains of being a single parent, took their toll on her. Most days, she would come home from work and would go to her room and cry for hours. I felt so helpless, not knowing what I could do or say to help her feel better.

The Lord finally answered her prayers by sending my step-dad into our lives. He loved my mother and was willing to take on four preteens, who had been without a father for eight years. However, as wonderful as it seemed in the beginning, it did not take long for the realities of merging two families, to take its toll on ours.

During my years in Junior High and High School, intense arguments became a way of life in our home. Family Home Evenings were better referred to as, "Prayer to Prayer Family Arguments". In fact, if I remember right, I am not even sure we made it to the closing prayer most nights before family members stormed off in different directions. It was not long before our family rarely had Family Home Evenings or family prayers.

When I was 17 years old, I could no longer take the contention in our home. Therefore, I decided to go to my Bishop for advice. However, to my utter dismay, his only advice was to leave home when I turned 18.

When I left his office, I was overwhelmed with feelings of hopelessness. Yet I knew there had to be ways to strengthen my family and draw us closer to each other, and I was determined to find those answers. Therefore, I turned to the One I hoped would help, and that was Heavenly Father.

I began to pray every day with all the energy of my heart that the Lord would heal my family, and that we would stay together. I have since come to realize, that in spite of all the growing pains of merging our two families, those experiences proved to be Celestial marriage training grounds for us, as I have been able to apply the things I learned in my youth, in my own marriage and family.

One of the things that kept me committed to sticking with my prayers when it seemed like they were falling on deaf ears, was that I knew that the Lord brought my step-dad and my mother together, and if their marriage failed, that each of us in the family would have to answer to Him for it, and I did not like to think about those options. I also knew that He sent us to Earth to succeed, not to fail. Because of that sure knowledge, I had great faith that He would help me and my family to succeed…but, I knew we had to do our part.

Not long after that, my mother told me that my step-dad had the impression while praying that morning, that it was my prayers that were keeping our family together. I was shocked and delighted, as I knew the only One who knew I was praying for our family to stay together, was the Lord.

However, in spite of that experience, and even though I continued to pray with all the energy of my heart for peace and harmony in our home, it continued to disintegrate. Then, one night while I was trying my best to focus on my homework, in spite of the arguing that was going on at the kitchen table, I heard my youngest brother yell, "Fine! Then I am leaving!"

As my brother got up to leave, my step-dad, who others had referred to as having the strength of a low-land gorilla, stood up to stop him with his fist. My mother quickly got in between my step-dad and brother, and took the blow that was intended for my brother. My mother fell to the floor like a limp rag, sobbing uncontrollably.

I felt like I was in the middle of a horrible nightmare, but was unable to wake up from it.

My step-dad and brother carried my mother to her bed while I called our Bishop to come to our aid. Like a good Bishop, he wasted no time in coming over. After giving my mother a priesthood blessing, he summoned the rest of our family (that was at home), to the living room.

He looked at each of us, and in as stern a voice as he could muster, he said, "I am going to ask you two questions and I want truthful answers! Number one, are you having Family Home Evening every week without fail?"

All sorts of excuses flew from their lips as to why we were not having Family Home Evening; ranging from arguments that always broke out, as well as work schedules, and school activities that got in the way.

He cut us off and said, "I do not want any more excuses! I do not want another one of you in my office until you can tell me you are having Family Home Evening every week without fail! I do not care if it is only two of you. You are to have it WITHOUT FAIL before any of you come to me for help!!"

Then he asked his next question. "Are you having family prayer night and morning without fail?"

The lame excuses started again. Then he cut us off, only this time, we could tell he meant business as he said, "Stop with the excuses!!! I do not want another one of you in my office until you can tell me you are having Family Home Evening every week, and family prayer night and morning, without fail!!"

That was a turning point for me and my family. Therefore, if my step-dad or mom did not plan one, I saw to it we had Family Home Evening every Monday night; and my step-dad saw to it we had family prayer every morning and night without fail. And, it was not long before peace and harmony started replacing the destructive, ugly spirit that had become so much a part of our home life.

My parents and family not only stayed together, but my parents served a number of missions for our Church before they died; and two of my brothers and I married in the temple, and are still active in the Church to this day. I am pleased to see that our commitment to follow our Bishop's inspired counsel continues to be practiced and passed on to future generations. And to think, it all started because my mother refused to give up the things she knew to be right, no matter how hopeless things seemed at times. I will be forever grateful to my angel mother for teaching me by example what it means to be a righteous wife and mother in the Lord's Kingdom.

Putting on the Whole Armor of God

When I was a child, I was terrified to do anything wrong and/or to go to sleep without saying my prayers. Believe it or not, I was sure if I messed up in those areas, that goblins would come and take me away while I slept, and that I would never see my mom and brothers again. Isn't that everybody's reason for being obedient and saying his or her prayers?

Okay, I can see that I need to explain what caused me to have such fear and trepidation about such things...so here goes: When I was a little girl, my mom used to read stories to my brothers and me before we went to bed. As much as we looked forward to that nightly ritual, there was a poem that she read a time or two that caused serious fear and anxiety for me. I have included it below, so you can see for yourself if it was my childish misunderstanding of its meaning, or if it was the intent of the author to scare the living daylights out of little kids, to get them to be good and say their prayers every night:

THE GOBBLE-UNS 'LL GIT YOU

EF YOU DON'T WATCH OUT!

(By James Whitcomb Riley (1849-1916)

Wunst they wuz a little boy wouldn't say his prayers, --

An' when he went to bed at night, away up-stairs,

His Mammy heerd him holler, an' his Daddy heerd him bawl,

An' when they turn't the kivvers down, he wuzn't there at all!

An' they seeked him in the rafter-room, an' cubby-hole, an' press,

An' seeked him up the chimbly-flue, an' ever'-wheres, I guess;

But all they ever found wuz thist his pants an' roundabout:

An' the Gobble-uns 'll git you

Ef you don't watch out!...

You better mind yer parunts, an' yer teachurs fond an' dear,

An' churish them 'at loves you, an' dry the orphant's tear,

An' he'p the pore an' needy ones 'at clusters all about,

Er the Gobble-uns 'll git you

Ef you don't watch out!...

I have no doubt that my mother's intent for reading that terrifying poem, was to help us kids want to behave, and to remember to say our prayers. I cannot speak for my brothers, but it worked well for me!! However, it took me years before I realized that there was no such thing as goblins, and that it was okay to let my arms and head be outside of my covers when I slept!

However, by the time I figured those things out, I had already gained a testimony of the blessings that come from being obedient for the right reasons, and for saying daily prayers... not out of fear, but because of wanting to stay close to the Lord.

The Lord told Joseph Smith, "And in nothing doth man offend God, or against none is his wrath kindled, save those who confess not his hand in all things..." (D&C 59:21)

King Benjamin told his people, "I say unto you, my brethren, that if you should render all the thanks and praise which your whole soul has power to possess, to that God who has created you, and has kept and preserved you, and has caused that ye should rejoice, and has granted that ye should live in peace one with another...I say unto you that if ye should serve him who has created you from the beginning, and is preserving you from day to day, by lending you breath, that ye may live and move and do according to your own will, and even supporting you from one moment to another—I say, if ye should serve him with all your whole souls yet ye would be unprofitable servants." (Mosiah 2:20-21).

One of the most important parts of family and individual prayers is to cultivate a spirit of love, devotion, and trust in God, and to dedicate ourselves to Him each and everyday, not just in words, but also in deeds. Besides, testimonies and love can be strengthened by hearing another family member's humble, sincere prayers for them.

We should take the time to really talk with our Heavenly Father, like we would a beloved earthly father. And we should not be surprised when He answers like a loving parent. We also should *not* get in the habit of saying a quick prayer, just so we can say we met our quota for the day. Rather, we should take time to ponder as we pray and be receptive to any impressions or feelings we may have. You may want to keep a pen and paper close by, so you can record those impressions and feelings, so you can refer back to them and not forget them.

Family Home Evenings should provide a setting where gospel principles are taught, and where family members learn to recognize good and praiseworthy things in each other. They should never be used to find fault with or tear down other family members, church leaders, teachers, or neighbors. When family members learn to safeguard against negative thoughts and words, then communication, loyalty and harmony will improve, bringing in its wake, an increase of love and respect one for another.

Parents want what is best for their children. They push them to excel scholastically, musically and in sports. They would do anything to insure their physical safety, teaching them at a young age, to never go with or to speak to strangers. They also make sure their children are well nourished and protected from harm, yet, why is it in those same homes, Family Home Evening and daily family prayer and scripture study, often get set aside as if they are not important?

With evil becoming more enticing and harder to recognize, why wouldn't parents want to see to it that they and their children have put on the whole armor of God before facing the world each day?

Beacons on the Top of Lighthouses

We are losing our youth and adults at record numbers to the evils of our day - which include pornography, sexual sins, drugs, alcohol, cigarettes, and apathy toward the things of God. Our minds are being indoctrinated daily with ideas and philosophies that cause many to lose sight of the Lord's doctrines and teachings, as well as to their divine missions that they were sent on earth to accomplish.

We have been greatly blessed with Church leaders and parents, whose job it is, to act like beacons on the top of lighthouses, providing safe passage through storm tossed seas. Without their guidance and direction, it would make it harder to see and recognize the jagged rocks of sin and complacency.

I heard a story years ago of a young woman who was blessed with parents who took their stewardships very seriously. The parents followed our Church leaders counsel to have meaningful weekly Family Home Evenings, as well as daily scripture study and family prayer. They also saw to it that their children went to church as well as Seminary. Yet, this young woman thought she knew better than her parents and leaders; thinking her choices, which were contrary to Church standards, were not that big of a deal. Dressing immodestly and hanging around others who had standards that were contrary to doctrines and principles that the Lord had set, did not seem to cause her alarm.

This precious young woman continued to ignore the teachings of her parents and Church leaders, moving further and further away spiritually, until she reached a point where she no longer felt guilt or remorse for choices she was making.

That loss of the Spirit nearly caused her to lose her church membership. Fortunately, she woke up and made the changes in her attitudes and choices, which helped her to find her way back to full activity in the Lord's Kingdom.

Give the Lord Equal Time

How is it, one can get to the point of becoming dull to the promptings of the Spirit?

Elder M. Russell Ballard illustrated how easy this can happen when he shared an incident from when he was a Mission President.

One day during an interview, one of his missionaries told him that he thought he was losing his testimony. President Ballard asked him how that could be; to which the Elder told him that he had been reading anti-Mormon literature. Then the Elder told him that he had some questions that no one else seemed to want to answer.

President Ballard then asked him what questions he would like answers to. As it turned out, they were the standard anti-Mormon issues. However, President Ballard said he needed some time to come up with some satisfactory answers. He then asked the missionary if he would be willing to meet with him in ten days so they could discuss the answers to his questions.

As the missionary started to leave the interview, President Ballard asked when the last time was that the Elder had read the Book of Mormon. The missionary dropped his head and said that it had been a long while since he had done so. Then President Ballard asked the Elder if he would promise to read the Book of Mormon for at least an hour a day, every day leading up to their meeting in ten days. The missionary agreed and left his office.

At the end of the ten days, the Elder returned to President Ballard's office. President Ballard pulled out the papers with the answers on them and started to go over them, but before he could begin, the Elder stopped him, saying that it was not necessary for him to continue, that he knew the Book of Mormon was true, and that Joseph Smith was a prophet of God.

President Ballard told him that it was great that he had gained his testimony back, but that he had worked a long time to find answers to his questions, and he was going to listen to them.

After answering all his questions, President Ballard asked the Elder what he had learned from his experience. The Elder replied that we need to give God equal time.[2]

Have Ye Inquired of the Lord?

Prayer is the way we communicate with our Heavenly Father. It is through sincere prayer that we receive Divine tutoring. It is only when we are humble and teachable, that the Father's mind and will, becomes our mind and will. The Father is always ready and willing to bless us with our righteous desires…but it is conditional on our asking. However, just asking is not enough, as we need to put in the work and effort to get the answers we desire. The following are ways to get the most benefit from our prayers:

1. Keep the commandments (Psalms 78:7).
2. Forgive others of their sins against you (Matthew 6:14-15).
3. Ask the Lord for forgiveness of our sins. We do not have to be perfect to receive answers to our prayers. However, we do need to be trying to overcome our sins and weaknesses (Psalms 32:1; 86:5; Luke 5:20).
4. Do not harden our heart. Hardening our heart will make it where we are not able to accept answers the Father gives (Mark 6:52).

5. Be humble and teachable and willing to act immediately with what you feel impressed to do (Psalms 1:17).

6. Study and ponder (think deeply) about it before you ask for it (Proverbs 4:26; 21:2). There are many prayers that go unanswered because we either do not ask in Christ's name (John 14:13–14; 15:7, 16; 16:23–24); or they are not the Father's mind and will, but come from man's selfish desires or the time is not right.

7. Be specific as you ask the Lord for what you or others need. I cannot help but wonder how many blessings are being withheld to those people who simply have not asked the One who is waiting and willing to give them what they desire and need.

8. Have faith, nothing wavering believing that the Lord will give the answers or help to our righteous desires (James 1:6).

9. Take time during and at the end of your prayer to listen for promptings and inspiration.

10. Be willing to accept the mind and will of the Father (Luke 22:42). He knows what is best. If He gave you want you want that is not right or the time is not right, it can keep you from greater blessings and growth.

11. Keep a paper and pen close by, and write down the answers and impressions, so you will not forget them, and can review them from time to time. You could keep a prayer and scripture journal to record your impressions and thoughts as you pray and read your scriptures. FYI: The scriptures are journals ancient prophets and scribes kept (John 19:35).

The first time I heard an adult say she did not know how to pray, I was very surprised, as I assumed that everyone knew how to pray. Therefore, in case any of you that are reading this book, are not sure how to pray, I have included these easy to follow steps:

1. **Address God** - We open the prayer by addressing God, because He is the One we are praying to. It is common to start by saying "Father in Heaven" or "Heavenly Father." We address Him as our Heavenly Father because He is the father of our spirits, and the One to whom we owe everything we have, including our lives.

2. **Thank Him** - After opening the prayer, we tell our Father in Heaven what we are thankful for. You can start by saying, "I thank thee..." or "I am grateful for...." We show our gratitude to Him by telling Him in our prayer what we are thankful for, such as our home, family, health, jobs, food, protection, the earth, our trials, etc.

3. **Ask Him** - After thanking Him, we can ask Him for help. Some of the ways we can do this is to say: "I ask thee..."; "I need..."; "Please help me..." We can ask Him to bless us with the things we need, such as knowledge, comfort, guidance, peace, health, our relationships with others, for protection for our family and friends, and that He will guide

and direct the leaders of nations to make right decisions, and to help family members and friends with problems they are having, etc.

4. **Close in the name of Jesus Christ** - We close the prayer by saying, "In the name of Jesus Christ, Amen." We do this because Jesus is our Savior and our mediator with Heavenly Father. He suffered and died for us that we may be able to return again to our Heavenly Father's presence. He is also the one we are commanded to have faith in. The Apostle John taught: "And whatsoever ye shall ask in my name, that will I do, that the Father may be glorified in the Son...If ye shall ask any thing in my name, I will do it." (John 14: 13-14.) We also close the prayer by saying "Amen" because it means we accept or agree with what's been said, whether by us, or by a person saying a family prayer; or in a meeting with other people.

Before a friend of ours was baptized, a family member found some anti-Mormon literature which he put many hours of study into. He used every opportunity to share what he was learning with her, as he was sure she had been deceived. However, she refused to read or listen to any of the material he presented to her.

When she could no longer take his constant attacks about the things that she held dear, she asked us how to deal with it. We reminded her that it was the Spirit who bore witness of the truthfulness of the Gospel to her, and that He would never mislead or lie to her. We then encouraged her to seek answers from the Lord in how to deal with her father. She therefore, learned to turn to the Lord in such matters, and gained an even stronger testimony of the truthfulness of the Gospel.

In 1 Nephi 15:7-11, Nephi asked Laman and Lemuel the cause of their disputations. Laman and Lemuel responded by saying, "Behold, we cannot understand the words which our father hath spoken concerning the natural branches of the olive-tree, and also concerning the Gentiles"

Nephi then asked them, "Have ye inquired of the Lord?" to which his brethren responded, "We have not; for the Lord maketh no such thing known unto us".

Nephi then gave them the pattern of how to gain their own answers to their questions, when he told them to:

1. Keep the commandments
2. Do not harden your hearts
3. Ask the Lord
4. Have faith, believing that "...surely these things shall be made known unto you." (1 Nephi 19:23)

We should liken this counsel to our day and our lives, as more times than not, many of us have very similar attitudes to Laman and Lemuel, in that, we will not put in the effort to petition the One that has *all* the answers.

Teach Correct Principles So Children Can Govern Themselves

What message are we sending to our children if we do not practice what we preach? Children need parents that are committed to setting good examples and teaching correct principles, and who have the courage to reinforce what they teach, like the following counsel given in the Doctrine & Covenants 121:41-44: "No power or influence can or ought to be maintained by virtue of the priesthood, only by persuasion, by long-suffering, by gentleness and meekness, and by love unfeigned; By kindness, and pure knowledge, which shall greatly enlarge the soul without hypocrisy, and without guile— Reproving betimes with sharpness [and/or clarity], when moved upon by the Holy Ghost; and then showing forth afterwards an increase of love toward him whom thou hast reproved, lest he esteem thee to be his enemy; That he may know that thy faithfulness is stronger than the cords of death." (Emphasis added)

It can be hard to discern if it is the Spirit prompting us to correct the actions of our children, or if it is from losing our patience or temper with them. That is why it is so important to daily seek for the Spirit to guide us, and then to have the courage to follow the promptings…*without hesitation.*

When our children were young and made poor choices, I would ask them if they had had any thoughts come to their minds, against making that choice. I was relieved when they said they did get those feelings, because I knew my prayers were being answered. Then I used those opportunities to teach them how important it is to follow those promptings for their physical, as well as their spiritual safety.

Teaching children correct principles when they are young, so they can learn to govern themselves in righteousness when they are older, is a dilemma that many parents deal with, as it can be an exhaustive struggle to know how to get our children to internalize and follow what they have been taught. Sometimes, it feels as if we as parents are talking to the wall. However, the counsel given in Proverbs 22:6 should give parents (and leaders) great comfort and courage: "Train up a child in the way he should go: and when he is old, he will not depart from it".

But remember, the working words there are, "when he is old". The counsel being, to never give up on your children…even and especially your adult children!

As the media and political groups keep trying to make behavior that the Lord has condemned, as acceptable and normal, it makes it difficult for parents to counter with the Lord's standards and have them stick in their children's minds and hearts.

There are many parents in and out of our church, who agonize over their rebellious children. The parents often feel they have lost their child to influences that they have no control over, and it seems there is nothing they can do to make a difference. It is President Boyd K. Packer's conviction, that there will come a time when those wicked influences will no longer be a challenge.

President Packer, Joseph Smith, Brigham Young, Wilford Woodruff, and Lorenzo Snow, all bore powerful testimonies that parents who have been sealed in the temple, who remain faithful to those covenants, will have their children with them in the eternities.[3]

Homes, where parents seek for and follow the Spirit in raising and training their children, will be seedbeds for Saints. The parents of those homes will improve their chances of being able to exclaim, "I have no greater joy than to hear that my children walk in truth" (3 John 1:4).

During my first year in Seminary, the teacher asked the students to read the Book of Mormon, as a family, by the end of the school year. Therefore, my dad got our family up at 5 am *every morning* for family prayer, and to read from the Book of Mormon, before we left for early morning Seminary.

I doubt any of us kids got much out of what we read on those early mornings, as we were so drowsy. However, the Spirit of that great book still had a profound impact on our family. In fact, in spite of how pitiful we were with our so-called "daily scripture study", the thing I noticed was how much better my family got along during that school year. I do not remember any fights, and my parents seemed more loving with each other. Our family even started doing better financially during that period of time.

Years later, one of my brothers, who had not attended church since he was a teen ager, said he remembered that when we read the Book of Mormon as a family, and had family prayer every day, that is when we got along.

Not long ago, we attended the sealing of a young couple in the temple. The Sealer told how most couples do not remember the advice they are given on their wedding day, but that this couple would if they would return to the temple often and pay close attention to the things they are taught in the ordinances, as well as the promptings they receive from the Spirit. He said the ordinances in the temple would help them find the answers and strength they would need to be able to build a marriage that will last the eternities. I thought that advice should be given to every couple who is sealed in the temple.

And again, the angel said: "Behold, the Lord hath heard the prayers of his people, and also the prayers of his servant, Alma, who is thy father; for he has prayed with much faith concerning thee that thou mightest be brought to the knowledge of the truth; therefore, for this purpose have I come to convince thee of the power and authority of God, that the prayers of his servants might be answered according to their faith" (Mosiah 27:14).

186

I want to repeat, never, never, NEVER give up on wayward or disobedient children!

Be Steady and Inspired

If your load seems too heavy to bear, there is One who can lighten it. In Mosiah 24, it tells the account of Alma and his people who were in bondage to the Lamanites, who were persecuting and heaping heavy burdens on them. When the Nephites repented of their sins, and submitted humbly and cheerfully to the will of the Lord, the Lord blessed them for their faithfulness: "And now it came to pass that the burdens which were laid upon Alma and his brethren were made light; yea, the Lord did strengthen them that they could bear up their burdens with ease, and they did submit cheerfully and with patience to all the will of the Lord."

The Adversary is working hard to destroy families and individuals. All one has to do is pick up a newspaper, turn on the news, or view the Internet to see the influence Satan is having on families and individuals. We have been warned in the scriptures and over the pulpit in General and Stake Conferences that conditions in the world are going to get much worse before the Second Coming. We need to be steady, and persevere, and seek for inspiration, so we will be able to obtain all that the Lord has promised to those who are prepared, and who seek for and do His will.

Perseverance means to continue in a given course until we have reached a goal or objective, regardless of obstacles, opposition, and other counterinfluences. Perseverance is a positive, active characteristic. It gives us hope by helping us realize that the righteous suffer no failure except in giving up and no longer trying (Dictionary.com).

The Lord needs righteous people to be the standard-bearers for truth and righteousness. We need to have the courage of Shadrach, Meshach, and Abed-nego (see Daniel 1-3). When King Nebuchadnezzar found out that Shadrach, Meshach and Aged-nego (who had been placed over the affairs of the providence of Babylon) were praying to their God instead of bowing down and praying to the idol he had commanded his people to worship, he had the young men brought before him.

Upon their arrival, he demanded to know whether or not they were following his orders to bow down to the golden image he commanded his people to worship. When he discovered that they had disobeyed his orders, he asked them, "Who is that God that shall deliver you out of my hands?"

Shadrach, Meshach, and Abed-nego, showed great courage and unwavering devotion to God as they boldly told the king, "If it be *so,* our God whom we serve is able to deliver us from the burning fiery furnace, and he will deliver *us* out of thine hand, O king."

And here is the point I wish to make, "But if not, be it known unto thee, O king, that we will not serve thy gods, nor worship the golden image which thou hast set up."

The king was so furious with them, that he commanded that his servants should build a fire and heat it seven times hotter than they usually heated it. Then he commanded the mightiest men in his army to bind Shadrach, Meshach, and Abed-nego and cast them into the fiery furnace. However, because the fire was so hot, the soldiers perished. As the king looked on, he was astonished that instead of perishing like his solders, Shadrach, Meshach, and Abed-nego were walking about in the fire unharmed.

Then the king asked his Counselors: "Did not we cast three men bound into the midst of the fire?"

They answered and said unto the king, "True, O king".

He answered and said, "Lo, I see four men loose, walking in the midst of the fire, and they have no hurt; and the form of the fourth is like the Son of God."

I thought it was interesting that King Nebuchadnezzar recognized that the fourth man was "like the Son of God" when he did not profess to believe in Him; and had just tried to have Shadrach, Meshach, and Abed-nego put to death.

The King then called out, "Shadrach, Meshach, and Abed-nego, ye servants of the most high God, come forth, and come hither."

Then the King and his counselors, princes, and governors noticed that Shadrach, Meshach and Abed-nego had not been burned any where on their bodies, and that their clothing had not been singed, neither was there any smell of smoke any where on their persons.

When the King realized he had been wrong, he said, "Blessed be the God of Shadrach, Meshach, and Abed-nego, who hath sent his angel, and delivered his servants that trusted in him, and have changed the king's word, and yielded their bodies, that they might not serve nor worship any god, except their own God. Therefore I make a decree, That every people, nation, and language, which speak any thing amiss against the God of Shadrach, Meshach, and Abed-nego, shall be cut in pieces, and their houses shall be made a dunghill: because there is no other God that can deliver after this sort."

The king then promoted Shadrach, Meshach, and Abed-nego over the province of Babylon (Daniel 3).

When the gentle breezes blow, and the sun is shining, and all seems to be well in Zion, it is very easy to have faith, hope and trust in the Lord. However, when the storms are raging and the tempest is tossing our small boat about with mountainous waves, and it seems that the very powers of darkness are about to succeed in destroying our peace and tranquility, how easy is it to say, "But if not, thy will be done", and mean it. Yet, that is exactly what Shadrach, Meshach, and Abed-nego did. They trusted in the Lord to preserve them, nevertheless, they were willing to submit to His will if He chose not to preserve them.

There is a similar account in the Book of Mormon, found in Alma 14, where Alma and Amulek were forced to watch, as the righteous, that would not deny Christ, were thrown into a raging fire. Only in that account, the lives of the righteous that were thrown into the fire were not spared.

After Amulek could no longer bear to watch the destruction of the innocent lives, he asked Alma: "How can we witness this awful scene? Therefore let us stretch forth our hands, and exercise the power of God which is in us, and save them from the flames."

Now remember, these were more than likely some of Amulek's family and friends. But Alma, showing forth the courage of Shadrach, Meshach, and Abed-nego, told Amulek: "The Spirit constraineth me that I must not stretch forth mine hand; for behold the Lord receiveth them up unto himself, in glory; and he doth suffer that they may do this thing, or that the people may do this thing unto them, according to the hardness of their hearts, that the judgments which he shall exercise upon them in his wrath may be just; and the blood of the innocent shall stand as a witness against them, yea, and cry mightily against them at the last day."

Then Amulek asked the question that any one of us might have been worried about: "Behold, perhaps they will burn us also."

Then Alma answered, "Be it according to the will of the Lord."

I have no doubt that that was NOT what Amulek wanted to hear from Alma. But then, Alma said something that I am sure eased Amulek's fears: "*But, behold, our work is not finished; therefore they burn us not* (Alma 14)."

How does a person overcome the fear of the, "But if not's", that we will all go through before the Second Coming? The way has been laid out very clearly in the scriptures, and by our Church Leaders, both past and present. Even with conditions in the world continuing to deteriorate, there is no reason to falter, lose hope, or loosen our grip on the Iron Rod. If we will but heed the counsels and admonitions of our Church leaders and follow their steady, valiant examples, we will have peace, joy and safe passage through the fiery furnaces and raging storms we may be called to go through.

Remember, in spite of the troubling times, the day will soon come when our Savior will reign. When that day comes, peace and righteousness will fill the earth, and all who have been valiant in their testimonies of Christ, and have remained faithful and true to the covenants they have made, will find joy beyond comprehension and they will dwell with Him forever.

So, ask yourself, "Is it worth the effort?" You and your family's eternal destiny depend upon your answer, as well as your commitment to stick with it.

Notes:

1. The quote associated with this can be found in: Joseph Smith, *History of the Church,* 2:23
2. M. Russell Ballard, "How to Find Safety and Peace", *New Era,* Nov 1997, 4
3. References to quotes: *Our Moral Environment, Ensign,* May 1992, 68; *Hope for Parents of Wayward Children, Ensign,* Sept. 2002, 11; quoted in Joseph Fielding Smith, *Doctrines of Salvation,* comp. Bruce R. McConkie, 3 vols. [1954-56], 2:90-91; (in *Collected Discourses,* comp. Brian H. Stuy, 5 vols. [1987-92], 3:364)

Section Three

Removing Relationship Inhibitors

The purpose for this section is for individuals and couples to be able to recognize where they are relationship-challenged. They will discover some hidden treasures that have proven beneficial in strengthening marriage and family bonds.

Chapter Fifteen

Removing Hidden Wedges

In his account, "Forgotten Wedges", Samuel T. Whitman (an aged, white-haired farmer), told how years before when he was a young man, living on his father's homestead, he was walking where a saw mill had recently been relocated. Scattered on the ground, were odd pieces of equipment and tools that had been left behind. To a young lad, such a find can be as valuable as finding a buried treasure.

On this particular day, he came across a feller's wedge, which is a 12", flat, heavy tool made out of iron, used to fell trees. Once the wedge is placed in a cut in the trunk of a tree (usually made by a saw or an ax), it is then hit with a sledge hammer to widen the cut, thus making it easier to fell the tree. The edge of this particular wedge was splayed (or split) from the many times it had been pounded by the powerful blows of sledge hammers.

Samuel told how he picked up his treasure, and being late for dinner, he quickly deposited it between the limbs of a young walnut tree near his house...intending to take it to the shed after dinner. Although his intention was good, the wedge remained between the limbs until after he had married and had taken over his father's homestead.

One day, upon noticing the wedge, he tried to remove it, only to discover that the tree limbs had started to grow up around it, making it impossible to remove it without doing damage to the tree.

Then, one winter's night while he slept, an ice storm covered the limbs of the now large tree. Usually, such storms did little more than bring down power lines and cause an increase of accidents on the highway. The massive limbs of the walnut tree usually bore up well under the weight of the snow and ice from previous storms. However, this time the weight of the ice was too much to bear, as one of the three major limbs split away from the trunk, causing it to crash to the ground. The other limbs, not being able to handle the imbalance and weight of the ice, fell, crashing to the ground as well. When the storm was over, nothing but a pile of splinters remained of the once mighty monarch.

In the early morning hours, the farmer went out to mourn his loss. As he looked over the remains of his once beloved tree, his eyes settled on something that caused him great remorse...for there, lying in the splinters, was the wedge that he had found in the field so many years before. It took only a moment for him to discover what had caused the demise of the tree. The wedge had been placed at the heart of the trunk where it prevented the limbs fibers from being able to knit together as they are supposed to.[1]

All of us have hidden wedges. However, too often, we go about life ignoring them, or refusing to accept that that little quirk, that annoying habit, that favorite sin or addiction, is of any consequence.

If these wedges are ignored, or allowed to remain for too long, they can cause serious damage to our lives and our relationships with others, especially in our own families. Then, when the storms come (as they always do), or if we allow Satan's fiery darts to pierce our armor, then like with the mighty monarch, with the wedge deeply embedded at its heart, we can find ourselves surrounded by the splinters of broken dreams and hopes for eternity.

Through obedience and faith, the Lord is able to purge from our lives all that is impure and unrefined. In such a state, the Spirit will be our constant companion (D&C 121:46).

When we have the Spirit as our constant companion, we will have a greater yearning to stand in holy places.

Standing in Holy Places

Regular temple attendance provides the holy places where we may find spiritual protection from the powers of darkness for ourselves and our families. Our homes should be an extension of the Spirit and holiness found in the temple. Therefore, anything that would detract from, or grieve the Spirit, should not be allowed in our lives, or our homes.

Years ago, in the August 1978 *Ensign*, under "Answers to Gospel Questions", I found a list similar to the one below. I keep the list in my scriptures, so I can quickly find it when I am having trouble recognizing the hidden wedges in my life:

WHEN YOU HAVE THE SPIRIT	WHEN YOU DON'T HAVE THE SPIRIT
1. You are happy, calm and your mind is clear.	1. You feel unhappy, depressed, confused, and frustrated most of the time.
2. You want to give of your time, talents and every other thing the Lord has blessed you with to help others and to serve in His Kingdom (Church).	2. You feel possessive, self-centered, or resentful of things others ask you to do, even in Church service.
3. No one can offend you.	3. It does not take much to offend you, and you are unwilling to get over it.
4. You realize that your thoughts and your actions are open to God.	4. You become secretive and avoid others, thinking it is only your business.
5. You love being with others and want to make them happy.	5. You avoid others, even your own family. You are critical of family members and Church leaders.
6. You prefer to give quiet service where others will not notice.	6. When you help others, your main desire may be to have your actions noticed, rewarded, or praised.
7. You are genuinely happy when others succeed.	7. You are jealous or resentful when others succeed, or are recognized.
8. You feel sorrow when others are suffering and try to help lift their burdens.	8. You may often question others motives and secretly delight when they fail or are having problems.
9. You are glad to attend your meetings and participate in church activities.	9. You don't want to go to church, go home or visiting teaching, or take the sacrament. You wish you had another church calling, or no calling at all.
10. You feel like praying and reading your scriptures.	10. You don't want to pray or read your scriptures, thinking they are boring or won't offer the help you need.
11. It grieves you because it is hard to keep all the Commandments all the time.	11. You find the commandments bothersome, restricting, or senseless.
12. You find strength in your resolve to avoid overeating and addictions. You prefer entertainment that edifies and invites the Spirit. You go to bed early and rise early. You are in control of your temper. You keep your passions in the boundaries the Lord has set.	12. You are a slave to your passions, you do not control them, and they control you. Hate, jealousy, anger, lust, and fatigue seem to be the only passions you feel, and you do not have any desire to be free of them, nor do you want to control them.

13. Your love for the Savior is in your heart at all times. You try to live each day as if He were beside you. You feel a deep sense of gratitude for His love and Atonement. You desire to be with Him and Heavenly Father in the Celestial Kingdom.	13. You have no desire to be like the Savior, thinking He has forgotten you. His teachings are foreign to you. You feel what He asks of you is too hard. You feel your sins are too serious and He will never forgive you, nor can He ever love or accept you because of them.
14. You have joy and peace every day of your life, even in the midst of serious trials. You have confidence in knowing you are a beloved child of God.	14. You get discouraged easily, and have a hard time believing that life is really worth it. You feel He does not exist or that He has forgotten you.

(See [2])

I have learned that it is the small efforts (that are rarely noticed by others) that we make in our marriages and families that contribute to the spirit that is felt in our homes. The biggest battles are fought in the recesses of our hearts, hidden from the view of others, but noticed by the One who matters most, and Who will bless us for those efforts.

In reality, there are actually no small efforts, when it comes to creating masterpieces, whether great or small. Think about what it took to sculpt the faces on Mt. Rushmore. Yet, that monument stands as a testament of each stroke of the sculpture's hand that helped to create it. It is a masterpiece which is enjoyed by countless awe struck admirers who come from near and far to see.

Just because the Lord reveals the hidden wedges in our personal lives, marriages and/or families, it does not magically make them go away. At first thought, one would be tempted to think that having Him make our weaknesses and sins magically go away, without much effort on our part, would be a great blessing. However, that is not the Lord's plan, as the ease of it would keep us from growing and having experiences that would strengthen us and make us more fit for His Kingdom.

Some wedges are easily discarded and never return. However, some may take a lifetime to completely remove, as they have been in place for so long, that we feel incomplete without them.

In those more difficult cases, it is too easy to keep running back to the garbage heap to retrieve the discarded wedge and put it back in its former place where it festers like a boil until we remove it again. The problem with that endless loop is that it gets harder and harder each time to leave the wedge in the garbage heap, as too often we give up, thinking that we will never overcome or be free of the wedge and its ill effects.

That vicious cycle has a way of making us feel like we are failures, and often affects other areas of our lives, as well as our relationships. The important thing to remember is to NEVER GIVE UP! You are only a failure when you quit getting back up each time you fall.

If a toddler, while learning to walk, does not get back up when he or she falls, they will never learn to walk. It is in the getting back up, that they not only master the skill of walking, but running and doing cart wheels as well. Even the fastest runner had to learn to walk before he or she could learn to run.

Some weaknesses or hidden wedges seem to be connected to us with an iron clad umbilical cord. However, like anything else in our lives, if we expect to succeed, we need to continue to apply what we are learning on a daily basis…with out fail, until the weakness or hidden wedge is no longer a part of us.

Thinking back to how the wedge hindered the walnut tree from being able to bear up under the weight of the ice on its branches, it should give more incentive to stay committed to permanently removing *all* the hidden wedges from our lives.

Do You Have the Courage to Pray for Correction Daily?

Karl Kern, one of our former Stake Presidents, shared a story from his first Stake Presidency training, where President Boyd K. Packer said he prays for two things each day: 1) Personal revelation; 2) Correction.

He said correction is much easier to receive when it comes from the Lord, but when it comes from peers, or family and friends; it is not easy to recognize it as coming from the Lord.

Our Stake President said the Apostle looked right at him and asked, "Do you have the courage to pray for correction daily?"

Our Stake President then looked at the members of our Stake and asked the same question. I remember as I sat there, a feeling of dread came over me. I wanted to think about the more pleasant messages I had heard in Conference, yet, I could not ignore the counsel from this humble, inspired servant of the Lord.

After pondering over what it would mean to pray for correction, I realized I needed to do so with all my heart, mind and strength, just like when I was challenged to thank the Lord for my trials. So, with all the conviction and sincerity I could muster, I managed to utter the words: "Please Father, bless me with correction. Help me to recognize it as coming from Thee, and help me have the understanding, courage, and strength to overcome my weaknesses."

I assume that since I asked for it while saying family prayer that morning that my family viewed it as a window of opportunity that might not open again. For, I no sooner said, "Amen", when gently and lovingly, they each let me know of something I did that they wished I would change. They were not unkind or hurtful about it, but it still hurt my feelings…until I realized that their comments were direct answers to my prayers. Oddly enough, as I allowed my mind to process that thought, I felt deeply loved and like I had great worth to the Lord. I knew He cared about me because of how quickly He answered my request.

However, just because we recognize a need to change something in our behavior, does not mean we will know *how* to accomplish it. That is where it takes effort to seek for the Lord's guidance and inspiration into how He would have us change. The rest is up to us to patiently follow through with, and not lose sight of those goals.

Let God be the Architect

Years ago when I was struggling with my self worth, I heard the following analogy by C. S. Lewis, titled "A Living House":

"Imagine yourselves as a living house. God comes into rebuild that house.

"At first, perhaps, you can understand what He is doing. He is getting the drains right and stopping the leaks in the roof and so on: you knew that those jobs needed doing and so you are not surprised. But presently, He starts knocking the house about in a way that hurts abominably and does not seem to make sense. What on earth is He up to? The explanation is that He is building quite a different house from the one you thought of — throwing out a new wing here, putting on an entire floor there, running up towers, making courtyards. You thought you were going to be made into a decent little cottage, but He is building a palace." [3]

After hearing that analogy, I immediately had an epiphany as I came to realize that my trials were actually opportunities that the Lord was using to help me become more refined. For the first time in my life, I felt loved and accepted by the Lord. Up to that point, I had no problem loving others unconditionally, but I could not imagine the Lord loving me, as I felt so imperfect, even though I tried hard to do what was right. I have since come to realize, when you feel like that, it is hard to love yourself, or to believe that the Lord can love you.

We are told to be perfect, even as our Father which is in heaven is perfect (Matthew 5:48). My husband and I are reading a book titled "The Beloved Bridegroom - Finding Christ in Ancient Jewish Marriage and Family Customs", written by Donna B. Nielson. The author helps the reader understand that in ancient Hebrew, to become perfect, meant you were perfect in keeping your covenants that you make with the Lord. Anyone of us can be perfect in something, whether it is being honest in all your business dealings, paying a full tithe to the Lord, etc. That explanation helped me feel a lot better about that scripture about being perfect.

Some of the struggles we go through come from choices we have made, whether they are from giving into temptations, or poor choices that have lead to setbacks or lost opportunities. Other struggles have to do with the sinful or poor choices made by others. We cannot always control everything that happens to us in this life, but we can control how we respond to them.

As I mentioned earlier, think of what a toddler goes through to learn to walk. He or she falls many times before they master the skill of walking and then running. It is amazing how quickly we go from saying, "Look Dear, Johnnie is walking!" to, "No, no Johnnie, don't touch that."

And sometimes it is my favorite Bill Cosby line: "Come here...come here...I said, COME HERE...HERE!!!", as the toddler continues on his/her merry way...while ignoring you.

Nevertheless, watching a toddler learn to walk is enlightening and exciting. The look on the toddler's face is priceless, as they stand without support for the first time...and then take their first wobbly steps, realizing they are not holding onto anything...and then tumble to the ground...only to get up and do it all over again.

It reminds me of when Peter was able to walk on the water towards Jesus, until he noticed the waves thrashing about his feet, and realized the impossibility of what he was doing, and began to sink (Matthew 14:25-31). It was then that the Master reached out His hand and pulled him gently and lovingly UP to safety (there is an analogy in the fact that he pulled him up when he was sinking) like a loving parent does with their wobbly toddler...until the child has mastered walking, and no longer needs the parent's helping hands to keep them steady on their feet.

Brother Philo Dibble gave an account that took place at Father Johnson's house in Hiram, Ohio, while Joseph Smith and Sydney Rigdon were working on the inspired version of the Bible. In Brother Dibble's account, a vision of the Three Degrees of Glory opened up to Joseph and Sydney (which was later recorded in D&C 76). There were other men present in the room, including Brother Dibble, but none of them saw what Joseph and Sydney saw, yet they felt the spirit and glory of the vision.

When the vision closed, Joseph sat calmly radiating a spiritual glow from what he had just witnessed while Sydney looked drained and limp like as a rag. With a smile, Joseph told the others that Sydney was not used to those experiences like he was ("Doctrine and Covenants & Church History Seminary Student Study Guide", Doctrine and Covenants 76; "Recollections of the Prophet Joseph Smith," The Juvenile Instructor, May15, 1892, 303–4).

For Joseph to come to know the ancient prophets as we know our good friends, he had to have had many encounters with them.

Like the toddler learning to walk, when we learn and grow in any area of our lives, we often step out into the black abyss of the unknown, falling and getting back up until we can move about with confidence (D&C 121:45). Think of it like Lehi's dream, where there is the need to hold fast to the Iron Rod to be able to find our way, because the mist's of darkness make it hard to see the Tree of Life at the end of the Rod. However, if we will trust that the Tree is actually at the end of the Rod, it makes it much easier to keep a tight grip until we reach the Tree.

Consider what Wladimir Kohanski (the noted concert pianist that I mentioned earlier in the book) told our son who asked how he became such an accomplished pianist. His words are an inspiration for any area we want to master in our lives, "Practice, practice, practice!"

Do not give up! Ether 12:27 gives hope that anything anyone desires to overcome or accomplish is within their power to do so: "And if men come unto me I will show unto them their weakness. I give unto men weakness that they may be humble; and my grace is sufficient for all men that humble themselves before me; for if they humble themselves before me, and have faith in me, then will I make weak things become strong unto them."

Another scripture that gives great promise and insight into helping us reach our goals, is Mosiah 4:27: "And see that all these things are done in wisdom and order for it is not requisite that a man should run faster than he has strength. And again, it is expedient that he should be diligent, that thereby he might win the prize; therefore, all things must be done in order."

Most anything anyone desires to overcome or accomplish is within their power to do so. However, be careful not to run faster than you have strength, or to take on more than you are able to handle. You are no good to anyone if you burn yourself out, or destroy your health in the process of working towards your lofty goals. Sometimes, it is our body that lets us know we need to slow down, when we do not use wisdom and good judgment in the use of our time and energies.

Remember, when we work like everything depends on us and pray like everything depends on the Lord, He will help our weaknesses to be turned into strengths, thus helping us to accomplish our goal(s).

The Parable of the Unwise Carpenter

There was once a very skilled carpenter, whose talents as a furniture-maker, became well known throughout all the land. One day the king sent for him, explaining that he desired to have a throne that would be the envy of kings from lands both near and far. The only catch was it had to be finished by the end of the week, in time for the grand ball where the King and Queen, Princes and Princesses, Dukes and Duchesses, and Lords and Ladies from the kingdom, as well as neighboring lands would all be in attendance.

Visions of fame and fortune filled the carpenter's imagination as he pondered what it would mean when it was noised throughout the land and abroad, that he now held the position as the King's royal furniture maker.

After locating the finest wood in the kingdom, he set to work designing a chair fit for a reigning monarch. After carefully constructing the beautifully contoured seat and back, he then attached the elegantly crafted arms. With four days left before the deadline, he decided to put his greatest effort and attention into the front legs that would be the most visible parts of the chair, leaving the less visible back legs until last.

Minutes turned into days as he tediously carved the intricate and delicate design into each of the front legs. As he worked, he imagined how he would be the envy of all the royal eyes that gazed upon his creation.

However, with putting so much time and focus into the intricate details of the front legs, he lost track of time until it dawned on him that it was the evening before the day of the ball, and he had not even started on the back legs. Therefore, he quickly set his greatest masterpieces aside, and looked for the wood to craft the back legs. To his horror, he discovered that he had miscalculated and did not have enough wood to make them the same length as the front legs.

Time was of the essence, so he quickly cut the pieces of wood for the back legs, along with the extra pieces to make up the difference in length, and then glued the pieces together. After making sure the back legs were the same length as the front ones, he quickly carved similar but less intricate designs into them.

As he then looked over his handiwork to make sure the seams would not be noticeable, he felt a since of pride as he realized that even a skilled carpenter would have a hard time being able to see where he had glued the pieces of wood together.

The morning sunbeams streamed through the shop windows as the carpenter polished the finished product. Truly, this was the most beautiful throne anyone had ever created!

There was no time for eating or sleeping, so he carefully loaded his beloved work of art into his wagon, making sure to protect it from being scratched or broken. Then, after meticulously placing it on the raised dais in the Throne Room, he walked around the massive hall, making sure that every royal eye, from any place in the room, would be able to see his masterpiece.

He then draped an elegant velvet tapestry over the canopy, and down the sides and back of the chair, and then stepped back for a final glance at his handiwork. Once satisfied that it was a picture of perfection, he quickly went home so he could get ready to attend the ball.

Upon arriving in the elaborately decorated hall, the overconfident carpenter chose to stand in the back of the room, where he would be able to see everyone as they gazed upon his work of art.

One by one, the royal guests entered…each gasping in amazement as the majestic throne caught their attention. A ripple of silence fell across the room as the king made his entrance. All eyes were fixed on the distinguished ruler as he slowly lower himself into his prestigious place of honor. Then, silence turned to shrieks of horror as the back legs of the throne gave way; and the king, along with his magnificent throne, fell backwards. Fortunately, for the craftsman, the king was able to escape serious injury because the tapestry acted as a cushion, softening his fall.

Because of wanting the honors of men, the carpenter had put most of his time and focus on the more visible parts of the chair, which allowed him little time to spend on the less visible parts. And due to lack of time and focus, the back legs were not able to bear up under the weight of the mighty monarch.

If the carpenter had put in equal amounts of time and focus on the visible, *as well as the less visible* parts of the king's throne, the less visible legs would have been able to bear the weight of the king, thus avoiding the throne's collapse and the disastrous outcome that resulted from a very angry and humiliated king!

Decide Now to Safeguard Against Emotional Divorce

Dr. Stephen Covey, in his best seller, "7 Habits of Highly Effective People", told about a man who came up to him, at a seminar, saying that he no longer loved his wife, and he did not know what to do about it. Dr. Covey simply replied, "Love her.", to which the man said, "You do not understand, I no longer love her!"

Brother Covey explained that *love* is not only a noun, but also a verb, and that our love grows for someone when we serve them. He reemphasized that the man needed to actively serve and love his wife for his feelings of love, to return and grow.

At Church, we all know people who are well respected in their church callings; who, through true discipleship, give tireless efforts and service, and have been instruments in helping to save many souls that have been under their watchful care.

In addition, there are countless faithful parents, who raise valiant sons and daughters who serve missions, marry in the temple, and go on to raise righteous families of their own. Yet, some of these same valiant leaders, parents, and spouses, find themselves in divorce courts, saying that they are clueless as to how they ended up there.

We spend endless amounts of time and money beautifying our homes, yards, and gardens, yet, we often invest little thought, time, or money into nurturing our own marriages. The well cared for house, yard, and garden, give nothing back. They cannot show us love and tenderness like a spouse and family members can. More importantly, from an eternal perspective, we cannot take our beautiful homes and yards with us when we pass on to the other side of the veil, like we can our families.

If we neglect our homes, they can become run down, lose their value, and be a source of embarrassment. Plants cannot grow without constant nourishment. Yards become unattractive when weeds are allowed to grow and trees and bushes go un-pruned. Likewise, love can die in a marriage and family when it is not nurtured on a daily basis.

My dad told me a joke, years ago, about a woman who asked her husband why he never told her that he loved her. The husband said he told her on their wedding day that he loved her, and if he changed how he felt about her, he would let her know. I did not think it was a very funny joke, as it was so tragic to think about a wife never hearing on a regular basis, that her husband loves her. And sadly, I fear that this is not so much a joke, but a prevailing attitude in far too many marriages.

A young wife once told me, "My husband's telling me he loves me as he's leaving for work, means nothing, unless he shows it at other times".

You husbands, I want you to think back to what you did that won your wife's heart when you were dating. Try capturing those feelings in a love letter to her...the *soppier the better*.

Jeeves, the manservant made famous by P. G. Wodehouse, said it best: "Soppiness is at the very heart of the successful love letter. Without a sufficient degree of soppiness, there is a danger of the communication being laid aside by the recipient to be read at some future date, together with the gas bill." ("Jeeves in the Cottage" from the "Jeeves and Wooster" series)

We can spend many hours studying and praying for help to gain the Lord's perspective about what to do to strengthen our marriage. However, if we do not put into practice what we are learning, then it will be in vain, and can do little to save *our* marriage if it is falling apart. "People [including spouses] don't care how much you know until they know how much you care".[4]

Go back to the lists that you made earlier about what makes you happy and unhappy. What do your lists show about what is important to you? If your list does not include being with your family (or if you are single, your future spouse and children) for eternity, then I would like for you to consider, what does it profit if you gain the world, but lose the things that should be the most important to you? Hint: that should be your family.

Notes:

1. Elder Spencer W. Kimball, an account written by Samuel T. Whitman titled, *Forgotten Wedges*. April 1966 General Conference
2. Adapted from Answer to Gospel Questions, Ensign, August 1978
3. C. S. Lewis, "Mere Christianity"
4. Attributed to Teddy Roosevelt

Chapter Sixteen

How do I Change my Spouse?

In his article, "Your Marriage and the Sermon on the Mount" [1], Rick Browning told about a couple who went to a counselor for help with their troubled marriage. However, their resentment and lack of forgiveness towards each other was so deeply rooted, that nothing he suggested seemed to be helping. As he contemplated on what to do next, he had an idea come to his mind. He opened the Bible to Matthew 5 and asked them to read the entire *Sermon on the Mount* (comprising chapters 5-7). Harold B. Lee referred to it as, "The Constitution for a Perfect Life" [2].

The counselor then challenged them as a couple, to read it three times over the next week. Then, with each reading, they were to focus on one thing that they must change to be in harmony with the principles the Savior taught. They were not to tell each other how to change, only to focus on their own weaknesses. At first, the couple seemed reluctant to do the assignment, but then agreed to the challenge.

At the next week's appointment, the counselor was pleased to see that they were much more relaxed and friendly with each other...which made it easier for them to discuss solutions and compromises to their marital difficulties.

Reading and studying the *Sermon on the Mount*, and seeing areas that they needed to change in their own lives, caused the spirit of contention to depart, and the Spirit of the Lord to come into their home and hearts.

Another couple sought the help of a counselor for their irreconcilable differences. The wife reported that her husband was cruel, manipulative, thoughtless, and had a bad temper. The counselor was surprised when the husband agreed with his wife's assessment of him.

Nevertheless, realizing his need to change, the husband made gradual strides over the next year to become kinder and more thoughtful with his wife and children. However, being unwilling to forgive and forget his wife chose instead, to file for a divorce.

Even in the Church, this scenario is far too common. When misunderstandings and hurt feelings are not resolved quickly, disgruntled spouses often choose to punish each other. However, such unchecked and careless behavior can stifle communication and may cause strained and volatile interactions between husbands and wives.

The Savior taught: "For if ye forgive men their trespasses, your heavenly Father will also forgive you: but if ye forgive not men their trespasses, neither will your Father forgive your trespasses." (Matthew 6:14-15)

Even the strongest marriages can collapse under the weight of unforgiven offenses. The Savior said, "Agree with thine adversary [or upset and angry spouse] quickly, whiles thou art in the way with him [or her]" (Matthew 5:25) (emphasis added).

The way to keep peace and harmony in our marriage, is to forgive *all* men (D&C 64:10) ...even a spouse who appears to be making little to no effort to change his or her hurtful or thoughtless behavior. This in no way means we should allow our spouse to be cruel or abusive towards us. It does however mean we should prayerfully seek for ways to express ourselves with clarity and kindness about how we feel in regards to their actions toward us (D&C 121:41-45).

A different couple (who also sought a marriage counselor's help) believed they each had to contribute fifty percent to have a successful marriage. The problem with that way of thinking is that each believes he or she is the only one giving their full percent. Thus, neither spouse is satisfied with the other's contributions to the relationship.

With this particular couple, the wife believed that love notes, cards, flowers, frequent thoughtful gifts, and words of love expressed on a regular basis, was the way to show their love for each other. Her husband, on the other hand, was a very practical and methodical person who believed he showed his love best, when he fixed things that were broken, kept the yard looking nice, and provided financial security for his family.

Each spouse worked hard to fulfill their own part of their agreement. However, it wasn't until they made the effort to figure out the differences in each other's love language, and then worked to fulfill those expectations, that their relationship started to improve.

Not everyone will behave in a Christ-like manner. So what are we to do when others say or do things that are very damaging or hurtful to us? The answers are at our fingertips: "If any man will sue thee at the law, and take away thy coat, let him have thy cloak also. And whosoever shall compel thee to go a mile, go with him twain. Give to him that asketh thee, and from him that would borrow of thee turn not thou away." (Matthew 5:40-42); "Therefore all things whatsoever ye would that men should do to you, do ye even so to them: for this is the law and the prophets." (Matthew 7:12); "...charity is the pure of love Christ" and that charity "seeketh not her own" (Moroni 7:45, 47).

False assumptions can lead to serious conflicts in marriage. It is amazing how Steven Covey's counsel to first seek to understand the other person's point of view before stating your own, can help the hurt or confusion to dissipate like dew in the morning's rays of the rising sun.

False assumptions and accusations can lead to resentment, anger, and bitterness that can be very difficult to repair and get over. The Savior warned, "Judge not, that ye be not judged. For with what judgment ye judge, ye shall be judged: and with what measure ye mete, it

204

shall be measured to you again. And why beholdest thou the mote that is in thy brother's eye, but considerest not the beam that is in thine own eye?" (Matthew 7:1-3)

When we judge our spouse unfairly or with harshness, it is often an indication that something is amiss in our own lives. It would be better to first stop and ask ourselves, *why does my spouse's behavior or attitude bother me so much?* Once we have discovered the beam in our own eye, and then cast it out, we will be less inclined to see faults in our spouse and others.

Anger is self-serving by nature

Anger is the antithesis to having the Spirit with us. Anger is self-serving by nature; so, why not make it an unwelcomed guest in your heart and home.

Nothing good comes from trying to resolve a misunderstanding or conflict if either spouse is so upset they cannot think straight. So, if you feel your temper getting out of control, it would be best to remove yourself from the situation until you can calm down sufficiently to be able to discuss the problem in a rational and loving manner.

The Savior said, "Contention is not of me, but of the devil" (3 Nephi 11:29). When we allow contention into our home, Satan can drive wedges between us and our spouse (and family members). The Savior, in the Sermon on the Mount, warned, "Whosoever is angry with his brother without a cause shall be in danger of the judgment: and whosoever shall say to his brother, Raca, shall be in danger of the council: but whosoever shall say, Thou fool, shall be in danger of hell fire" (Matthew 5:22)

The Lord uses strong reproof for those who belittle or call each other names, especially when done in anger. Yet often, spouse's and family members think nothing of making fun of, or calling each other names when they are playing around, or are upset with each other.

We should never allow another person to treat our spouse (or family member) with derision or disrespect. However, we should use self-control when we defend our loved one(s), remembering that it is the offensive behavior, not the person that we do not like.

As I mentioned earlier, when reproving others, we should do so early on with gentleness, meekness, and clarity, when the Spirit of the Lord prompts us to do so; and afterwards, we should show forth an increase of love towards the person we have reproved, so he or she does not think of us as an enemy. (D&C 121:41, 43)

I found the following poem years ago, that is a good reminder of how our actions and words can make a difference in the lives of our children. I added "spouses" to it, because it is also true for them:

Children [*and Spouses*] Learn What They Live
[By Dorothy Law Nolte - modified by Terry Olsen]

If children [*and spouses*] live with criticism,

They learn to condemn.

If children [and spouses] live with hostility,

They learn to fight.

If children [and spouses] live with ridicule,

They learn to be shy.

If children [and spouses] live with shame,

They learn to feel guilty.

If children [and spouses] live with encouragement,

They learn confidence.

If children [and spouses] live with tolerance,

They learn to be patient.

If children [and spouses] live with praise,

They learn to appreciate.

If children [and spouses] live with acceptance,

They learn to love.

If children [and spouses] live with approval,

They learn to like themselves.

If children [and spouses] live with honesty,

They learn truthfulness.

If children [and spouses] live with security,

They learn to have faith in themselves and others.

If children [and spouses] live with friendliness,

They learn the world is a nice place in which to live. [3]

Now, before your tongue gets worn out from licking your wounds, I would like to point out that there is not a person alive today that would feel good about themselves after reading that poem (whether it has to do with the way they have treated family members or because of the way they have been treated by parents and/or their spouse). So why share it? Because it makes you stop and think about how what you say and do can positively or negatively affect your spouse and children. This would be a good poem to put in a prominent place in your home as a gentle reminder for family members to see.

Recently, while babysitting some of my grandkids, they kept taking toys from each other, and each time a tug-o-war broke out. Using the situation as an opportunity to teach and build bridges, I asked, "Is that the way you treat someone you love?"

Because of their young ages, I really did not expect them to grasp what I was saying. However, after the second or third gentle reminder, the offender handed back the toy to the one they had taken it from, and then muttered a pitiful sounding, "Sorry". It did not take much to figure out that their parents had taught them well, but it also helped me to realize that even at an early age, children have the capacity to understand the importance of treating others the way they want to be treated.

It can be hard to overcome the negative effects of abuse and unrelenting criticism. Low self-esteem is not the only painful outcome of living in such a home. Struggling to overcome the mentoring of a poor role model can bring about much anguish of soul to the one who is striving to be like our Savior.

It is no secret that the road to becoming Christ-like is not an easy one. Disappointments and setbacks are a way of life for the weary but determined traveler. However, if the dedicated student is persistent and trusts in the sculpting hands of his Master, then a Christ-like demeanor and countenance is within the reach of even the weakest of Saints. When such a transformation takes place, family members and friends will consider it a great blessing to have such a person in their home and lives. Often, family members and friends will become better people because of their unconditional love and acceptance of them, even in their imperfect states.

Learning to treat others the way we want to be treated is not so difficult a task when our efforts involve people we hardly know or have very few dealings with. However, when it involves a spouse or child who may not have the same desire for spiritual refinement, it can be a serious challenge. We have been told that we should never give up on our wayward children, but the same can be said of spouses who seem reluctant to overcome un-Christ-like behavior.

Never Lose Sight of What Makes Your Spouse Special to You

Why is it that before marriage, couples can spend endless hours trying to get to know everything they can about each other? Yet, after they have tied the knot, they often lose their interest in the very things that they found so alluring about one another.

I am sure that there is no single answer to that age-old problem. Nevertheless, there are tools that have helped countless couples bring back those loving feelings. Don't worry you do not have to be a skilled tradesman to use them.

So, let's start at the beginning. List all the things that attracted you to your spouse (or if you are single, do this about the person you are considering marrying or someone you are attracted to). Take as long as you wish to write your list, and make sure to put a line or two in between each trait. Next to those traits, write how you felt when you first discovered those things about them.

The next assignment is for those who have been married a while. On a separate piece of paper, I want you to write down all the traits from the first list. Next to them, I want you to write down what caused your feelings to change, making sure to be as honest as you can. It may take a few days to analyze.

This last list is NOT for posterity, nor for your spouse to see. It is for you alone to analyze what might have brought about your change of attitude. The reason for putting the second list on a separate piece of paper, is once you have figured out what brought about the change, you may not want to bring those attitudes back to your memory because of the temptation to go back to that way of thinking.

Once you have figured out what changed on your part, NOT your spouse's part, it should help you realize where you got off course so you can look for ways to make course corrections to be able to get the spark back into your marriage.

Now, find a place where you can be alone without any distractions. Then, pull out your first list and think back to how you felt with each of those magical moments of discovery. Let the ocean waves of what you felt back then, return with full force. Once you have recaptured those feelings (no matter how hard they may be to hold onto at that moment), I want you take one or two of those traits and write a love letter to your spouse expressing how much you love him or her, and how much you admire those traits. Remember, the soppier the better.

If you continue to do this periodically, choosing different traits each time, you will notice the sparks returning, and your spouse should be much happier and more pleasant to be around.

If after following the steps above, you are still struggling with this assignment then read the following scripture to give you some inspiration. Sometimes we just need to get the *desire* back into our hearts; even if we don't feel like doing something…especially if it has to do with strengthening our marriage.

"But behold, if ye will awake and arouse your faculties, even to an experiment upon my words, and exercise a particle of faith, yea, even if ye can no more than desire to believe, let this desire work in you, even until ye believe in a manner that ye can give place for a portion of my words" (Alma 32:27)

So there you have it! If you truly want to gain back what you had when you were dating, then start with a SINCERE desire, and then follow the rest of the recipe found in Alma 32:27-43. And remember, you cannot have a beautiful garden just because you plant seeds and do nothing more than pray for them to grow. Likewise, unless you are willing to plant the seeds and nurture them…then buying the finest seeds, and studying the best books on gardening, will do little to produce a beautiful garden. In addition, nurturing the seeds alone is not enough, unless you nurture them with the proper nutrients. After all, if you put plant food intended for rose bushes, on your citrus trees, the citrus fruit might come out tasting odd, if the tree does not die first.

One summer, many years ago, one of our sons was given the assignment to take care of someone's yard while they were away for an extended period of time. Since he was too young to drive, I drove him to their home, and while he watered their yard, I waited in our van, reading a book. I never bothered to check on his work, because I felt he needed to fulfill the assignment without my micromanaging him.

One day, he told me that the grass was dying, even though he had followed the homeowners' instructions. I had been there when the instructions were given, and from what I was able to assess, he had done as he was instructed. However, upon further investigation, I discovered that instead of putting out a good amount of water, the sprinkler was emitting nothing more than a fine mist.

Our son would have had to leave the sprinkler in each section of the yard for hours, instead of the 15 minutes he had been instructed to do. So, the obvious thing to do was to make sure to give each section of the lawn more water. However, the grass continued to look more malnourished. Then, I got the idea to put fertilizer on the lawn. He enlisted one of his younger brothers to fertilize the lawn while he mowed and watered. The false assumption on the part of the younger brother was if a little fertilizer is good, then a lot would do a much better job.

Imagine our horror when we returned the next day to see a dead lawn!

I raced to the store and bought a huge bag of grass seed in hopes of resurrecting the lawn before the homeowners returned. However, when we got to the house, we were shocked to see that they had returned earlier than anticipated.

No amount of apologies would take away the sick feeling I had every time I thought of that brown lawn; for every attempt we made to reseed and try to get the lawn back to the condition it was in before the homeowners left, were graciously declined.

The homeowners did not appear to harbor any ill feelings, but it did not take away the feeling that we broke their trust and could not restore their confidence in us.

I have since learned many lessons from that experience, but the most important one is to first get educated about the plant(s) you want to grow, and then to follow through with the proper care and nutrients.

The importance of learning to speak each other's love language, takes on new meaning when we realize that love can die between spouses when it is not nurtured properly. Sometimes, the lack of interest in one's spouse can come from the diversities between them. What is very desirable and interesting to one, may be painfully boring or lack luster for the other. So, what can be the solution to that challenge?

When a favorite food is consumed on a daily basis, it often loses its desirableness. Likewise, if you play a favorite tune on a piano for too long, the once beautiful tune can become annoying and even nerve racking. Diversity can keep foods enjoyable to the taste, and music pleasing to our ears. Therefore, making the effort to appreciate each other's diversities can help to bring the excitement back into your marriage.

My husband's and my taste in movies is sometimes light years apart. I realized a long time ago, if I left the room when Eric put on a movie that I did not want to watch, he would usually turn it off and come looking for me, wondering why I had left the room. I did not want to make him feel like my dislike for those movies was in any way connected with how I felt about him. Therefore, I learned to endure movies that were sometimes painful for me to watch.

A few years ago, one of Eric's birthday gifts (from our youngest son), was the movie "Duel", which was Steven Spielberg's first movie. Previous viewings of the movie were as much fun for me, as listening to someone scratching their fingernails down a chalkboard. However, about the time he was given that movie, I read about the importance of spouses learning to speak each other's love language. So that was when I decided that for his birthday, I would speak his love language, by offering to watch "Duel" with him. I let him know that I was doing it as a birthday present, and that I would not fall asleep (not an easy feat for me when watching any movie), and not complain (also not an easy feat me when watching that movie).

Since it was a special edition of the movie, Steven Spielberg's commentary was included, so we chose to watch that first. Did you know a technique that Steven developed in the making of that movie, revolutionized the movie industry; and that he made the movie in a week's time? Did you also know that he used the sound from one of the scenes in the movie, for the noise the shark made in "Jaws"? You will have to watch the commentary as well as the movie, to figure out the filming technique he developed and which sound was duplicated for the sound the shark made.

Hearing Steven's insights beforehand, gave more value to the movie, and helped me to see it with different eyes. I'm still not a fan of the movie, but I now have an appreciation for the genius and artistic talent that went into the making of it. Also, my efforts with trying to speak my husband's love language opened the door to his being more willing to learn my love language...and I did not have to lay a guilt trip on him to get him to do it.

Making the effort to discover your spouse's hidden talents, interests, and love language, may not be easy. It will require paying closer attention to what your spouse shows an interest in. If your spouse is shy and insecure, it may take a lot of patience and effort, and even prayer to get them to share those things with you.

There are many who possess amazing talents and abilities which are waiting to be given the opportunity and/or a safe place to let them shine through. Take for example, Susan Boyle,

210

(when she made her début on "Britain's Got Talent"), knocked the world off their seats, along with Simon (the judge who is the hardest to please). Her incredible voice, and the video clip of her début being put on YouTube (where millions viewed it), made her name a household word as she became an overnight success.

It is interesting to note the amazing transformation that took place with her appearance and confidence as she has been given many opportunities to share her talents with thousands, and possibly millions of fans.

If strangers can do that for Susan, think what an adoring husband or wife would do for a spouse who is encouraged and praised for their talents; or from a spouse who has made sterling efforts to learn and then speak their love language. My husband's sterling efforts to speak my love language, has made me feel like a queen. When I call him on the phone and he answers, "Hello beautiful!", I want to throw my arms around him and cover his face with kisses.

You may find yourself being pleasantly surprised as you take the time to really get to know your spouse's hidden talents and abilities. After all, just because you have been married a number of years, does not mean that you know everything about them.

Think of how many wars and rumors of wars would dissipate, and how many divorces could be avoided, if more efforts were made to better understand one's supposed enemy...even, and especially if at times, it is your spouse.

Through those efforts, you might come to better understand the following scripture: "Be not forgetful to entertain strangers [or your spouse]; for thereby some have entertained angels unawares" (Hebrews 13:2) (emphasis added).

My mother was masterful at letting offenses (even when they were intended) roll off of her back. She had a gift of making friends with everyone she met, even people who in the beginning had no intention of becoming her friend. No one remained a stranger for long if she was in the room.

One day, after visiting a family member in the hospital, I left my mother in the waiting room while I went to get the car. When I came back for her, she was chatting with a woman that she met when I left to go get the car; and even though my mother was over 40 years the woman's senior, they had made instant friends, exchanged e-mails, and made plans to meet for lunch...all within the 15 minutes I had been gone!

This was not an uncommon occurrence for my mother. She had a knack for quickly finding common grounds with others, and making them feel like they were the most important person in the room. I have no doubt that her ability to put people at ease, as well as make friends easily, kept the two of us from harm one day while traveling on a lonely backwoods road in Idaho.

We had just dropped off some friends and were headed home when we saw a man walking along the lonely dirt road. Therefore, being the Good Samaritan that she was, she offered him a ride. As we drove further into the secluded woods, I noticed the man taking the cover off a long gun that he had been carrying. Not knowing what else to do, I immediately started saying a silent prayer for our safety. In an instant, my mother looked in the rear view mirror and said, "That is a beautiful gun. Where did you get it?"

The man did not respond, so she repeated herself. The man shook his head as if coming out of a trance, and said, "Huh?"

My mother, once more in as friendly a voice as she could muster, said, "That is a beautiful gun. Where did you get it?"

The stranger then said the name of the city where he had gotten it. Then my mother asked where he wanted to be dropped off. His response that where we were was fine, brought a silent sigh of relief from inside of me. My mother then stopped the van and bid him a cheery "Goodbye".

As we drove off, I told my mother, "Don't you ever pick up a stranger again!"

However, true to her nature, she continued to be a friend to all, including the homeless, stranger, and destitute. One day, after I was married, I called home, and a voice answered that I did not recognize. Thinking I had misdialed, I asked if Joy was there. Imagine my surprise when I heard the unknown voice call out, "Mom, it's for you."

When my mother got on the phone, I inquired to whom the unfamiliar voice belonged. She told me that he was a stranger that did not have a place to stay, so she and my dad took him in. They obviously had made him feel like one of the family.

I prayed for their safety on a daily basis, partly, because I worried that one day, they would pick up a stranger that did not have their best interest at heart. I am grateful that the Lord heard my prayers!

Thank Heaven for people like my parents, who take literally the Savior's counsel to feed, clothe, and take in the stranger, fatherless, and homeless! However, I would *strongly* counsel the reader to make sure to seek for and follow the Spirit when taking on such charitable acts, as I have known people who have picked up hitchhikers that had tragic endings.

In an effort to get a spouse to change, some have used tactics that have not brought about the outcome they desired. I saw a *Cosby* show once, where Claire and Cliff Huxtable kept arguing over a difference of opinion. Each time they made up, one or the other would say something, and another argument ensued.

Finally, Claire suggested that they write down what was upsetting them, then read and discuss what each had written. Cliff briefly jotted down a few words, and then put his paper down while Claire continued to fill her paper as fast as her hand and pen could write. When Cliff saw how many things she was writing about him, he picked up his paper and started writing frantically. Claire, supposing Cliff was doing it just to be spiteful, asked to read what he was writing.

She became even more upset when she discovered that the only thing Cliff had written was how dumb that idea was. It came out that he could not come up with anything more that upset him about Claire.

In the September 1999 *Liahona* magazine (which was repeated in the January 2011 *Ensign* magazine), Lola B. Walters told how she learned early in her marriage, how much sweeter life was if she did not focus on her husband's faults. She told how as a young wife, she had come across an article in a magazine that recommended couples discuss truthfully and candidly the habits and mannerisms they found annoying about each other. The theory the author put out, was if partners know of such annoyances, they could correct them before resentful feelings develop.

Lola told how it made sense to her, so she decided to talk with her husband about the idea, and even though he was hesitant, he agreed to try it.

They were each supposed to come up with five things that they found annoying about each other. So, she chose as one of her husband's annoying habits, how he ate grapefruit. She could not stand that instead of cutting it in half and eating it with a spoon he peeled it and ate each section as one eats an orange. Her complaint was that no one else ate grapefruit like that [she never met my husband].

She stated how painful it would be for him to expect her to spend a lifetime, and even eternity, watching him eat grapefruit that way. She said she could not remember what the other items were on her list, but she was sure they were of equal importance to her.

She reported that even though it had been 50 years since that painful event, she still remembered his puzzled, thoughtful expression as he looked at her and said, "I can't think of anything I don't like about you."

She said she had to turn her back to him to be able to hide her tears, as she had found fault over trivial things about him while he had not noticed any of her annoying habits.

That painful experience taught her the need to keep her perspective, as well as how we should ignore the small differences in our spouse's habits and personalities. She noted that now when she overhears a husband and wife finding fault with each other, she refers to it as, "The Grapefruit Syndrome".

It is interesting that those two scenarios seem to be common in many marriages, as it is usually only one spouse that will focus on the failings and imperfections of the other, when the other spouse rarely has any complaints about their imperfections.

I have never been part of, nor understood why some wives find great delight in joking about and confessing their husband's failings with family and friends, as well as strangers. Such behavior is detrimental and unfair to the husbands who are not present to be able to defend themselves. The same advice could be given to husbands, who, when with other guys find great delight in belittling and making fun of their wives. If the tables were turned in either case, it might take speaking a lot of love language and apologies to convince the wounded spouse that they are still valued and loved.

Treat Your Husband like the Righteous Priesthood Holder That He Is

Why is it, so many Latter-day Saint wives, are reluctant to let their husband's be the priesthood leaders and patriarchs in their homes; and refuse to treat them with the respect and dignity that should be shown to a patriarch? Could it be that the traits one associates with priesthood holders and patriarchs are barely discernable in so many young (and not so young) Latter-day Saint husbands and fathers?

Just because a husband and wife are working hard towards exaltation, is not proof that either of them is perfect. Becoming perfect takes time, and will never take place on this side of the veil. So lighten up on each other, and focus on the diamond in the rough, instead of the thorn on the rose.

Therefore, while her knight in shining priesthood armor takes time to immerge on a more regular basis, it would pay big dividends, if the fledgling wife treated her equally fledgling husband, as if he already possesses the wisdom and spiritual strength of King Benjamin, until he actually does.

She should make sure to be patient and forgiving of his weaknesses as he grows into the "spiritual patriarch" that she thought she married. Likewise, it would be beneficial if the husband would be patient with his wife as she learns to trust and have faith in him as the leader of their home; and as she overcomes her weaknesses, while growing into the refined daughter of God that he thought he married.

Behind every prophet, has been a dedicated and courageous woman, who had to be patient and supportive of him as he was taught line upon line and precept upon precept, as he grew into the man that the Lord could trust to lead His Kingdom on the Earth.

I have no doubt that each of those wives have stories of their own, of how the Lord tutored them as well, and helped them to stretch and grow, so they could fill the role of a prophet's wife (D&C 25).

I love the movie "My Fair Lady", because it shows the example of when you treat a person the way you want them to be, they often become the person you dreamed of. The story is about a very snobbish Professor, named Henry Higgins, who is an expert in phonetics and the dialects of England. He brags to his new friend and colleague, Colonel Hugh Pickering, that within six months, he can take Eliza Doolittle (a filthy, unrefined flower girl with a strong Cockney accent), and pass her off as a refined lady, bread in high society.

After six long months of agonizing tutoring and training, Eliza is transformed into an elegant and genteel lady, who is able to fool everyone at the society ball they attend, including King George V, and the prince of Transylvania, who believed her to come from a royal bloodline.

The true beauty of the movie is not just the transformation that takes place with Eliza; but while trying to transform her into a refined lady, Professor Higgins falls in love with her, and starts his own transformation into a more compassionate person.

Another story of how one person's efforts can bring about amazing transformation in others is the story of Don Quixote de la Mancha, which is about Miguel Cervantes, a poet, writer and actor, who had been imprisoned while awaiting trial with the Spanish Inquisition for charges of heresy against the Catholic Church. Some of the guards had discovered Cervantes preaching (by way of his plays) that men did not have to depend on their clergy to read the Bible to them, but could do so on their own.

While awaiting trial, Cervantes' fellow prisoners steel his costumes and props, and come close to burning his unfinished manuscript. He stops them from burning the manuscript, by asking that he first be allowed to defend himself by the story, and then let them judge whether he is guilty of heresy or not.

Not having anything else to do with their time, the prisoners agree to his petition, and he, along with the prisoners, act out the play; which is about Alonso Quixano (a retired country gentleman in his fifties), who lives with his niece and housekeeper, in La Mancha.

In the story, Alonso has become obsessed with books about brave knights and chivalry. After refusing sleep and food, so he could continue to read his books, it is not long before he has lost his senses, and believes himself to be a knight.

Because of all the injustices in the world, he decides to go out as a knight-errant with the intent to right the wrongs in the world…no matter how hopeless and difficult his quest may be. He puts on an old suit of armor and renames himself "Don Quixote de la Mancha". Then, mounting his skinny carthorse (that he has renamed, "Rocinante"), he sets out on his quest. However, before taking off on his journey, he decides to take along his good friend and neighbor, Sancho Panza, to act as his squire, by convincing him that they will bring back treasures from their conquest.

They no sooner start out on their adventure than Don Quixote sees a windmill that he imagines to be a large monster with four arms. After loosing the battle with the monster, he sees a run down roadside inn (that in his disillusioned mind, he believes to be a castle). It is there that he meets Aldonza (a combination kitchen maid and harlot).

From the moment he sees her, he becomes smitten with her beauty; insisting that her name is "Dulcinea", a noble and high borne lady. Because of his kind treatment, and insisting she is Dulcinea, not the whore that she insists she is, her life is transformed, and she becomes the more modest and genteel Dulcinea.

There are others in the story, whose lives become more refined as well, because of the kindness, respect, and dignity Don Quixote shows them. But, the true miracle in this story, takes place with Cervantes' fellow prisoners as they act out their parts in his play. The evidence of this, comes about as Cervantes and Sancho Panza are going up the stairs to be tried by the Spanish Inquisition; and the prisoners who are left behind, start to sing, "To Dream the Impossible Dream", which was lead out by the prisoner who played Aldonza (who is shown with her head and shoulders covered by a shawl, and whose features have softened greatly). She and the rest of the prisoners are crying as they sing with increasing conviction, about holding onto their dreams, no matter how hopeless, and no matter how far...

Each time I watch that movie, I wipe away streams of tears as I witness the transformation that comes not only to the actors and actresses in both the play and the play within a play, but also because of the feelings that lift me up and give me hope and increased strength to hold fast to my dreams...no matter how hopeless and difficult they may seem at the time. I also come away feeling like I want to go out on my own quest to right the ills and wrongs in the world, no matter how hopeless and no matter how far...even if it is only *one heart at a time*...that is the main reason for writing this book.

Remember the story Stephen Covey told about the woman, who after attending his seminar, worked hard to apply the principle of "being a light, not a judge"; and how her efforts helped to transform her husband into the priesthood leader and patriarch of their home, that she desired? Her husband's comment showed the depths of his wife's commitment when he said, "It is hard to live with an angel, and not change."

Can you see the transforming power of treating others as if they are already the person you wish them to be? The important thing is not to become discouraged if the transformation is not obvious right away, or does not happen for a long period of time. I have seen it take sometimes four or more decades before a husband, wife, or wayward child grows into the person their loved one(s) prayed for. So, keep praying with faith for them, and never give up! If you get discouraged, read and reread the story of Alma the Younger, found in Mosiah 27.

The Atonement Has Power to Transform Hearts and Heal ALL Wounds

A few years ago, the right sleeve of my mother's sweater caught fire while she was cooking her breakfast. The skin on her entire right arm was so seriously burned that the doctor removed it and replaced it with fake skin. When that procedure failed, they removed skin from her abdomen and placed it on her arm.

The skin graft was actually healing quite nicely, but after her first surgery, she became violently ill, not being able to keep any thing inside of her that she ate or drank. This continued for 17 days; and in that time, she lost 14 pounds and looked emaciated. We tried everything to coax her to eat and drink, but her condition worsened.

Amazingly, she never complained the whole time. She was very happy and cheerful and had a gift for making everyone who visited her, feel like the most important person in the world. Even though that was always her nature, it was inspiring to see her continue to do so in spite of being terribly ill, and suffering from terrible pain.

On day 17 of her ordeal, I once again asked the nurse if they could check and see why my mother could not keep food or liquids inside of her. We were actually concerned that she would die if something did not improve soon. Fortunately, they finally granted my request. I have no idea why they ignored our family's requests previously, but maybe seeing that my mother had lost 14 lbs in two weeks, was enough to get their attention.

The test results showed that she had Clostridium Difficile, also known as C Dif., which is a serious bacterial infection that often attacks people who are hospitalized. It resembles a bad case of the flu, causing the person to suffer with serious bouts of diarrhea and vomiting. It is also highly contagious and it can be life threatening if it is not caught in time and treated with the proper medication.

The doctor immediately started my mother on medication, which removed the bacteria from her system within 24 hours. However, by the next evening, she went into shock, and was taken by ambulance to the hospital, where she died within 30 hours.

Her last few days were almost too unbearable…as she was delirious, and in and out of consciousness. I was deeply concerned about her being so malnourished, that I convinced the nurse to insert a feeding tube into her stomach. We even tried to get her to eat some Jell-O® and applesauce, but it was too difficult for her to swallow with the feeding tube down her throat.

It was obvious that she was in terrible pain, and that there was nothing we could do but pray and try to comfort her.

Then, in the very early hours of the 22 day of her ordeal, the nursed called to say we should get to the hospital as quickly as we could, and then immediately called again to say we did not need to hurry.

Nothing could have prepared me for the scene that I saw when I entered her hospital room…as it was obvious that her last hours were pure torture for her. I could not bear to look at her, as it made me realize how badly she had suffered. Guilt swept over me because I had not been there for her during her greatest hours of need. I had wanted to stay with her the night before, but my family and the nurse talked me into going home to get what they felt was much needed rest. I don't think any of us expected her to die that night, or I would have stayed against their protests.

I struggled to find peace of mind and comfort over the next few days, yet, no amount of praying and pleading for it, would bring it. Then, on the day of her funeral, we got word that my paternal grandfather (who meant the world to me), was in the hospital, dying of kidney failure. I was unable to go see him, which added greatly to my grief and heartache.

Then, in an attempt to get a message to a self-estranged family member that I will refer to as George, one of my brothers called the police and the operator, to see if they could get a message to one of George's neighbors, as no one in the family had George's phone number, nor any idea if he was still living at his last known address.

My brother's efforts proved to be a success, as George was able to speak on the phone to my grandfather before he died. However, within two days, I received two threatening messages on my answering machine; one from George's spouse, and the other from their adult son, threatening me with what they would do if I ever tried to contact them again.

Because of George's son's violent behavior, and frequent run-ins with the law, as well as threats to kill people (and no, I was not one of them), I had no reason to take his and his mother's threats lightly. Needless to say, I was scared out of my mind for me and my family. I realized if George and his family could find my phone number, they surely could find where I lived. To top it off, my family and I had no idea what their son looked like, which made it even more terrifying.

A few nights later, I was praying for safety for me and my family, as well as for relief from all the fear and grief that was consuming my weary mind and heart. I no sooner petitioned the Lord, when I heard the words, "The Atonement can heal ALL wounds."

Immediate peace washed over me like a warm ocean wave; and the overwhelming fear and unbearable grief (that had seconds before been a constant companion) left, and has not returned, to this day.

If the Lord could heal my unbearable heartache and fear; and help Eric's great uncle to transform into the person his great aunt would want to spend eternity with, He can do the same for those who feel like their marriage/family is too damaged to be healed.

Notes:

1. "Your Marriage and the Sermon on the Mount", Rick Browning, *Ensign*, August 1991

2. "Decisions for Successful Living", Salt Lake City: Deseret Book Co., 1974, p. 56

3. Author Dorothy Law Nolte approved the use of the short version

Section Four

We are all Gods and Goddesses in Embryo

My reasons for including this section is to help the reader to better understand the divine roles of men and women, as each has a distinct and individual role in the Lord's Plan.

Chapter Seventeen

Reaching our Full Potential as Husbands and Wives

After the Lord created Adam, He saw that it was not good that he should be alone. Therefore, He caused a deep sleep to come over him, and while he slept, the Lord removed a rib from his side; and from it, He formed a woman. When the Lord brought her to him, Adam said, "This I know now is bone of my bones, and flesh of my flesh; she shall be called Woman because she was taken out of man" (Genesis 2:23; Moses 3:21-23).

"Therefore shall a man leave his father and his mother, and shall cleave unto his wife …and they were no more twain but one flesh" (Matthew 19:5-6).

Have you ever wondered why the Lord chose to describe the creation of woman in this way? I wonder if it had to do with getting the idea across of the man and woman not being complete or perfect without the other. Together, they create a whole. Likewise, they cannot enter into the highest degree of the Celestial Kingdom without each other.

In Genesis 2:18 (King James Version of the *Bible)*, it refers to Eve as a "help meet" to Adam; where as the Hebrew text refers to Eve as "a partner worthy of him"; The LDS footnote refers to *help meet* as: "*helper* suited to, worthy of, or corresponding to him". Likewise, the Hebrew word for *helper* implies that the woman is not to be thought of as a subordinate or of having a lesser status than the man; but rather, of one who is his *equal.* The Lord's design for men and women is for them to be equal and complimentary to each other in status. Yet, even though their roles are equal in importance – each role is very different and unique.

This life is meant to be a preparatory time for when exalted husbands and wives will reign in their respective stations, in their own family kingdoms. In Roman architecture, the keystone at the top is what keeps the arch from caving in. In fact, there are antique arches that are thousands of years old, which are still standing strong, while the walls around them, have crumbled to the ground. The Lord created the heavens and the earth, and then filled the earth with animals of every kind. He then created man, which was His greatest masterpiece. However, as wonderful as all His creations were, they all would have been for nothing without the woman; for she, as Elder Russell M. Nelson said, was the "keystone" in the priesthood arch of creation.[1]

Even though the power of the priesthood is given to men, women should not feel like their role in His Divine Plan, is of less importance. Elder James E. Talmage said that women hold a position all their own in the eternal plan of the Creator; and that both the husband and wife, make up the governing head of the family, while each has separate duties and responsibilities that the other is not qualified to fulfill.

Weaknesses on the part of either spouse should not take away from, or interfere with the delicate balance of home and society.[2]

Woman has a role that no man will ever fill; and that is of being a co-creator with God. Man provides the seed, but woman is the vessel in which bodies are prepared to house the spirit children of our Father in Heaven.

 Mother Eve set the pattern for all women, by providing bodies for spirit children who were entrusted into hers and Adam's care. She nurtured the children, while Adam taught his sons to work by the sweat of their brow—teaching them how to provide food and shelter for the families they would have in the future. In addition, Adam provided protection for his family, both physically and spiritually, as well as setting the pattern for presiding as a righteous priesthood leader in their home.

The Lord has entrusted men to be His standard bearers in holding and exercising the power of the priesthood, even as young as 12 years of age. He has placed great trust in the hands of fathers; for it is their responsibility to teach and set the proper example for future generations to emulate.

The man being the head of the wife, like Christ is the head of the Church, in no way means dictatorship—or that he should be domineering or overbearing (Ephesians 5:23). It takes great humility and heroic efforts for a man to seek for, recognize, and then follow the counsel of the Lord and His leaders in regards to his role as a husband and father. In addition, it takes strength of character and great trust for the wife to learn to rely on her less-than-perfect spouse as the spiritual leader of their home (Ephesians 5:23-25).

However, both the husband and the wife can find comfort in Ether 12:27, in regards to their own, as well as each others imperfections and weaknesses: "And if men come unto me I will show unto them their weakness. I give unto men weakness that they may be humble; and my grace is sufficient for all men that humble themselves before me; for if they humble themselves before me, and have faith in me, then will I make weak things become strong unto them."

Our Father in Heaven knew it would not be easy for us to gain insight and understanding between His teachings and the world's in regards to the roles of men and women. Therefore, He has provided us with easy to understand teachings and guidelines that can be found in the scriptures and from our Church leaders.

There is an excellent guideline that was intended for priesthood quorums to follow, that a wise husband and/or father would do well to utilize, to make it much easier for his wife and children to learn to trust in him as the leader of their home. It can be found in D&C 107:30-31: "The decisions of these quorums…are to be made in all righteousness, in holiness, and lowliness of heart, meekness and long suffering, and in faith, and virtue, and knowledge, temperance, patience, godliness, brotherly kindness and charity...Because the promise is, if these things abound in them they shall not be unfruitful in the knowledge of the Lord" [3] (Emphasis added).

A perfect pattern for this counsel is set by the First Presidency and the Twelve Apostles. When an idea or suggestion is presented in those meetings, each person is given the opportunity to share his views (when moved upon by the Holy Ghost). Each member of the council shows the courtesy of being a good listener, while the others take their turns in sharing their views.

When a decision is made in their council, it is not by a popular vote, but by each member individually and collectively seeking the mind and will of the Lord. An atmosphere of harmony is encouraged in those meetings, so the Spirit of the Lord can guide them in their decisions. If even one member of the Quorum is not in agreement with the others, the discussion is tabled and set aside until all the members of the council have had time to study it out and seek for further inspiration on the subject before discussing it again.

Husbands and wives, as well as fathers and mothers, would be wise to adopt this counsel as they strive to magnify their individual and collective roles.

Can you imagine a home where that example is followed? Family Home Evenings would be edifying for all, and would no longer be referred to as "Prayer to Prayer Arguments". Every family member would feel like a valued and beloved member of that family, whose views are not only allowed to be shared, but listened to by all the others. However, if you know of such a family who accomplishes this 100% of the time, I would like to meet them to congratulate them. The truth is we are all gods and goddesses in embryo, who have weaknesses and imperfections. And, most parents would be grateful if their family can get through a Family Home Evening (or Family Council) without getting into an argument, and are still talking to each other by the end of the evening.

In a marriage, the line of divine authority (where the husband answers to the Lord, and the wife answers to the husband), is the design the Lord has set for all of His children. In other words, the Lord has placed each of his children, whether male or female, in a hierarchical chain. In His wisdom and order concerning those respective roles, He requires the follower to pay close attention to the counsel of those who are placed over them.

There Must Needs be Opposition in All Things

Have you considered why the Lord planned for families to treat each other with kindness and love, as well as to allow unpleasant or hurtful behavior with one another? I think part of it has to do with having opposition in all things so we can learn to appreciate the good, and to savor the sweet experiences in our lives. Might it also be for us as individual family members, to learn to love each other unconditionally, no matter what the other family members say or do to us? Adopting this attitude and refinement, helps us in overcoming the natural man, and to gain attributes that will make it easier for others to know Christ through our actions and countenances.

When we lose ourselves in the service of others, rather than expecting others to meet our needs, then we will gain greater insights and understanding into the heart of our Savior. It is the interaction with other family members, where our greatest tutoring for godhood takes place. In other words, the Lord's design and purposes for the family is to be a seedbed and schoolhouse for His Saints.

There is Beauty all around *because* there's Love at Home

I have been a wife and mother for over three decades; and in that time, I have had many opportunities to see what works, and what does not work when trying to maintain a loving and harmonious environment in my home. The following are some suggestions intended to help spouses recognize, and to hopefully avoid common pitfalls that occur in all marriages:

A wife that chooses to focus on her husband's faults and frequently stands in opposition of him can cause to unravel the delicate fibers that make up the fabric that holds their marriage together. As justified as she may imagine the reasons for her attitude, the fact is, that her reasons are often inspired or fueled by the one who makes it his greatest effort to destroy families.

If the destructive attitude is allowed to simmer long enough, it can reach the point of boiling over, and when that happens, the marriage can be lost, along with the couple's original dream of being together forever.

Husbands are usually clueless when it comes to knowing what is bothering their wives when they are upset with them. Comments I have heard have ranged from, "What have I done now?" to, "Does anyone understand women?"

The truth of the matter is men and women do not think alike. Once the husband or wife quits expecting the other to think like them, or, as we like to call it, "The right way", half of the battle is won.

Since men and women are not mind readers…even though many would like to think they are…passing blame for unfulfilled expectations in marriage and family life, can be disastrous to a Celestial bound family.

When unresolved issues, disagreements, or misunderstandings go unchecked, and course corrections are not made, then couples can go for years, living what some refer to as "parallel lives"; where they live in the same household and never connect emotionally, socially, physically, or spiritually. It has been said, "Silence is golden", but in marriage, it can be deadly.

Each hour and day that silence between the couple continues, it drives one more nail in the coffin of their dying marriage. Misery is the only outcome of such a marriage, not only for the couple, but also for any children, or extended family members and friends.

Latter-day Saints are not exempt from these challenges. In fact, the last time I read the statistics, the divorce rate among members of our Church was 40%. This is unacceptable! It is a trend we must STOP if we are to be prepared to meet the Savior when He comes!

How can a man or woman who is unkind or critical to their spouse (and/or family), be allowed to live in a Zion Society that we are told will exist during the Millennium? In addition, how can either expect to be allowed to live in the Celestial Kingdom with such attitudes?

There is a sanctifying influence that takes place when a husband and wife are committed to expressing selfless love through word and deed, and exercising forgiveness one for another as they partake of the emblems of the Sacrament each week. A couple, who has committed themselves and their marriage to these sanctifying attitudes, will come to know what Heaven on Earth is like. Their homes will be refuges from the storms that their family will face on a daily basis, and the Spirit of the Lord will be felt by all who enter their home.

Creating such an environment, takes the efforts and deep commitment of each spouse and member of their family. Moreover, it is possible to accomplish this even when it is only one member of the family who is making the sincere effort to be Christ-like, which should not to be confused with being self-righteous.

A couple, who makes the sacrifices to create a Christ-centered home, builds the kingdom of God in ways they cannot begin to imagine. Such a family will experience great joy and blessings that will flow forth into the eternities.

However, the couple who has allowed discord and self serving practices to be a way of life, can only diminish or destroy their chance of filling the measure of their creation as husband and wife, and as an eternal family. The wife who chooses to withhold physical intimacy from her husband, to punish or manipulate him to do what she wants, will oft times set up conditions that may cause the husband to seek solace in places that can block his ability to obtain exaltation, and has the potential to break trusts that should exist between a husband and wife.

The wife who will show forth grace (forgiveness and acceptance) towards her husband, especially when he deserves it least, will set the stage for him to reciprocate when she least deserves it. *Grace* is an enabling or strengthening power given to another who cannot provide it for him or herself, but needs it.

Women, by nature, have great capacities to show forth *grace*. Women have great abilities to strengthen and uplift the sometimes, weakened knees and wearied minds of their battle weary husband's and family members. If she will forgive and forget all real or imagined annoyances she feels towards her husband, and replace such thoughts with what he does that is right and noble, and then *work* to love and fill his needs physically, emotionally, socially, and spiritually—without expecting anything in return, then he will come to view her as an angel, and will most likely wish to repay her through his own acts of *grace*.

Christ shows *grace* for us in our weakness. We should follow His example if we wish for Him to continue to show forth *grace* for us...even when we least deserve it...but desperately need it. *Grace* is one of the most over looked, yet most powerful traits of godliness.

The Apostle Peter gave the following wise counsel to wives and husbands: "Ye wives, *be* in subjection to your own husbands; that, if any [husbands] obey not the word, they also may without the word be won by the conversation of the wives...While they behold your chaste conversation coupled with fear...Whose adorning let it not be that outward adorning of plaiting the hair, and of wearing of gold, or of putting on of apparel...But *let it be* the hidden man of the heart, in that which is not corruptible, even the ornament of a meek and quiet spirit, which is in the sight of God of great price...Likewise, ye husbands, dwell with *them* [the wife] according to knowledge, giving honour unto the wife, as unto the weaker vessel [less strong physically, not lesser in importance], and as being heirs together of the grace of life; that your prayers be not hindered...Finally, be ye all of one mind, having compassion one of another, love as brethren, *be* pitiful [having compassion], *be* courteous: Not rendering evil for evil, or railing for railing: but contrariwise blessing; knowing that ye are thereunto called, that ye should inherit a blessing" (1 Peter 3:1-4; 7-9). (Emphasis added)

Patriarchy and Matriarchy are Apostate Forms of Government

It is common in today's world, for women to compete for or usurp authority, and for men to abuse authority, "...hence many are called, but few are chosen" (D&C 121:39-40).

Hugh Nibley pointed out that both *Patriarchy* and *Matriarchy* are apostate forms of government. [4]

Dictionary.com defines *Patriarchy* as "A form of social organization in which the father is the supreme authority in the family, clan, or tribe and descent is reckoned in the male line, with the children belonging to the father's clan or tribe."

Likewise, Matriarchy is "A form of social organization in which the mother is head of the family, and in which descent is reckoned in the female line, the children belonging to the mother's clan or matriarchal system."

In "The Family: A Proclamation to the World", the First Presidency said that it is by divine design that fathers are to preside over their families in love and righteousness. It is their role to provide for the necessities of life and protection for their families. It is the role of mothers to be the primary nurturer of their children. Moreover, it is through their sacred responsibilities, that fathers and mothers are to help each other as equal partners.

Even though their roles and responsibilities can differ greatly, the Lord views men and women's roles with equal importance. It is with great alarm that the Lord's designs for marriage and for the family are being redefined and erased one vote and pen stroke at a time in the courts and halls of Congress in the United States and throughout the world.

There are strong warnings and consequences all throughout the scriptures to those who promote such destructive ideologies and practices. In The Family: A Proclamation to the World", the First Presidency warned that individuals who fail to fulfill family responsibilities as the Lord designed for them, will stand before God and have to give an accounting of their actions. Strong warnings are given throughout the scriptures by ancient and modern prophets about the calamities which *will* happen to individuals, communities, and nations who do not protect, but contribute to the disintegration of the family. All one has to do, is to read the headlines in the news to know that the Lord keeps His promises!

Elder James E. Talmage said that the difference between men and women was established in our pre-mortal state, which has carried over into this life, and continues after this life, both as spirit sons and daughters, and as resurrected beings." [2]

In the October 2010 General Conference, President Boyd K. Packer made it clear that no vote can change the Creator's plan or design for men and women.

The temple ordinances provide keen insight and enlightenment into the Lord's purposes and designs for marriage and the family, as well as men and women's roles in His kingdom on the Earth and in eternity. Every temple ordinance provides its own unique tutoring that is designed to instruct and edify the humble and teachable patron who comes prepared to be taught the higher order of things that exist within and are a requirement for entrance into the Celestial Kingdom.

The trust the Lord has given to women, to serve as counselors and supports to their husbands, is a Divine indenture (D&C 25). If the wife, will approach her assignment from the Lord, in the spirit of humility and love, seeking for unity with her husband, and aligning her will with the mind and will of the Lord in regards to her divine role, her efforts will act as a springboard for continued mutual respect, and spiritual growth, individually, as well as collectively, with her husband and their family.

The Lord has placed great trust in giving men the authority to act in His name through the power and authority of the priesthood. Perfection is not a requirement for being allowed to hold the priesthood. However, as the man strives for perfection, and allows his wife and family to be the recipients of the blessings the priesthood offers, and his wife makes the effort to be a support, comfort, and counselor to him in righteousness, then he and she will be equal beneficiaries in this preparatory stage of learning to rule and reign together in their own family kingdom.

In fine tuning their individual and collective roles as husband and wife, the couple is able to align their lives and hearts with the Lord's. This sanctifying process will allow them to reach a point where the one who seeks to destroy the family unit, will have no power over them. Even with evil being evident nearly every where we look, or try not to look, there are those who *choose* daily to keep sacred ordinances that they have made in the temple.

Partaking of the Sacrament on a weekly basis, and participating in the sacred temple ordinances, opens the way for the Lord to purge from the heart and mind those things that are incompatible with Celestial glory.

I love the promises that are given in the temple ordinances for those who are true and faithful to their temple covenants. It is hard to comprehend such glories and majesties, yet each time I hear them repeated, it gives me great hope, that if I endure valiantly the trials and hardships of this life, then one day, they will all be worth it! In fact, I know without a shadow of a doubt, that the blessings that await us in the Celestial Kingdom are greater than anything our finite minds can comprehend or conceive.

The Lord sent us to Succeed, Not Fail!

We have been commanded to be perfect like our Father in Heaven is perfect (Matthew 5:48). Easier said than done, right? Remember, the Lord sent us to succeed...not to fail! He has provided tools to help each of His children to find their way back to His presence. However, we need to do our part in discovering those tools and resources; and then wisely put them to use for the benefit of those in our sphere of influence, as well as in our own lives.

The Lord will never deny the humble, teachable seeker of truth, safe passage back to Him.

The Price of Eternity

What price are you willing to pay to have the blessings of eternity?

In a costume shop window, at a Renaissance Faire that my husband and I attended over 20 years ago, there was a sign which read, "Pay like a pauper - dress like a pauper. Pay like a Prince - dress like a Prince".

I thought at the time that it was a sermon in and of itself. Yet, I have since had very few opportunities to use it. However, it fits very well with the point that I want to get across in trying to explain how the level of commitment and effort that each spouse is willing to put into their marriage, will be proportional to the blessings and Divine intervention they receive. This can also include comfort and peace of mind when the journey is long and difficult, or when the reasons for the trial seem too hard to understand.

If a couple strongly desires miracles in their marriage (and/or family), then they need to apply the principles of faith and works, along with their prayers (James 2:20). However, there are many who give up before they see their objectives and desires come about. Often, it is when we reach that point, if we will just put forth one more effort, or one more ounce of faith, that the answers and blessings come, and sweet peace and joy will fill our hearts. Gratitude to the One, who willingly gives the sweet relief and answers, can bring tears to the recipient as well as the Giver. Then why is it, so many individuals and/or couples lack the staying power, and give-up before crossing the Celestial Finish Line?

The following are some observations that I have come up with that might explain why this occurs:

- An unwillingness to hand over the reigns to the Lord, due to lack of complete trust or faith, can also cause us to fail at accomplishing our desired goals. We pray for His help, but are unwilling to give the problem back to Him. In addition, we often lack the patience to let the answer or blessing come in the Lord's way and time.

- Doubt and fear can also get in the way. They are *temptations* that we should not allow ourselves to give in to. When we doubt or fear, we deny ourselves blessings that the Lord would otherwise be more than willing to shower down upon us (James 1:3-7; Alma 32:21-43; Alma 56:47; D&C 6:36).

- Some of us lack confidence. The following scriptures offer great insight and enlightenment into gaining the confidence we need to see our worth to the Lord, and to be able to do what He requires of us: D&C 121:34-46; Ether 12:27; 1 Corinthians 1:27; D&C 35:13; D&C 124:1; and Abraham 3:22-23. After reading and pondering on those passages of scripture, how can anyone feel like they do not have worth to the Lord? Once we feel of His love and acceptance of us, our confidence will wax strong...not to be confused with false pride, self-righteousness, or arrogance. D&C 121:34-46 is very clear on that subject. When we let the Lord guide us, *we will have* confidence that He will lead us back to His presence.

- Impatience is often a saboteur of being able to accomplish our goals. You did not gain your testimony and understanding of the Savior and His Gospel over night...did you? It came a little bit here, and a little bit there, like everything else we learn in this life. 2 Nephi 28:30 teaches, "...thus saith the Lord God: I will give unto the children of men line upon line, precept upon precept, here a little and there a little; and blessed are those who hearken unto my precepts, and lend an ear unto my counsel, for they shall learn wisdom; for unto him that receiveth I will give more; and from them that shall say, We have enough, from them shall be taken away even that which they have."

- We must *never* give up. We must continue to believe and have faith, and trust in the Lord's ability to bless us with the righteous desires of our hearts...even when it seems like our prayers go unanswered for long periods of time; or when we cannot see the fruits of our labors.

The poet, Robert Browning, wisely stated, "A man's reach should exceed his grasp, or what's a Heaven for?" [5]

So reach with all you're reaching! Stretch a little farther, and cross the finish line that you started before coming to the earth!

What a choice blessing it is to know that with the Lord, we can do all things that He requires of us...even in seeing to it that our Celestial dreams can become a reality.

Now, what will you do differently in your marriage, because of what you learned today?

Notes:

1. Russell M. Nelson, "Lessons from Eve," *Ensign*, Nov 1987, 86
2. James E. Talmage, "The Eternity of Sex", pp. 600, 602
3. "Prophets", *Ensign,* May 1991, p. 28
4. Hugh Nibley, "Patriarchy and Matriarchy, in Old Testament and Related Studies" [Salt Lake City and Provo: Deseret Book/FARMS, 1986], p. 96
5. Robert Browning - (May 7, 1812 – December 12, 1889) was an English poet and playwright

Bibliography

Brotherson, Laura "Strengthening Marriage through Sexual Fulfillment"

--------.   "From Honeymoon to Happily Ever After", MeridianMagazine.com, LDS Marriage

Network

Dictionary.com

Lewis, C. S., "The Chronicles of Narnia"

--------.   "Mere Christianity"

Marek, Norma Cornett, a tribute to a beloved child (author passed away 18 July, 2004),

BreaktheChain.org

Nolte, Dorothy Law, "Children Learn What They Live", 1972/1975

Riley, James Whitcomb, "The Gobble-Uns 'll Git You Ef You Don't Watch Out!" [1849-1916],

Google online search

Roosevelt, Teddy, a quote attributed to him found on a Google search

Wikipedia.com

Citations

Adler, Shannon "300 Questions LDS Couples Should Ask before Marriage"

Ballard, Russell M., "How to Find Safety and Peace", *New Era*, Nov. 1997, 4

Bednar, Elder David, "Things as they Really Are", CES Fireside for Young Adults, BYU Idaho,
May 3, 2009

"Brigham Young University Speeches of the Year", 1973, "Marriage is Honorable", BYU Press,
1974, p. 263

Brinley, Douglas, MD, Marriage Seminar in Tucson, AZ, Spring 2007

Brown, Robert, - (May 7, 1812 – December 12, 1889) was an English poet and playwright

Cannon, George Q., "Journal of Discourses", 11:230

Corbett, Don Cecil, "Mary Fielding Smith: Daughter of Britain" [1966], 228; 237

Turnbull, Agnes Slight, "When Queens Ride By" [Published in 1888; 1930 award winning story];
revision by Terry Olsen

Distribution Center for The Church of Jesus Christ of Latter-day Saints, *Video item* #53061000

---------.   "Strengthening the Home", pamphlet, 1973, p. 7

Ensign, Sept. 2002, p. 11, "Hope for Parents of Wayward Children"

---------.   "When You Have the Spirit vs. When you Do Not Have the Spirit", Answer to
Gospel Questions, Aug. 1978

---------.   "Prophets", May 1991, 28

Evans, Richard L., *Area Conference Report* (England) 8/71:71

Featherstone, Vaughn J., taken from an address given during the Manti Temple Rededication events of April 1987

Hafen, Bruce C., "The Atonement: All for All", *Ensign,* May 2004, 97

Hinckley, Gordon B., an address given to the Regional Representatives of the Church of Jesus Christ of Latter-day Saints, 6 April 1984

----------.   "The Women in Our Lives", *Ensign,* Nov. 2004, 84

History of the Church", *Mary Fielding Smith,* 5:355

Intellectual Reserve, Inc, www.LDS.org, 2002

Kimball, Spencer W. "Oneness in Marriage", Ensign, March 1977

----------.   "Marriage and Divorce", BYU Devotional given on 7 September 1976

----------.   "The Teachings of Spencer W. Kimball", ed. Edward L. Kimball, (Salt Lake City: Bookcraft, 1982), p. 311-312

----------.   *Ensign,* Nov. 1978, p. 103

----------.   "Be Ye Therefore Perfect", devotional address, Salt Lake Institute of Religion, 10 Jan. 1975

LaHaye, Tim and Beverly "The Act of Marriage - The Beauty of Sexual Love" (1998)

LDS.org, "Provident Living": *Chastity; Morality*

--------.   "Family Living"

--------.   "A Parents Guide"

--------.   "Temple Preparation Seminar Teacher's Manual", Lesson 7, 31

--------.   "The Family: A Proclamation to the World"

--------.   "Young Women Manual 2", Lesson 33

McConkie, Bruce R., Collected Discourses, 3 vols. [1954-56], 2:90-91

McKay, David O., *Conference Report*, Oct. 1942, pp. 12–13

McLean, Michael "Hold on the Light Will Come" - title to a song

Nelson, Russell M., "Lessons of Eve", *Ensign,* Nov. 1987, 86

Nibley, Hugh, "Patriarchy and Matriarchy, in Old Testament and Related Studies", [Salt Lake and Provo: Deseret Book/Farms, 1986], p. 96

Packer, Boyd K., "Our Moral Environment", Ensign, May 1992, 68

Romney, Marion G., "The Book of Mormon", Ensign, May 1980, 65

Smith, Joseph Jr., "History of the Church", 2:23

Smith, Joseph F., Improvement Era, vol. 20, p. 739

Smith, Joseph Fielding, Doctrines of Salvation, comp.

---------.   "Life of Joseph F. Smith", 1969, p. 131

Talmage, James E., "The Eternity of Sex", pp. 600-602

Wheat, Ed, MD and Wheat, Gaye "Intended for Pleasure" (1997)

---------.   "Before the Wedding Night: Pre-Marriage Counsel" (CDs)

Whitman, Samuel T., "Forgotten Wedges", General Conference Address given by Spencer W. Kimball, April 1966

Worthlin, Joseph B., "The Restoration and Faith", *Ensign*, Jan. 2006, 35)